POSTCARD HISTORY SERIES

Martinsville

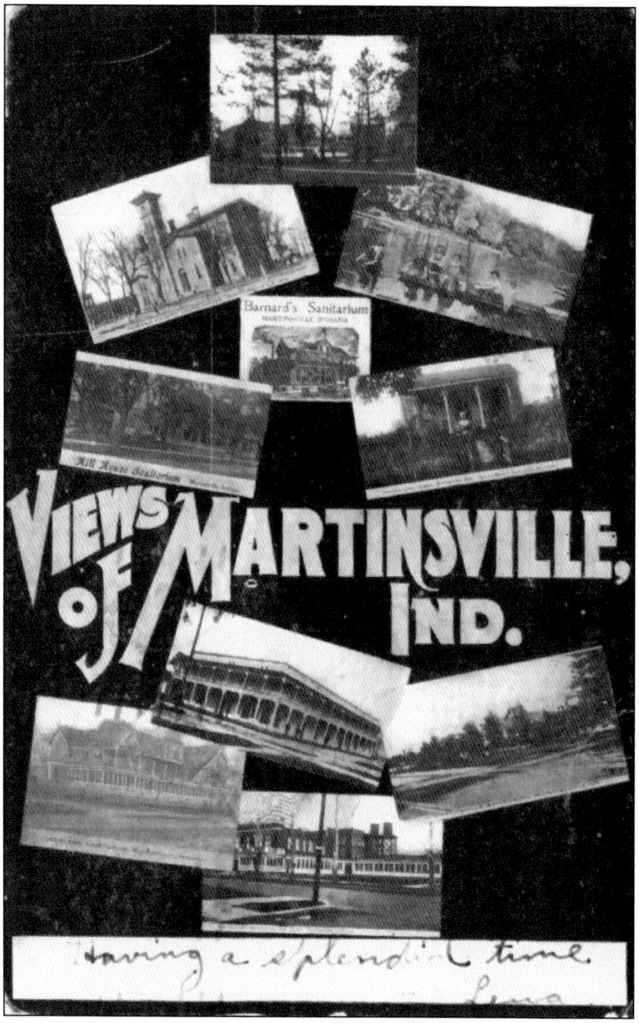

MARTINSVILLE MULTIVIEW, 1908. Seen here, clockwise from top, are Home Lawn Sanitarium, Blue Bluffs resort, Celestina Phelps (also known as Aunt Tiny, she was the inspiration for a character in *Lovey Mary*, a popular novel), Martinsville Sanitarium, Colonial Sanitarium, Highland Sanitarium, National Sanitarium, Hill House Sanitarium, Morgan County Courthouse, and Barnard's Sanitarium.

On the front cover: **SANITARY BARBER SHOP, *c.* 1915.** Harry Preston operated a barbershop at this location for a few years before moving to the north side of Morgan Street. Born in 1878, Preston began working in barbershops at the age of 12 and stayed in the profession until he died in 1942. The identity of the black shoe shine boy is unknown. The photographer of this card is Michael Cohn.

On the back cover: **SERVING TABLES ON JEFFERSON STREET, CENTENNIAL CELEBRATION, 1922.** On October 12–13, 1922, county residents thronged the courthouse square to celebrate the 100th anniversary of Morgan County's founding. Slices from a 630-pound birthday cake were distributed from these tables. Following the event, real-photo postcards produced by Ennis Brothers sold for 15¢ each, two for 25¢, or a complete set of 16 for $2.50. Today one card will easily command much more at auction.

POSTCARD HISTORY SERIES

Martinsville

Joanne Raetz Stuttgen and Curtis Tomak

ARCADIA
PUBLISHING

ISBN 978-0-7385-5230-9

Published by Arcadia Publishing
Charleston SC, Chicago IL, Portsmouth NH, San Francisco CA

Printed in the United States of America

Library of Congress Catalog Card Number: 2007942457

For all general information contact Arcadia Publishing at:
Telephone 843-853-2070
Fax 843-853-0044
E-mail sales@arcadiapublishing.com
For customer service and orders:
Toll-Free 1-888-313-2665

Visit us on the Internet at www.arcadiapublishing.com

We dedicate this book to local historians, both past and present, who have provided a record of earlier times through their research, memories, writings, collections, and advocacy.

CONTENTS

Acknowledgments

We are indebted to the generosity of many postcard collectors who graciously shared their collections with us. Some are friends we have known for a long time (and bid against at auctions). Others are people we had never before met but who answered our call for postcards. Still others include eBay sellers who e-mailed us scans of cards when we somewhat sheepishly asked. Thank you to the following people, institutions, and organizations: Academy of Hoosier Heritage, Robert Barnard, Nancy Bennett, Del Chafey, Michael Gorham, Kevin Kent, Bill Kirk, Pam Lanham, Morgan County Historic Preservation Society, Morgan County Public Library, Tim and Camilla Morris, Elmer and Viola Reynolds, Joe Seiter, Keith Steinway, Bob Strader, Joanne Raetz Stuttgen, Bruce and Virginia Throckmorton, Curtis Tomak, and Jim Whitaker.

Furthermore, we are beholden to the following local residents, historians, and organizations whose passion for and commitment to preserving and recording the past have enriched this book immeasurably: Albert "Dutch" Allen, Wanda Allen, Kimberly Bright, Harry Brown, Alice Burns, Sam Cline, Dale Drake, Charles Finney, Alma Fraker, Mae Kivett Gano, Richard Hamilton, Becky Hardin, John E. Hurt Sr., Lloyd James, Virginia "Gin" Lewis, Morgan County Historic Preservation Society, Morgan County History and Genealogy Association, Bette Nunn, Elmer Reynolds, Lucille Sadler, Margaret Sedwick, and Phyllis Walker.

INTRODUCTION AND HISTORY OF POSTCARDS

This book is a sequel to our *Morgan County* Postcard History Series book published by Arcadia Publishing in 2007. Like the Morgan County book, the present book is a history based upon postcards. It greatly benefits from Joanne's extensive knowledge of local history and her research experience. My postcard collection was a primary resource for this book, but we also utilized other collections. We are very grateful to the contributors listed in the acknowledgments. Over 200 postcards are pictured in this book. Dates given in the captions refer to the postmark date or are based upon other information on the card with circa dates being an estimate based upon the type of card.

With a population of about 13,000, Martinsville is the largest town in Morgan County. From the beginning, it has been the county seat, being founded and designated as such when Morgan County was established in 1822. Morgan County is located in south-central Indiana immediately southwest of Indianapolis. It is a rural area of about 409 square miles with a population of approximately 70,000.

Well known for its mineral water sanitariums, Martinsville acquired the nickname "City of Mineral Water." The earliest sanitarium, the Barnard, opened in 1888, and the last in operation, Home Lawn, closed in 1968. Over the years, there have been 12 different sanitariums, known by numerous names.

Martinsville has other claims to fame as well. The Old Hickory Chair Company began business in Martinsville in the 1890s. The name was changed to Old Hickory Furniture Company in 1921, and the company remained in business until 1978. Old Hickory furniture was well known and sold nationwide. Today it is much in demand and highly collectible.

Grassyfork Fisheries was started in Martinsville in 1899. It developed an international market, and the company was billed as the "World's Largest Goldfish Hatcheries." When Grassyfork was sold to Ozark Fisheries in 1970, it is said to have been producing some 40 million goldfish per year.

Two Indiana governors were from Martinsville. Emmett F. Branch was governor from 1924 to 1925 and lieutenant governor from 1920 to 1924. Paul V. McNutt governed from 1933 to 1937. McNutt was an extraordinarily accomplished individual who became known internationally. Among other things, he was dean of the Indiana University Law School, national commander of the American Legion, U.S. high commissioner to the Philippines, appointed to a number of extremely important federal positions by Pres. Franklin D. Roosevelt, and a contender for the Democratic nomination for president in 1940.

John R. Wooden, the famous basketball coach, is from Martinsville. He coached the University of California, Los Angeles to a record 10 NCAA National Basketball Championships, was an All-American at Purdue, and played on the Martinsville team that won the state high school basketball championship in 1927. The Martinsville boys also won the state high school basketball championship in 1924 and in 1933.

The Martinsville girls have also contributed much to the athletic success of the high school, especially by their exceptional achievements over the past 17 years. During that time, they have won 16 state championships: 10 golf, 2 basketball, 2 volleyball, and 2 softball titles.

Martinsville High School also has a most impressive record in academics. Competing annually in the Large School Class in the Academic Decathlon, Academic Super Bowl, and Academic Spell Bowl competitions, Martinsville has won the most state championships (21), has won at least one state championship for 13 consecutive years, has won the decathlon state championship each of the past 11 years, is the only school to win all three championships in the same year, and is the only school to have won multiple state championships in each of the three competitions.

The formal term for the study and collecting of postcards is *deltiology*, which derives from a Greek word referring to a small writing tablet. Over the years, the terms *postcard* (post card) and *postal card* have been used in various ways and contexts. However, in a technical sense *postcard* has come to mean a privately printed card to which a postage stamp is affixed, whereas *postal card* refers to a government-printed card that has a preprinted stamp.

Deltiology has become one of the most popular collecting activities in the United States. This is evidenced by the large and continually growing number of postcard collectors, dealers, and organizations such as the Indianapolis Postcard Club (IPC). Organized in 1975, the IPC has about 115 members, holds monthly meetings, and now hosts two shows per year where postcards are bought, sold, traded, and exhibited. The volume of postcard business conducted on the Internet further attests to the interest in postcards.

People collect postcards for various reasons. Some collections reflect an interest in a particular topic: for example, trains and depots, sports, schools, Route 66, restaurants, occupations, politics, parks, postal history, famous people, theaters, royalty, holidays, children, advertising, courthouses, and animals.

Many collections are based upon an interest in the history of certain places or events, memories, experiences, associations with people and places, and/or personal and family history. For example, someone may collect just the city of Wabash, anything Morgan County, or a combination of hometown and current place of residence. Some places, such as French Lick and West Baden, may be collected just because they are interesting or unusual.

Many postcards are desirable as objects of art. Often cards are sought that have been illustrated by a particular artist, with those that are "signed" (printed signature) being more desirable. Some people search for postcards manufactured by a particular company or taken by a specific photographer. For instance, the white-, gray-, and silver-bordered view cards (see page 22, top) made by the Wayne Paper Box and Printing Corporation of Fort Wayne from the early 1930s to the late 1940s are favored by some collectors. Others, for example, may collect the fine real-photo postcards made by J. Inbody of Elkhart from about 1907 to 1915.

Some people are interested in postal history and collect old postcards because of their cancel marks and postmarks from post offices that no longer exist. The image on the front of the card or the type of card is usually of little or no real importance.

Collections may also focus on certain categories of postcards as exemplified by the following three kinds of cards.

Real-photo postcards are actual black-and-white photographs printed onto photographic paper having a postcard back (see page 119). They are quite popular because of the quality of the image. Although actual photographic postcards of one kind or another are still produced, those typically thought of as real-photo postcards date from approximately 1900 into the 1920s.

View cards are postcards that basically show scenes or views of such things as towns, buildings, and landscapes (see page 80). This is a standard and popular kind of card. The time span for what are regarded as view cards is from the 1890s to the present.

A multiview postcard is a card that has from 2 to at least 19 separate views on it (see page 2). Typically the views are images of individual view cards for a particular place. Examples are multiviews of towns or university buildings. Multiviews are collectible cards with the general time span of vintage examples being from the 1890s into the 1930s.

Although there may be a primary reason for the composition of a postcard collection, many collections result from a combination of factors. Some are based upon an interest in history combined with an association with a particular area. Halloween cards may be collected because of the subject matter, beautiful colors, and artistic quality.

It takes more than an interest in a topic or a place to collect postcards. Some people collect many different kinds of things related to their subject area but do not have much interest in postcards. However, many people think that postcards themselves are so nice and so enjoyable to collect that they concentrate on them to satisfy their area of interest basically to the exclusion of other things. For instance, it may be that a person does not have much interest in photographs pertaining to their subject area or is not really interested in collecting relevant trade cards or blotters even though the images or text on them are as good or better than on postcards. Assembling an outstanding postcard collection becomes an important goal that is reinforced by the good feeling that comes from a sense of accomplishment.

A number of postcard companies distributed postcards that advertised their products. One side of the card is a sample of a type of postcard being advertised, and the other side has ordering and price information. This is exemplified by a printed white-border view postcard produced by the Auburn Postcard Manufacturing Company of Auburn, Indiana, during the 1915–1930 period. The stated price for 500 copies of the printed view cards is $3.75 and that for 100 "full size photo post cards" of local views is $1.50.

Some postcard photographers put their name on the front of their postcards and/or advertised their business on the back. For instance, "J. Inbody, post card artist, Elkhart, Ind." is on the back of a card postmarked 1907. Another example is M. L. Photo, who signed as such on the front of 1907–1915 real-photo postcards and often had some version of "M. L. Photo Company, Chicago" on the back. M. L. Photo produced good-quality cards of many places in Indiana, including some towns in Morgan County.

Several Morgan County photographers produced postcards during the first two decades of the 20th century. Those from Martinsville include A. G. Bergen, Michael Cohn, Ennis Brothers (Edward and Harry), and Paul Kelso.

In addition to professional photographers, it was a common practice for anyone to take photographs of family members, homes, places, and events and have them printed as postcards. Beginning about 1906, this was aided by the availability of small affordable cameras for postcard photography.

Postcards came into use during the last half of the 19th century as a convenient means of sending a brief message. The earliest postcards were privately published. Evidently the first card that qualifies as a postcard in the United States is the Lipman Postal Card designed and copyrighted by John Charlton and H. L. Lipman of Philadelphia in 1861. Not many of these cards are known. The oldest mailed example is dated October 25, 1870, and that card is the earliest-known mailed American postcard.

The U.S. government entered the postcard business in 1873 when the U.S. Postal Service began the production of prestamped, 1¢ mailing cards referred to as postal cards. From 1873 until 1898, only the U.S. government could produce the 1¢ cards. During this time, privately published cards with a written message were required, like letters, to have a 2¢ postage stamp affixed to them. The interval from the Lipman card to 1898 is often referred to as the pioneer period (era) of postcard history.

On May 19, 1898, the Private Mailing Card Act became federal law. This act permitted privately published mailing cards with a written message to be mailed domestically for 1¢ like the government-printed cards but required that a postage stamp be used. The private cards had to have the words "Private Mailing Card Authorized by Act of Congress of May 19, 1898" printed on the back (address/postage side) to distinguish them from government cards. As before, the message on government cards and on privately published cards was to be confined to the front. The time from the 1898 act to 1902 constitutes the private mailing card period.

The December 24, 1901, order of the U.S. Postal Service rescinded much of the 1898 act and allowed privately published cards to have "Post Card" (Postcard) printed on the back instead of "Private Mailing Card." As before, the back of government and private cards was an undivided area to be used solely for the address. Although undivided backs were the norm prior to 1902, the period from about 1902 to 1907 is considered to be the undivided-back period. The message was still to be confined to the front in a space provided at the side or the bottom of the card and/or written anywhere on the front, including over the picture. It was during this period that real-photo postcards came into prominence.

As of March 1, 1907, the U.S. Postal Service permitted the back of postcards to be divided by a vertical line with the message to the left and the address to the right of the line (see page 38). This initiates the divided-back period which, for the purpose of postcard history, is considered to last until 1915 (the beginning of World War I). During this time, hundreds of millions of postcards were mailed each year in the United States. People not only used postcards for messages but also generally viewed the cards as desirable as souvenirs and pictorial records. Collecting postcards (both unused and mailed) and keeping them in albums had become a craze. People exchanged cards as collectibles, and sometimes the message on a card included a request to be sent a view card in return. This period plus the preceding few years is commonly referred to as the golden age of postcards. During this time, Germany was the world leader in postcard production, largely due to its superior printing and production technology, and most U.S. postcards were printed in Germany.

World War I brought the postcard business with Germany to an end, and then most American postcards were made in the United States. In an effort to reduce production costs by saving ink, postcards manufactured from about 1915 to 1930 had a white border around the front (see page 39). Although the use of white borders continued later, the period from about 1915 to 1930 is termed the white-border period.

Beginning about 1930, great quantities of postcards were printed with brightly colored inks on paper having a high rag content and a linenlike textured look (see page 30). Although the image covers the entire card on many linen postcards, they often have a white border, a carryover from the previous period. Also, it is not unusual for a white-bordered linen card to have the same view as appeared earlier on a postcard from the white-border period. The linen period is considered to date from about 1930 to 1950, although linens were made well into the 1950s.

Chrome (photochrome) postcards (see page 112) are the familiar glossy, colored photographic postcards of recent times. They first appeared in 1939 and by the late 1940s had become the most common or the standard type of postcard. The chrome period overlaps the linen period and is considered to extend from about 1940 to the present time.

A word about postage rates: from the passage of the Private Mailing Card Act in 1898 until 1952, the rate was 1¢, except during the World War I years when postage was raised to 2¢. In 1952, postage was again raised to 2¢, and rates have continued to increase since then.

This book was written because of our interest in postcards as pictorial records of the past and our strong interest in Martinsville and Morgan County history. We hope you find the book to be as enjoyable, interesting, and informative as it has been for us to prepare it.

—Curtis Tomak

One

Lesser-Known Sanitariums

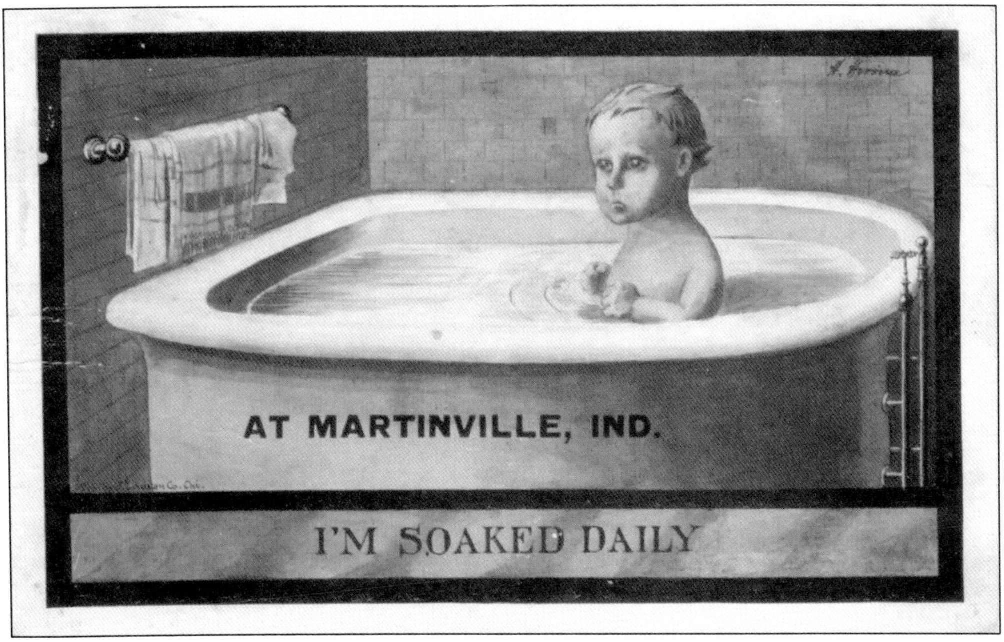

"I'm Soaked Daily," *c.* **1910.** The missing *S* on this comic card did not throw off a local postcard collector who knew this tyke in the bathtub and the tongue-in-cheek caption referred to Martinsville's mineral water sanitariums. Once- or twice-daily baths in the water, plus medicinal swigs and an amazing array of other period treatments supervised by a physician, were the standard treatment for a variety of physical ailments.

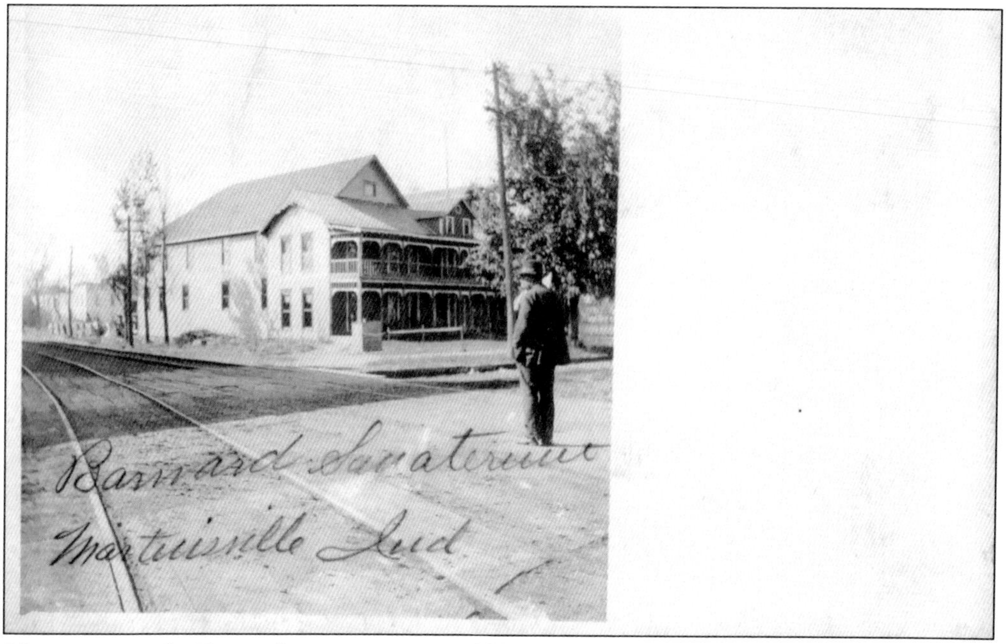

MARTINSVILLE'S FIRST SANITARIUM, *c.* 1905. In July 1887, water was discovered while drilling for gas on property owned by Elizabeth Barnard on the south side of Morgan Street west of the railroad. Disappointment turned to advantage when scientists praised the water's medicinal properties. A year later, Elizabeth's husband, Sylvanus, constructed a bathhouse with a pool, steam room, and small rooms with tubs. The man in the photograph may be the Barnards' son Henry.

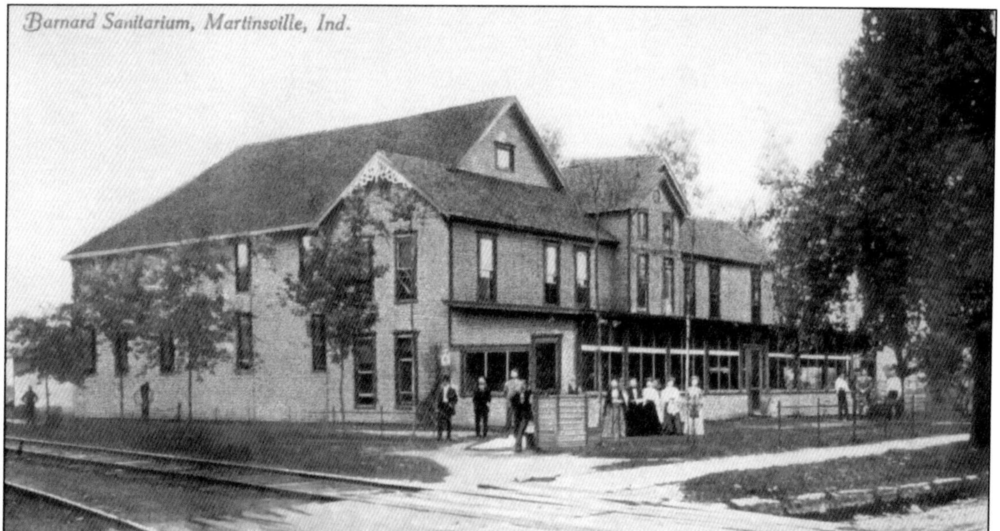

BARNARD SANITARIUM, 1908. Following a fire in 1889, a new two-story bathhouse was built. Guests, who lodged in the city's hotels, boardinghouses, and private homes, sought relief from a variety of ailments—tuberculosis, cancer, digestive disorders, kidney and bladder diseases, acne, alcoholism, depression, impotence, constipation, rheumatism—by bathing in and drinking the water.

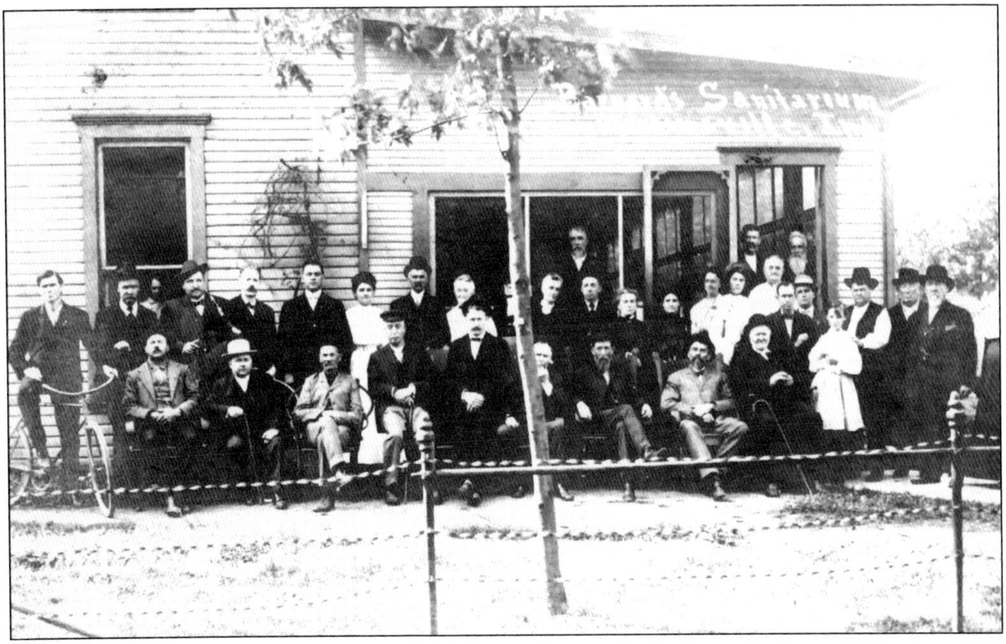

GROUP PHOTOGRAPH OF GUESTS, 1907. According to the *Indianapolis News*, "[Martinsville's mineral water] was certainly nasty enough to cure anything, if nastiness is what makes a good remedy, and, as everybody knows, the chief characteristic of medicine is its offensiveness." So successful was the bathhouse that Sylvanus Barnard enlarged and renovated it in 1890.

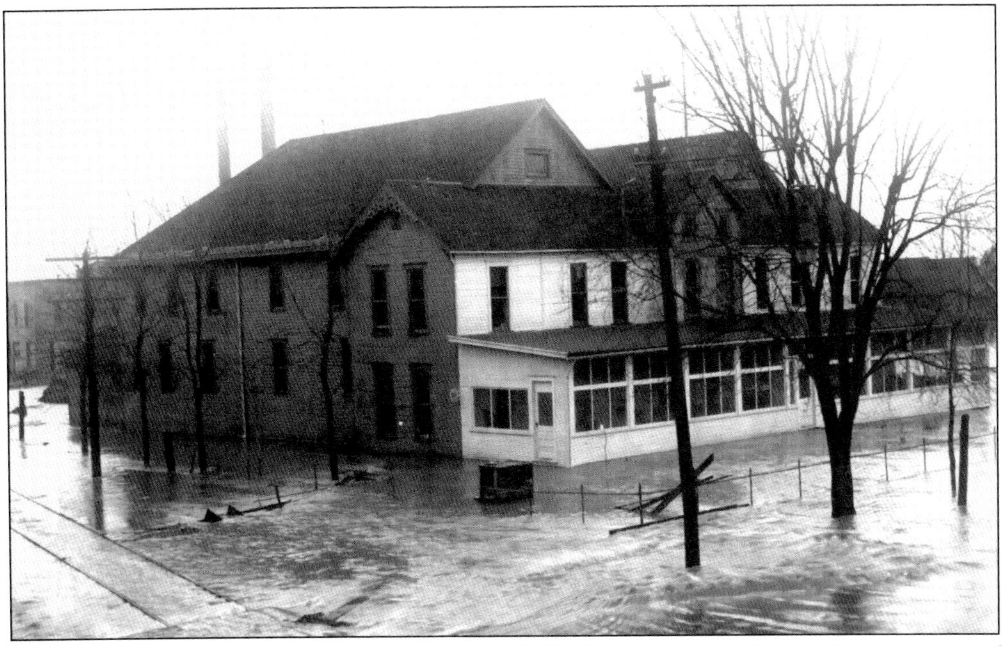

BARNARD SANITARIUM IN FLOODWATERS, 1913. On March 25, 1913, after two days of heavy rain, the White River overflowed its banks, submerging northwest Martinsville. Guests at the Barnard Sanitarium were evacuated to the city's other sanitariums and private homes that had been spared. On page 113 is a second flood photograph showing the Barnard Sanitarium from the rear.

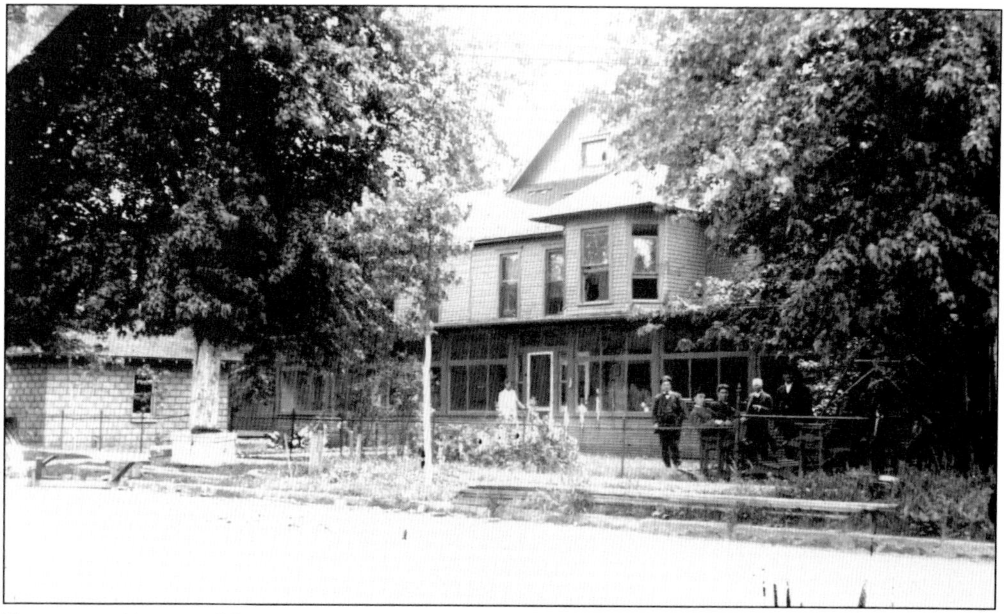

Barnard Family Members in Front of Sanitarium, 1920. Martinsville resident Bob Barnard is the great-great-grandson of Sylvanus Barnard. This real-photo postcard is part of a large collection of papers passed to him from his father. The white-haired gentleman in the middle of the group of men appears to be Sylvanus's son Henry, who retired in 1924. He died a year later.

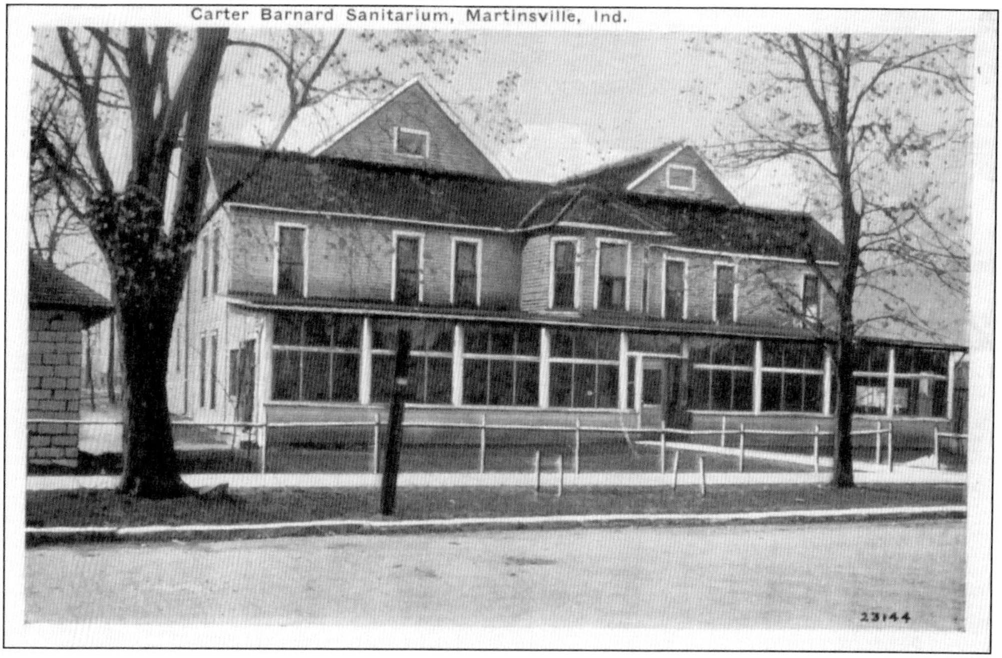

Carter-Barnard Sanitarium, *c.* 1925. Henry Barnard sold the sanitarium to Dr. O. M. Carter and two partners in 1924. Remodeling included the addition of a kitchen and dining room, laboratory, and private baths and lavatories. The small block building shown at the left in both cards on this page is the well house, said to have been used as a shelter by the railroad watchman who stopped automobile traffic at the Morgan Street crossing.

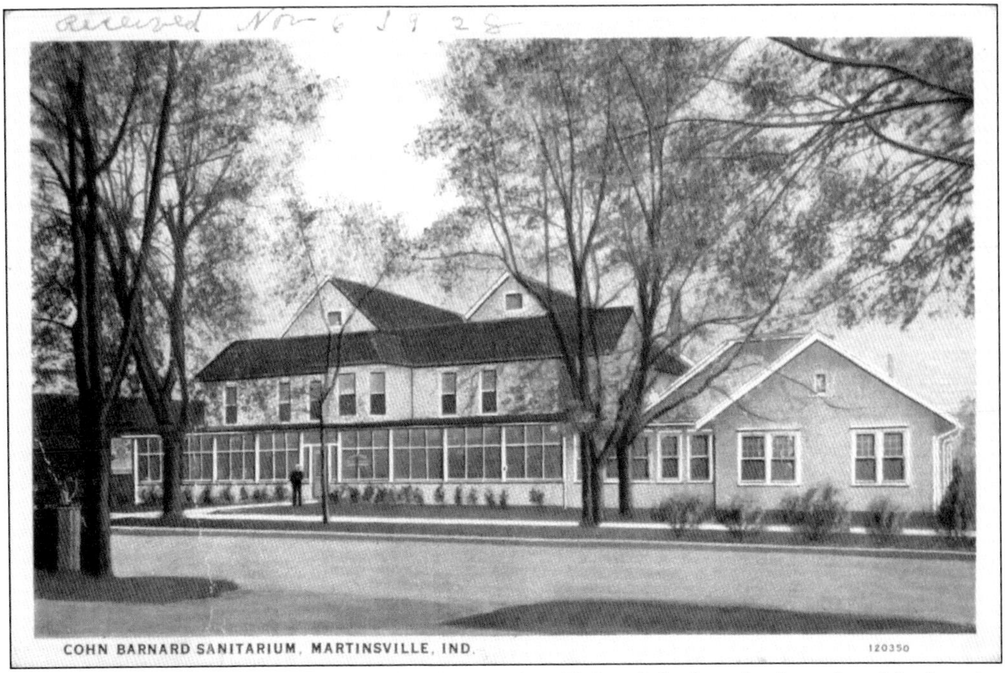

COHN-BARNARD SANITARIUM I, 1928. Martinsville's original sanitarium flourished under the ownership of David and Michael Cohn, father and son, who purchased the Carter-Barnard Sanitarium in 1926. The Cohn family came to Martinsville in 1903 and entered the sanitarium business. Upon David's death in 1933, Michael and his wife, Dolly, took over operations of the Cohn-Barnard Sanitarium. It was destroyed by fire on February 4, 1940.

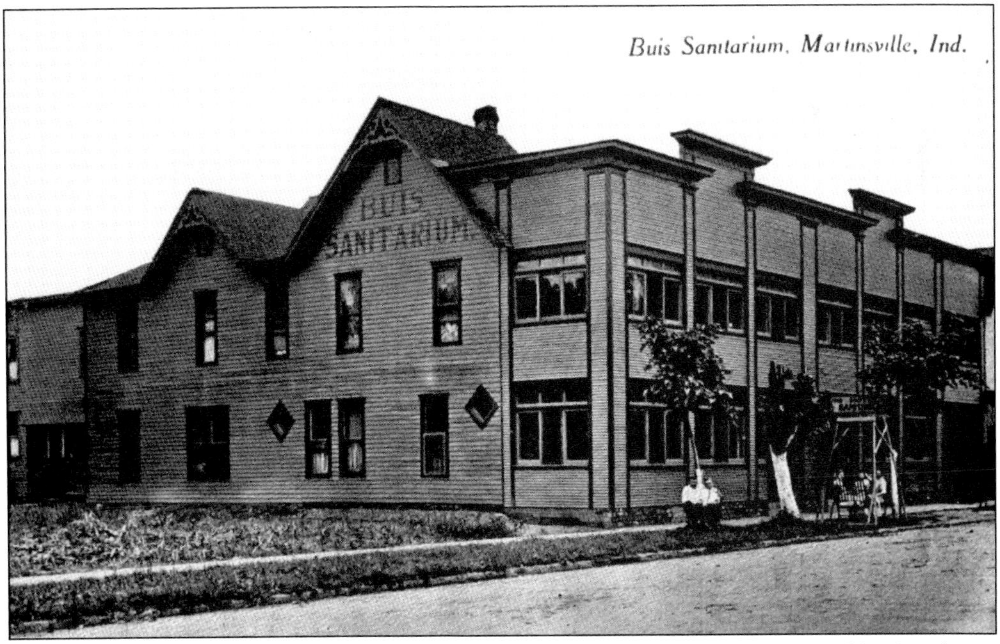

BUIS SANITARIUM, C. 1915. In 1915, Reason Buis drilled a well and converted his hotel into the Buis Sanitarium, located on the southeast corner of Marion and Pike Streets. The original frame hotel is easily distinguished from the two-story sunporch addition facing north.

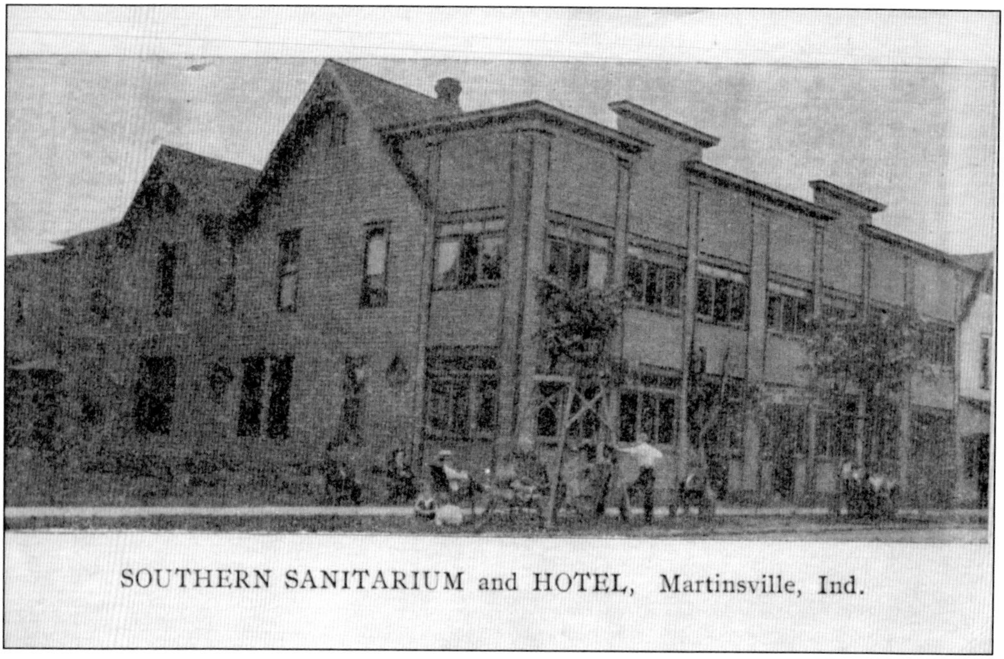

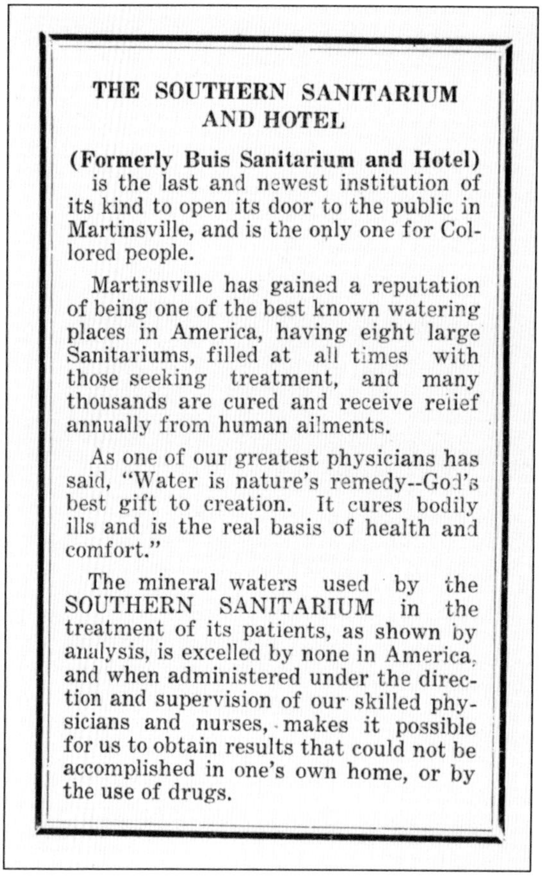

THE SOUTHERN SANITARIUM AND HOTEL

(Formerly Buis Sanitarium and Hotel) is the last and newest institution of its kind to open its door to the public in Martinsville, and is the only one for Colored people.

Martinsville has gained a reputation of being one of the best known watering places in America, having eight large Sanitariums, filled at all times with those seeking treatment, and many thousands are cured and receive relief annually from human ailments.

As one of our greatest physicians has said, "Water is nature's remedy--God's best gift to creation. It cures bodily ills and is the real basis of health and comfort."

The mineral waters used by the SOUTHERN SANITARIUM in the treatment of its patients, as shown by analysis, is excelled by none in America, and when administered under the direction and supervision of our skilled physicians and nurses, makes it possible for us to obtain results that could not be accomplished in one's own home, or by the use of drugs.

SOUTHERN SANITARIUM AND HOTEL, C. 1920. Four years after opening, the Buis was sold, renamed, remodeled, and reopened as the Southern Sanitarium and Hotel, which catered to blacks. Closed in 1926, it was purchased by the Branch Grain and Seed Company and razed. This card is a trade card not intended for mailing; however, both the front and back sides are shown, as this is the only known image of the Southern Sanitarium.

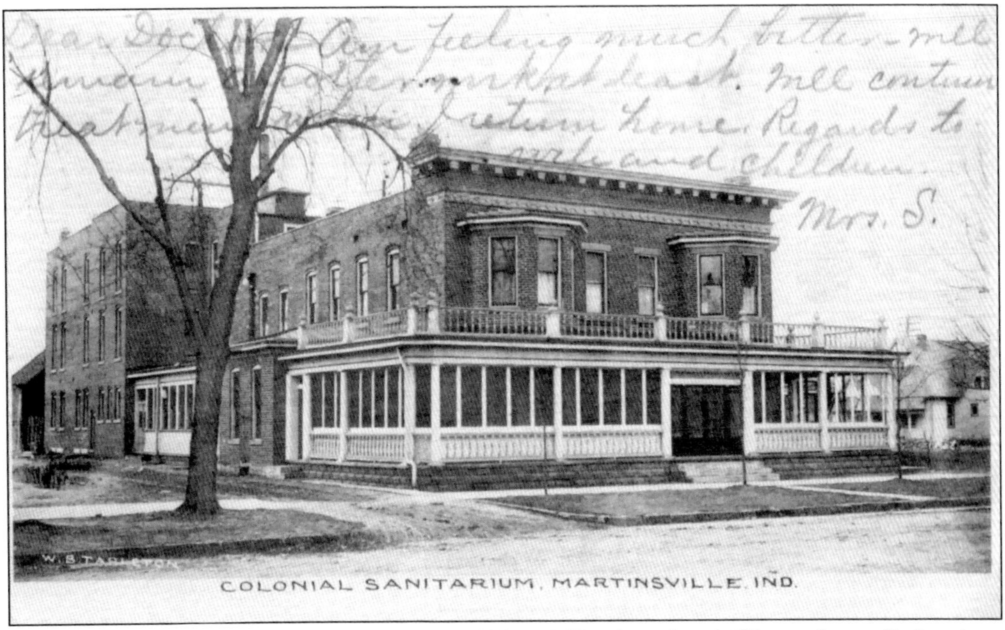

COLONIAL MINERAL SPRINGS HOTEL, 1907. Following the drilling of a well, brothers James V., Charles J., and Edgar V. Mitchell refitted a brick apartment building as a 65-room sanitarium, celebrating its grand opening on February 4, 1906. Mrs. S. writes, "Dear Doctor, Am feeling much better—will remain another week at least. Will continue treatment when I return home. Regards to wife and children."

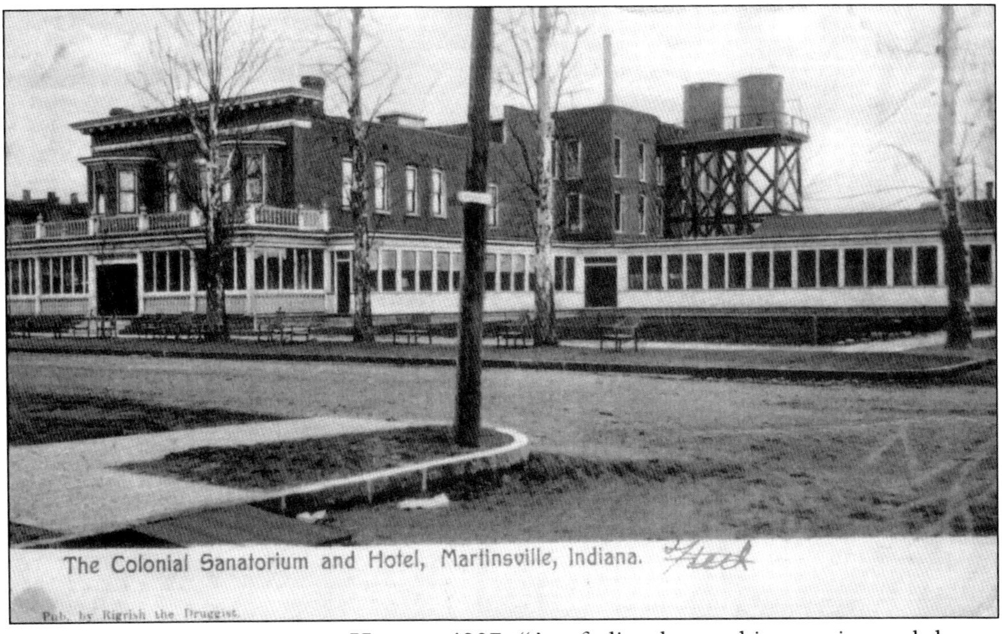

COLONIAL SANITARIUM AND HOTEL, 1907. "Am feeling better this morning and do not think I'll be home until next week," writes Harry. "Had an all night rain last night. Are having a full house now met two people that I knew . . . Two came here yesterday from West Baden in very bad condition. One of them took ten mud baths with no results and now he is here And of course he expects help."

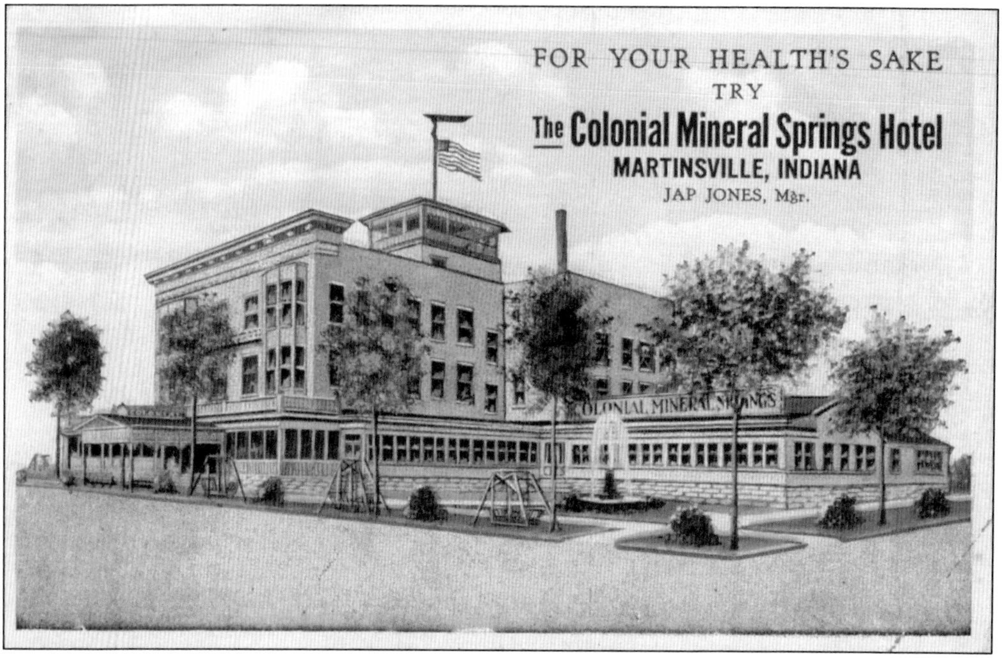

COLONIAL SANITARIUM, *c.* 1908. Located at the southeast corner of Washington and Mulberry Streets, the sanitarium underwent extensive improvements in early 1907, including the addition of a third floor, a coat of pale yellow paint, and the landscaped grounds shown here. Guests enjoyed mineral baths, vapor baths, a cooling room, and Turkish baths.

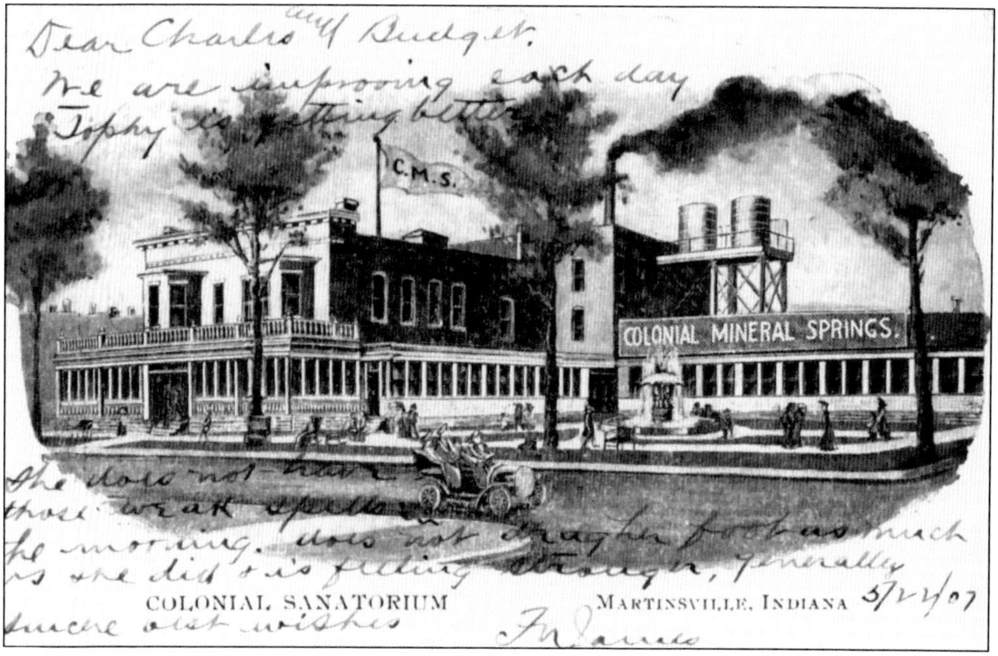

COLONIAL SANITARIUM, 1907. F. W. Jones, the sender of this card, writes, "Dear Charles and Bridget, We are improving each day. Sophy is getting better. She does not have those weak spells in the morning, does not drag her foot as much as she did, and is feeling stronger, generally. Sincere best wishes."

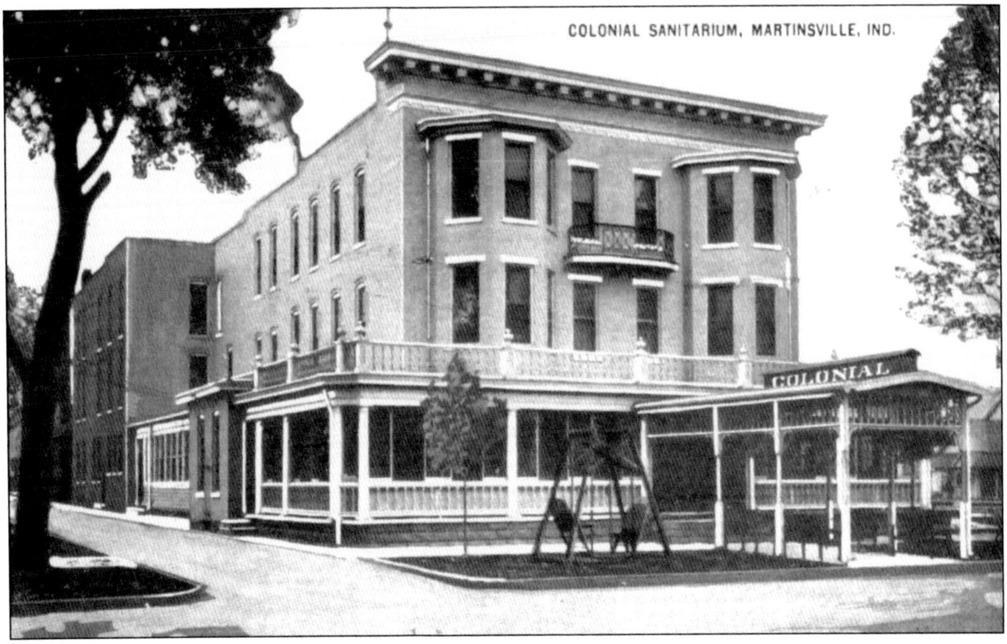

COLONIAL SANITARIUM, *c.* 1910. Martinsville's booming sanitarium industry contributed to the city's prosperity, providing reliable employment and spawning the development of important allied food-, retail-, and service-oriented businesses. With the promise of year-round work at good wages, the industry also attracted new residents. Between 1890 and 1900, the population of Martinsville doubled. In 1900, more than 200 new houses were built.

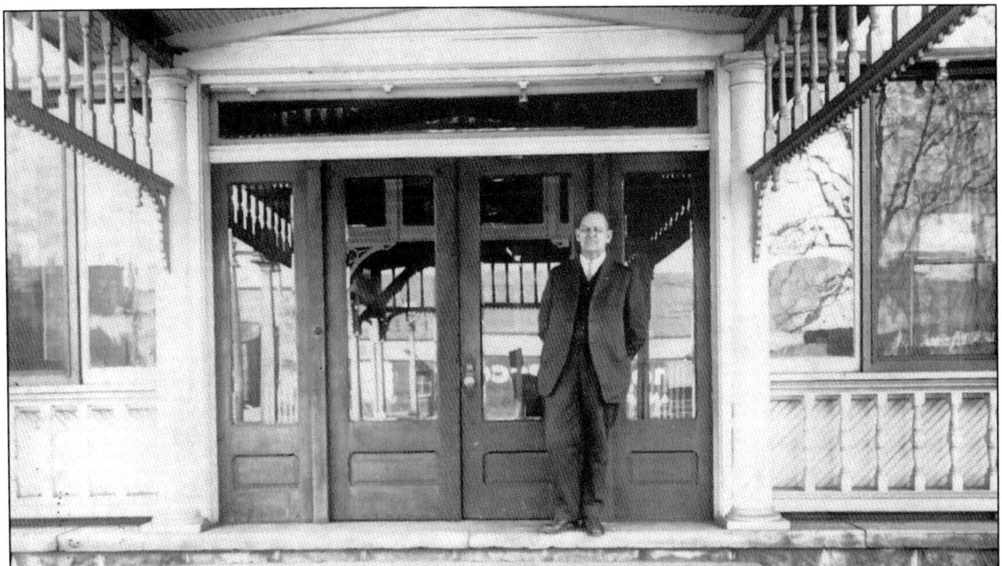

DR. BENJAMIN W. TILFORD, *c.* 1915. Born in Martinsville in 1859, Tilford was a graduate of the Medical College of Indiana, receiving his Morgan County license in 1897. During his lifetime, he served as city clerk; was employed at Tilford Drugstore, owned by his brother Roy; and was clerk at the Colonial Sanitarium. He is seen here at the front entrance. When he died in 1932, he was secretary of the Home Building Association.

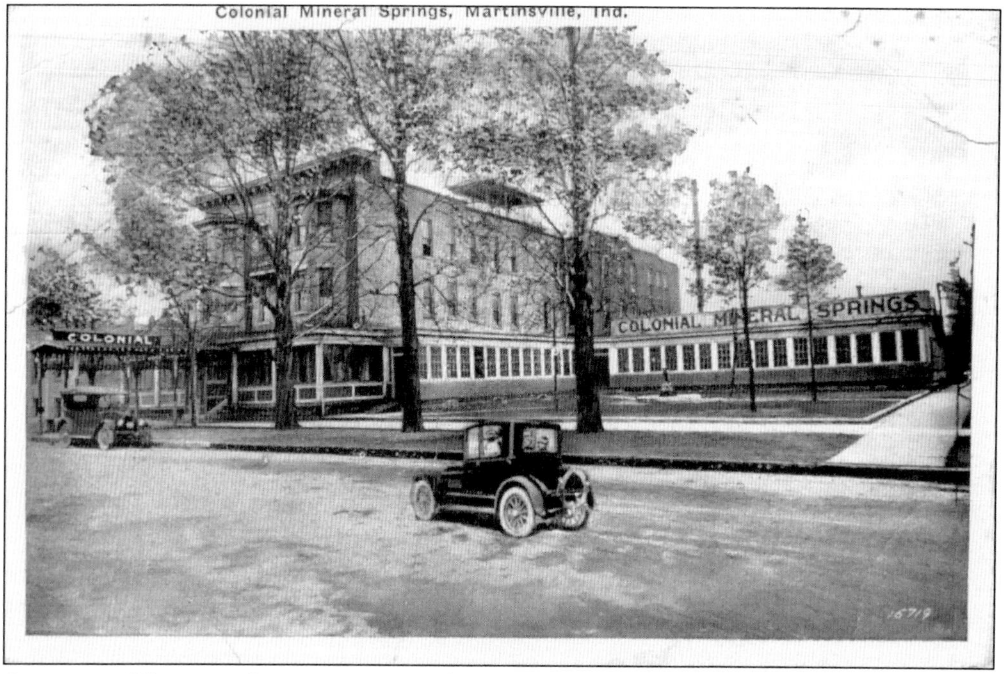

COLONIAL MINERAL SPRINGS, 1924. The personal automobile made Americans no longer dependent on the train or interurban. While the automobile made it easier for Americans to travel on a whim, it also made it possible for them to go anywhere they desired. Many fell out of the habit of a one- or two-week stay in Martinsville.

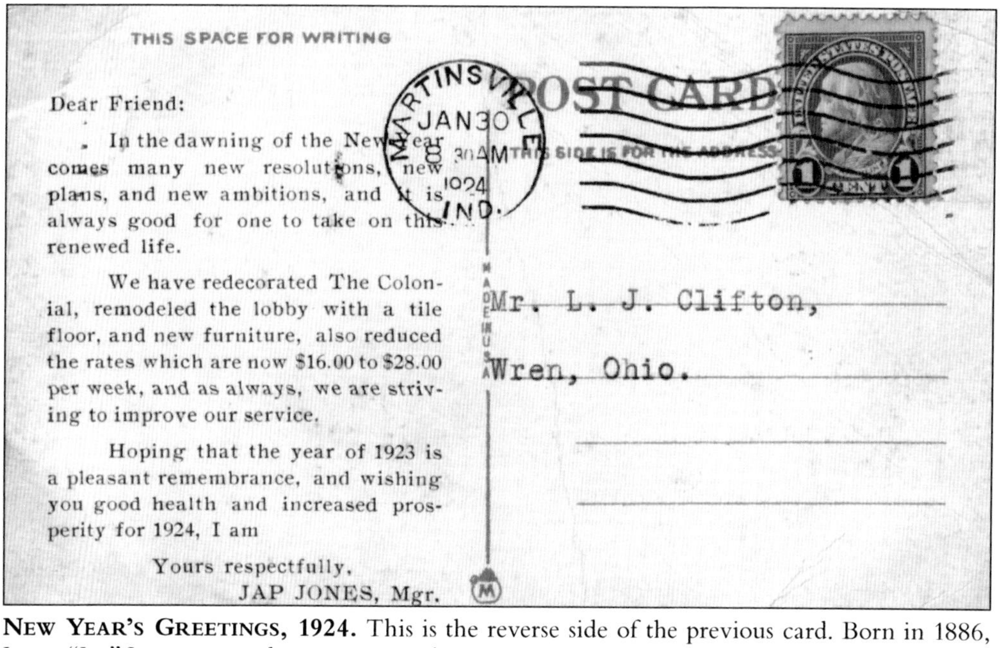

THIS SPACE FOR WRITING

POST CARD

THIS SIDE IS FOR THE ADDRESS

MARTINSVILLE JAN 30 8 30 AM 1924 IND.

Dear Friend:

In the dawning of the New Year comes many new resolutions, new plans, and new ambitions, and it is always good for one to take on this renewed life.

We have redecorated The Colonial, remodeled the lobby with a tile floor, and new furniture, also reduced the rates which are now $16.00 to $28.00 per week, and as always, we are striving to improve our service.

Hoping that the year of 1923 is a pleasant remembrance, and wishing you good health and increased prosperity for 1924, I am

Yours respectfully,
JAP JONES, Mgr.

Mr. L. J. Clifton,
Wren, Ohio.

NEW YEAR'S GREETINGS, 1924. This is the reverse side of the previous card. Born in 1886, Jasper "Jap" Jones operated stores at Waverly, Mooresville, and Martinsville before managing and owning several sanitariums. He went on to establish the Jap Jones chain of hotels. He was elected to the Indiana House of Representatives on the Democratic ticket and served as chairman of the Indiana State Highway Commission under Gov. Henry F. Schricker. Jones died in 1965.

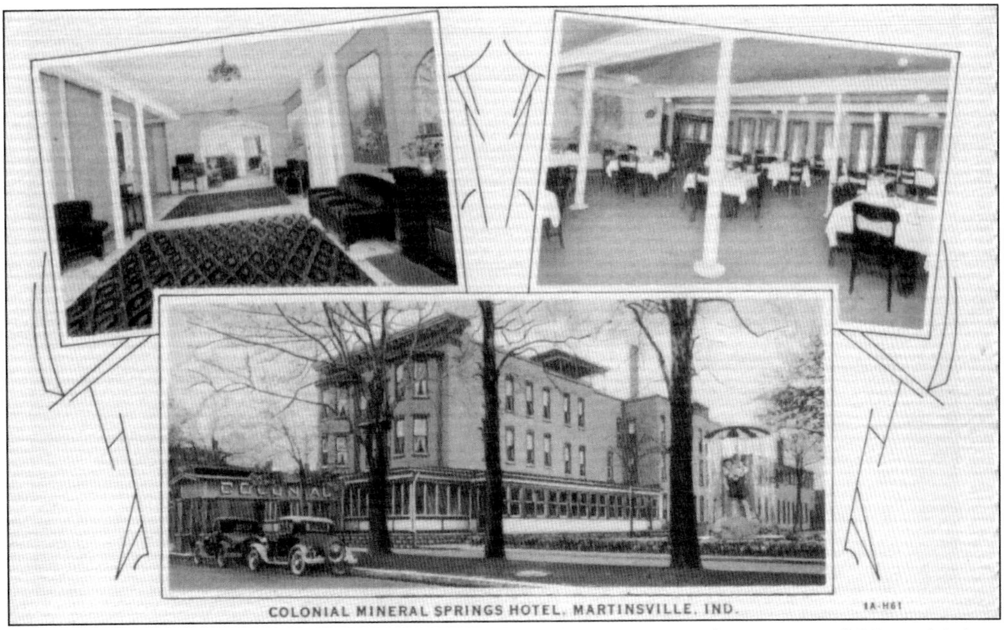

Colonial Mineral Springs Hotel, c. 1930. The caption on the reverse of this multiview postcard reads, "The Colonial Mineral Springs Hotel and Sanitarium (That home-like place). Delicious Food. Courteous Service. Moderate Rates. Famous Mineral Baths under the supervision of an ethical qualified Medical Staff. Scientifically heated and ventilated Bath Department. We recommend the Colonial."

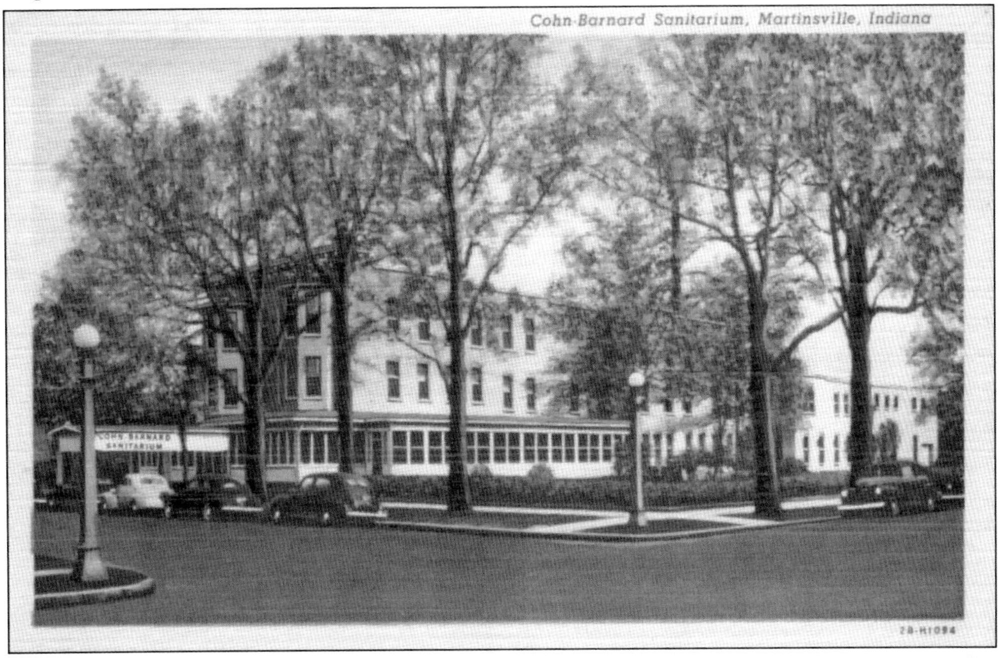

Colonial as Cohn-Barnard Sanitarium II, c. 1940. Following the February 1940 fire that destroyed the Cohn-Barnard Sanitarium, Michael Cohn purchased the Colonial Sanitarium, which had been vacant for several years, and renamed it Cohn-Barnard. Two months of extensive repairs, redecorating, and refurnishing were followed by a May 30 grand reopening.

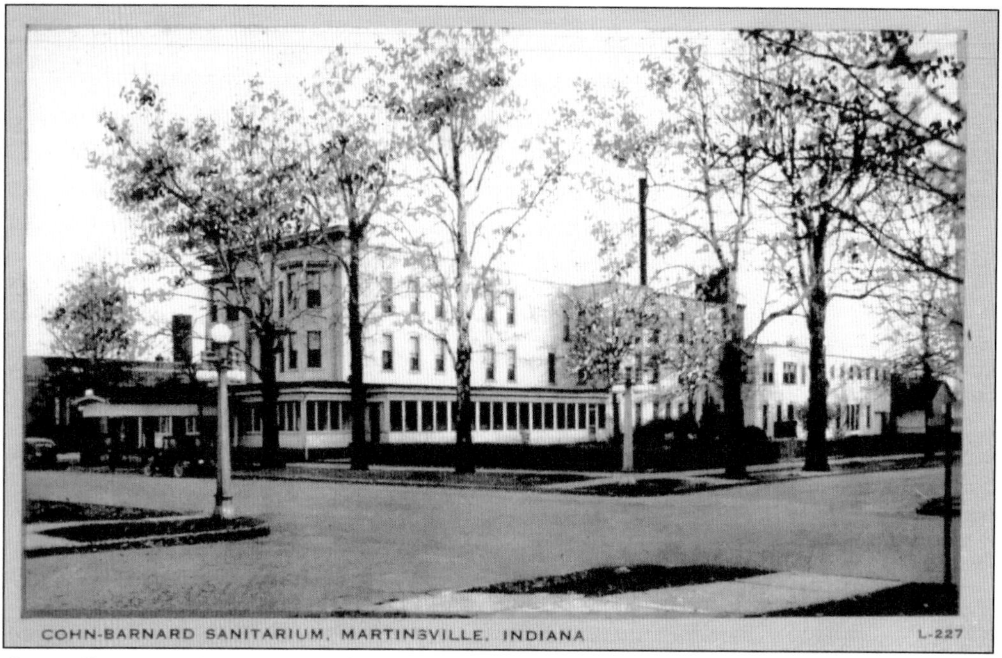

COHN-BARNARD II, *c.* 1945. The new Cohn-Barnard contained 50 rooms, public and private dining rooms, sun parlors, and second-floor bathing facilities. Rooms for card playing featured rustic furniture made by Martinsville's Indiana Willow Products Company. A memorable feature of the lobby was a pair of identical fireplace mantels decorated with mirrored glass and colorful pottery. Mahogany staircases had white trim and blue carpet.

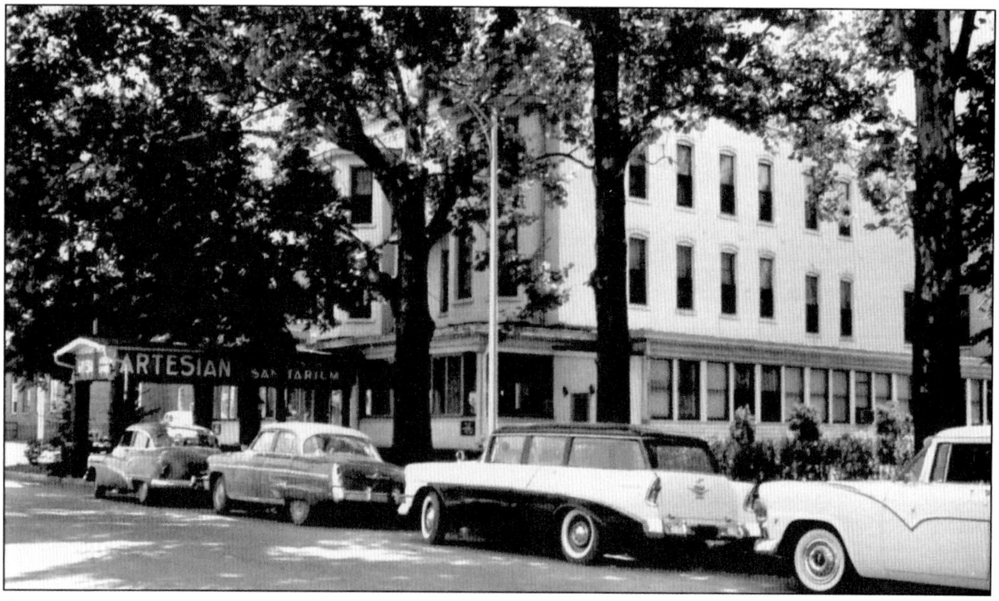

ARTESIAN SANITARIUM, *c.* 1955. The post–World War II years were marked by a dramatic decline in the sanitarium industry, owing to advances in medicine and transportation and changes in Americans' recreational interests. In 1955, after a 50-year career, Michael Cohn sold the Cohn-Barnard II to Dr. David Eisenberg, former owner of the Whiting Sanitarium. Eisenberg renamed it the Artesian. It closed in 1962 and was torn down a year later.

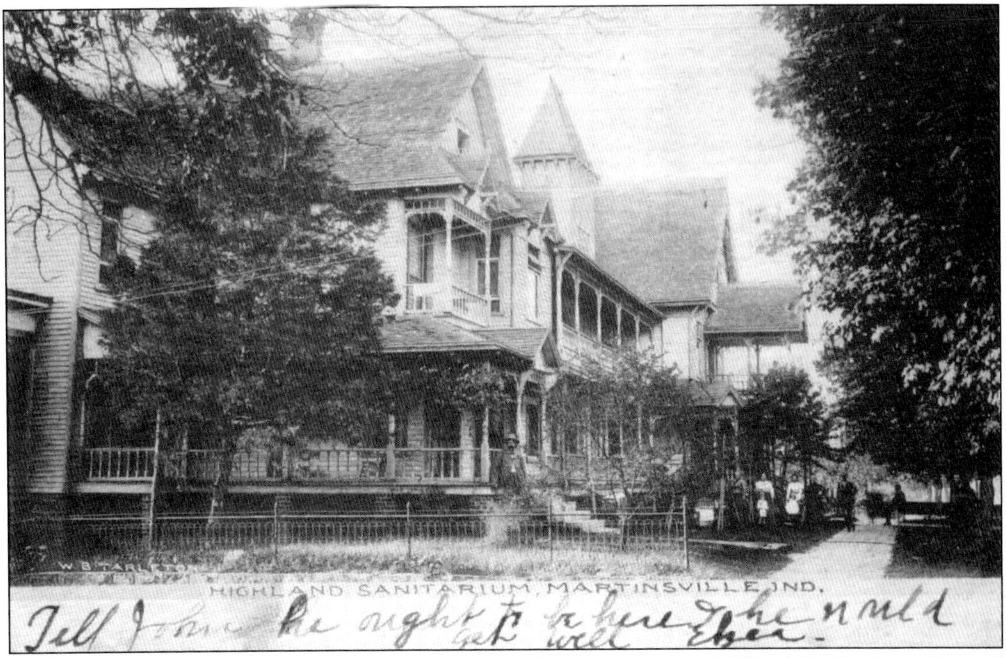

HIGHLAND SANITARIUM, 1907. Built in 1896, the three-story Highland Sanitarium, located on the west side of Main Street north of Highland Street, boasted 70 guest rooms, 10 bathrooms, electric lights, steam heat, indoor recreation rooms, and an expansive east porch. "Tell John he ought to be here and he would get well," writes the sender of this undivided-back card.

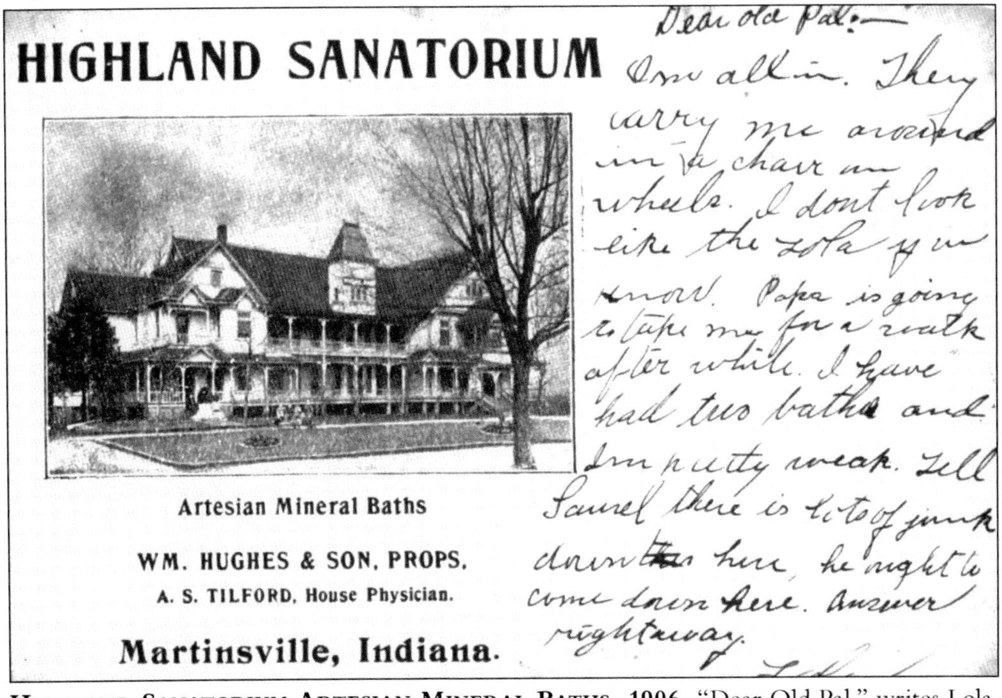

HIGHLAND SANATORIUM ARTESIAN MINERAL BATHS, 1906. "Dear Old Pal," writes Lola. "I am all in. They carry me around in a chair on wheels. I don't look like the Lola you know. Papa is going to take me for a walk after while. I have had two baths and I'm pretty weak.

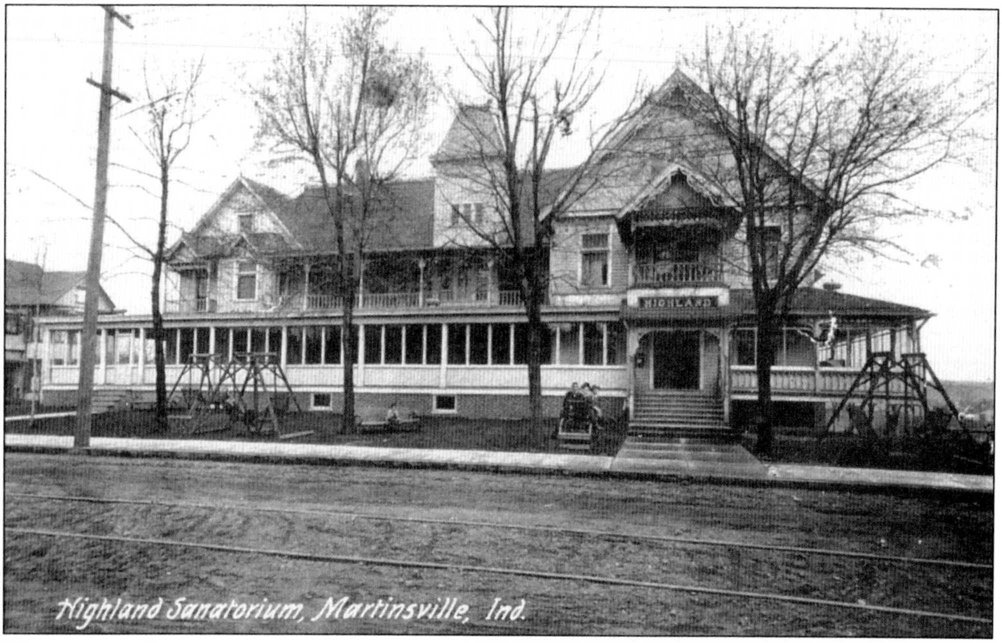

HIGHLAND SANATORIUM, 1908. Situated on the west slope of Cunningham Hill and overlooking the White River valley, the Highland faced Main Street and the interurban tracks, which are clearly seen in this view. Early postcards alternate in the use of *sanatorium*—a long-term health care facility—and *sanitarium*—a health resort. Seemingly, Martinsville's mineral water industry was struggling to define itself and its clientele.

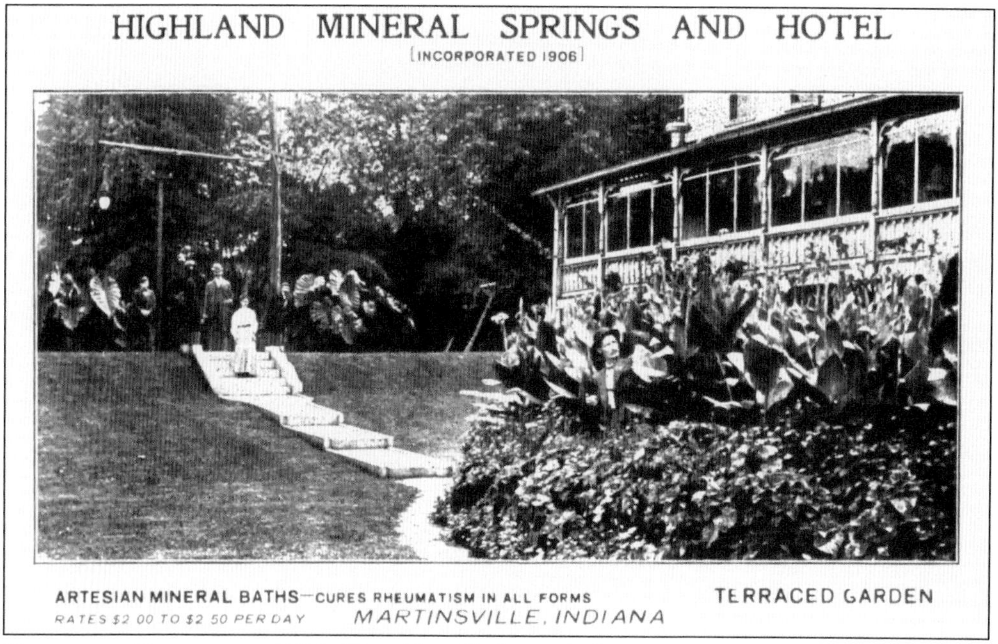

TERRACED GARDEN, C. 1908. The sidewalk descends from Main Street along the north side of the sanitarium. Note the suspended streetlamp above the elephant ears planted along the street and the man hidden in the bed of cannas. To many guests, Martinsville's quiet, rural character was a much welcome respite from the noise, filth, and commotion of the city.

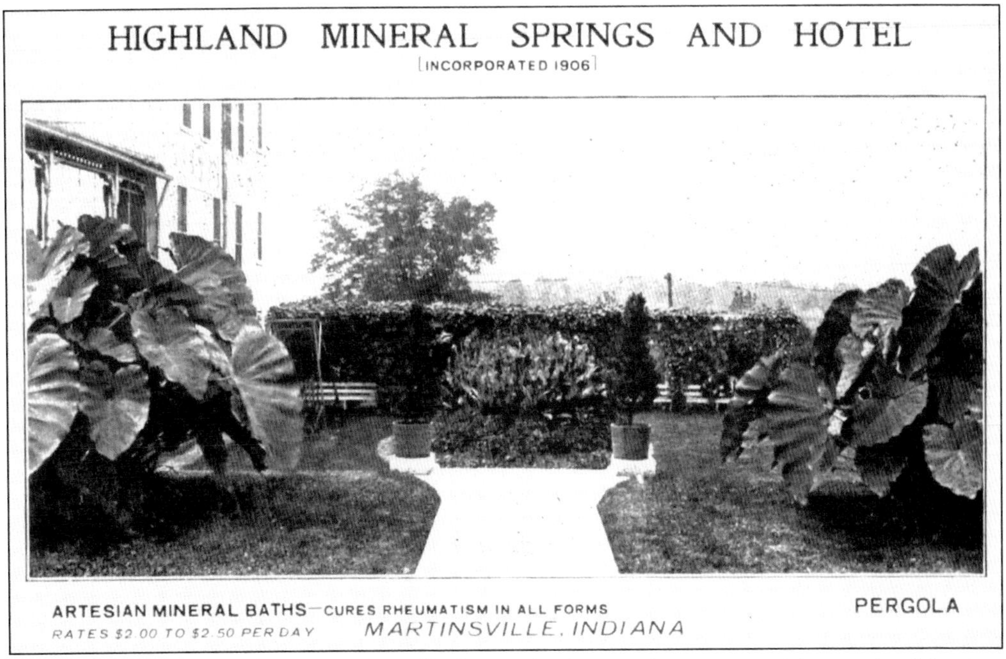

PERGOLA, C. 1908. The same sidewalk shown in the previous postcard is seen in this view looking west toward White River. "Together with its magnificent wooded hills, and with the lovely flowers, stately trees and cool fountains this site is unsurpassed for sanitarium purposes," gushed the *Daily Reporter.*

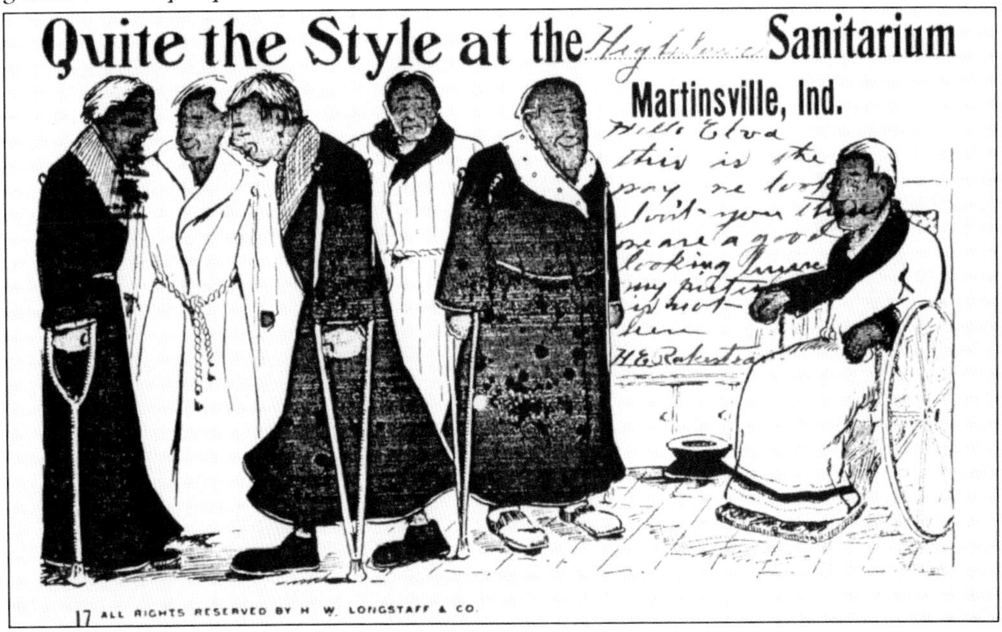

QUITE THE STYLE AT THE HIGHLAND SANITARIUM, C. 1906. H. E. Robertson, the sender of this comic card, writes in 1911, "Hello, Elva. This is the way we look, don't you think we are a good looking bunch. My picture is not seen." The fill-in-the-blank style of this card made it suitable for sale by any of the city's sanitariums. A guest merely had to write in the name of the spa he or she patronized.

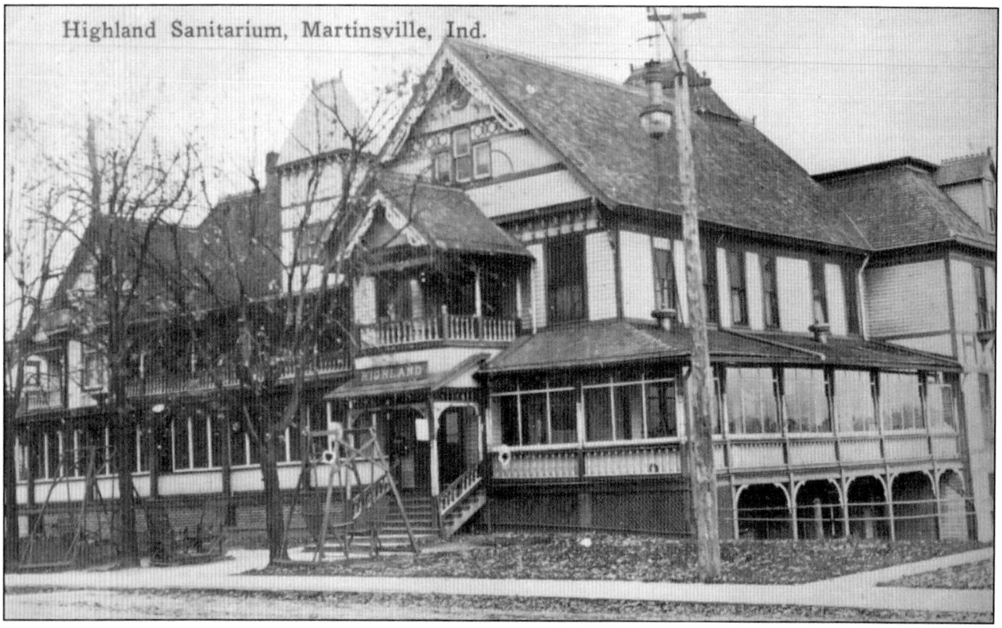

HIGHLAND SANITARIUM LOOKING SOUTHWEST, *c.* 1915. The Highland had many owners during its first 30 years. In 1923, Dr. Simon P. Scherer bought the sanitarium. According to the *Daily Reporter*, he brought "a broad vision of the possibilities for the institution . . . to be run as an intermediate between the family physician and the hospital."

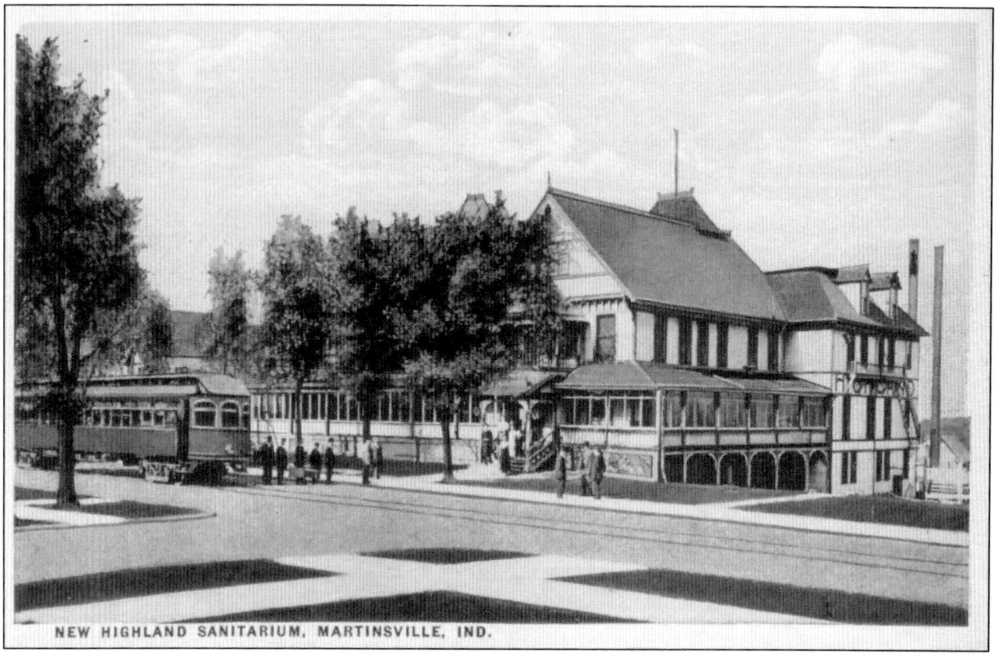

NEW HIGHLAND SANITARIUM AND INTERURBAN, *c.* 1923. Conveniently located on the interurban line, the New Highland enjoyed its own stop. Many guests walked on their own to the front entrance. Others arrived in such ill health that crutches, wheelchairs, and even gurneys were required to transport them the short distance. Still others were shuttled to the sanitarium from the Vandalia station a few blocks away.

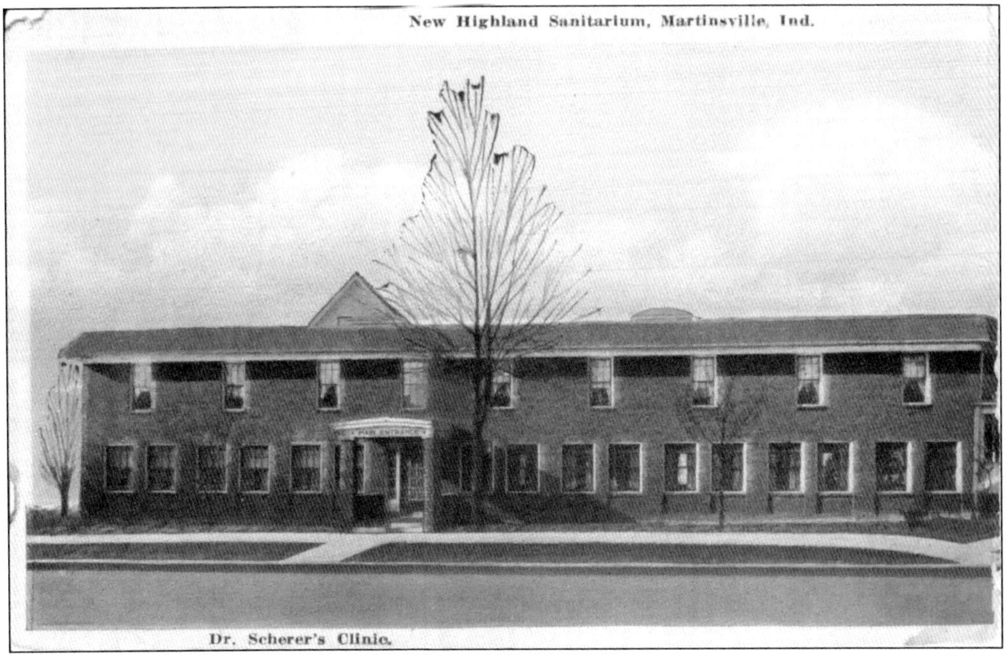

Dr. Scherer's Clinic, *c.* 1925. Scherer expanded the sanitarium along Main Street almost to Highland Street. The brick annex included a modern medical clinic with examination rooms, laboratory, physical therapy and x-ray departments, and a dental office. The "old run down institution" was entirely updated. This view is the left half of a bifold card.

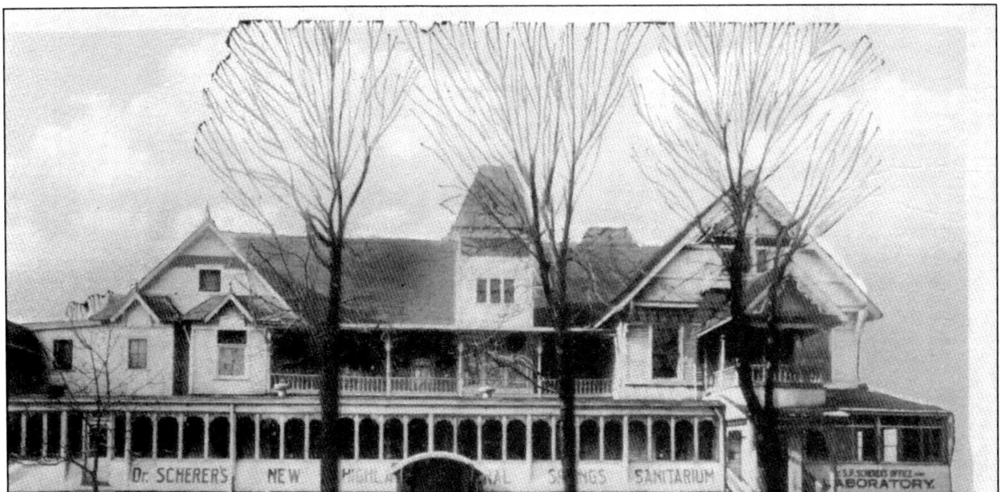

Dr. Scherer's New Highland Sanitarium, *c.* 1925. The card's right half shows the original sanitarium. Dr. Scherer provided "the burden bearers of the commercial world" and "captains of industry" with treatments that would "better enable them to conduct the work appropriate to their support."

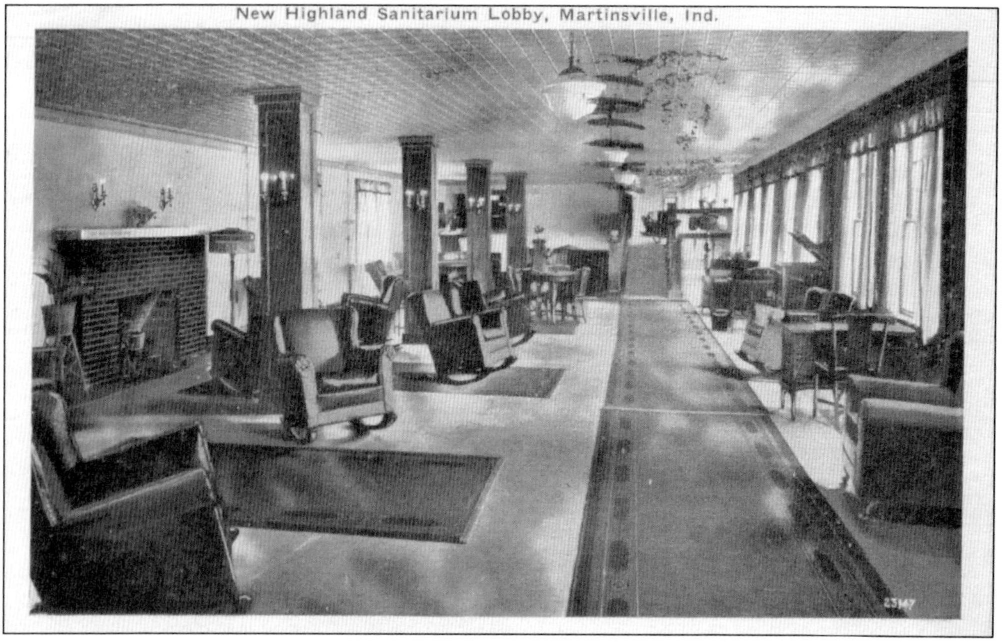

New Highland Sanitarium Lobby, c. 1925. Located in the annex, the "new up to the minute lobby with a grand old fireplace" was linked to the "sanitarium proper" by an "inclined plane passageway." The color scheme included walls tinted in "mellow straw color," natural woodwork, an ivory ceiling, gray and brown floors, tan furniture, and gray and black draperies.

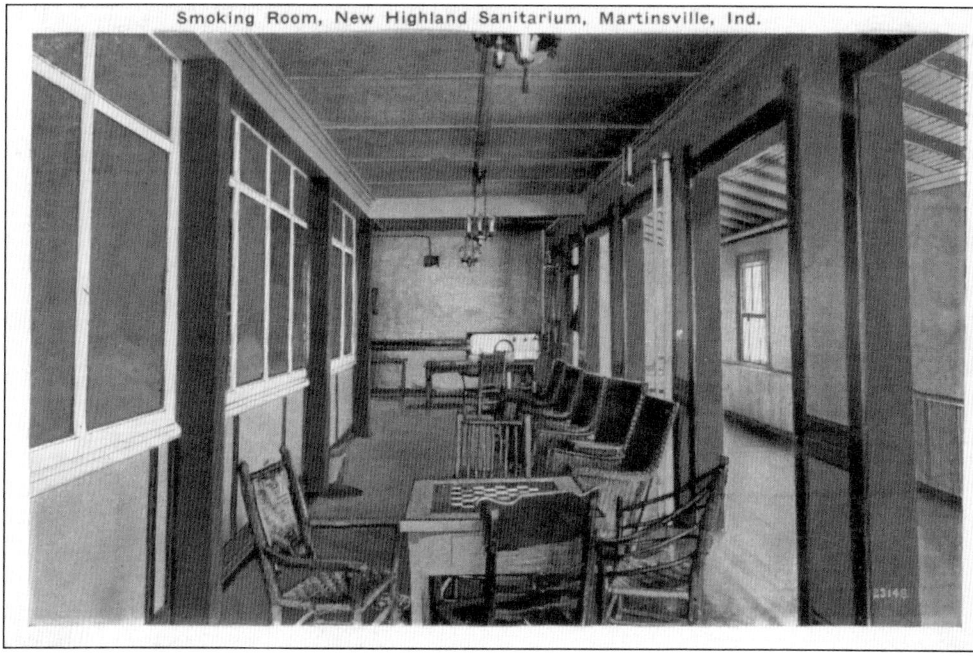

Smoking Room, c. 1925. A hickory chair, a game of checkers, and a fine cigar or hand-rolled cigarette were the perfect closure to a day spent in the pursuit of health and wellness. "God forbid that any should fail to get relief who come in Spirit and Truth," said period promotional literature. "Come to the 'Water of Life' and drink freely."

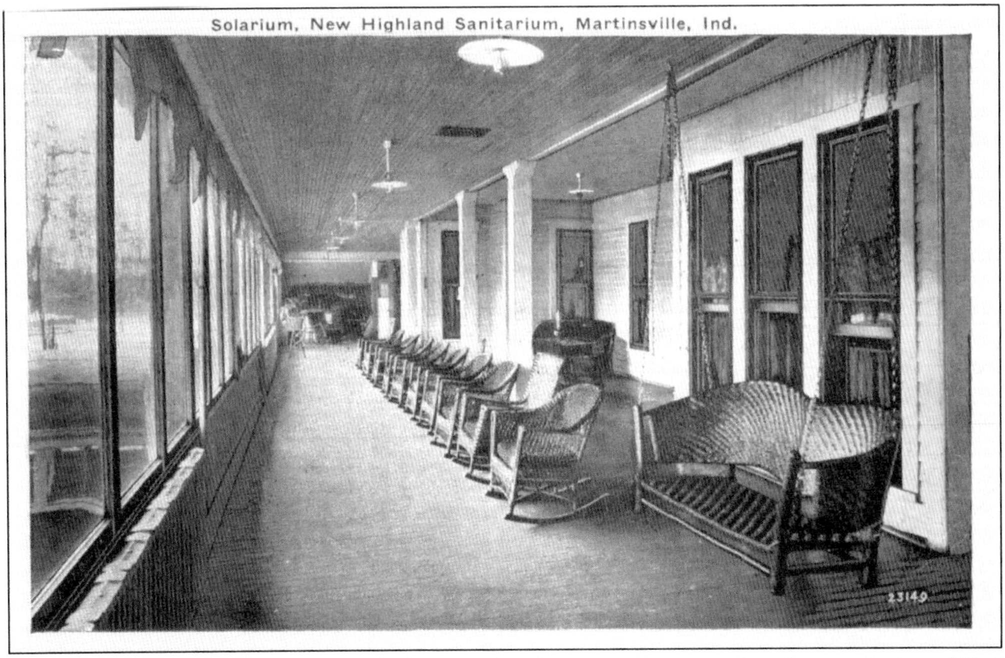

Solarium, c. 1925. The original glass-enclosed sunporch was updated as a solarium filled with comfortable wicker rockers facing Main Street. Radiators against the front wall heated the room for cold weather. A Martinsville-made Old Hickory settee is suspended by chains from the ceiling. The clapboard siding of the original sanitarium can be seen on the back wall.

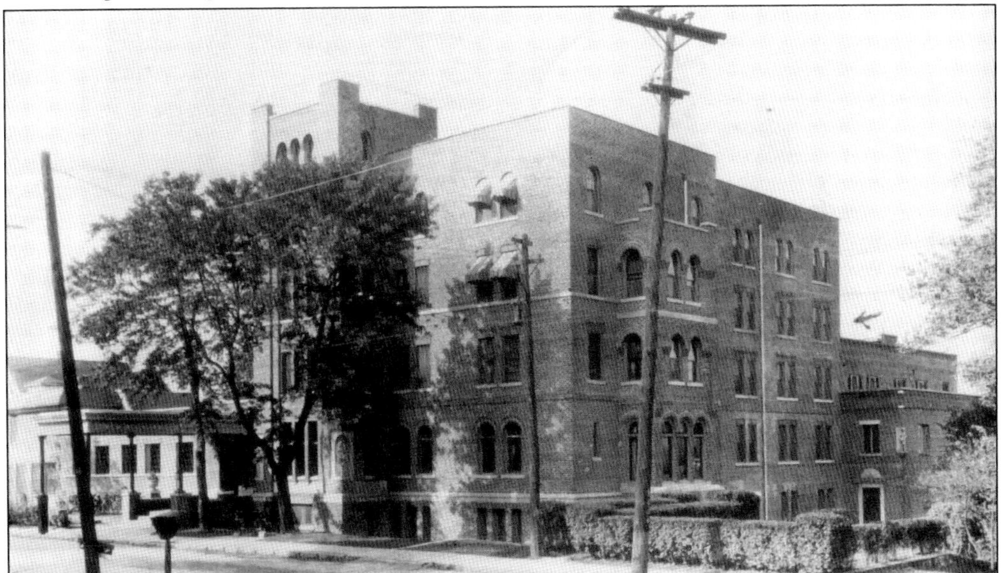

New Five-Story Addition, 1930. In 1928–1929, a Spanish Revival–style, five-story building replaced the northern third of the original sanitarium. The new building's "quaint atmosphere" was derived from the adobe finish of the walls, enamel tile wainscoting, "Terrazza [*sic*] floors," and Mediterranean light fixtures and furniture. Tragedy followed triumph a month later when on March 11, 1929, the remainder of the frame building, which Scherer planned to eventually raze, was destroyed by fire.

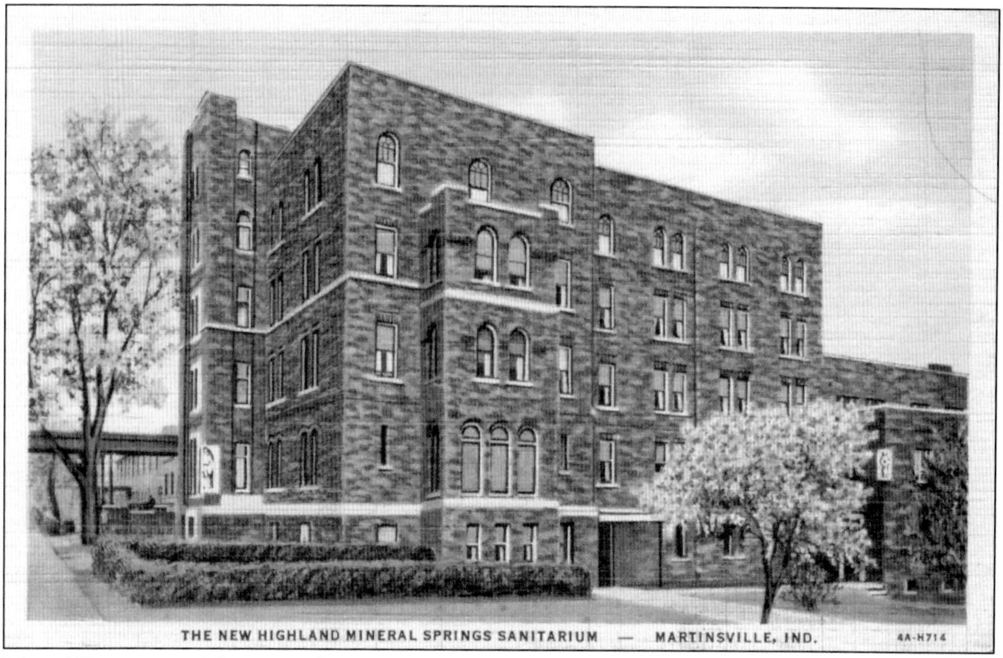

New Highland Mineral Springs Sanitarium, Front and Reverse, c. 1940. The 1929 building was championed as "the most modern hotel and health clinic in the central states" by the *Indianapolis Medical Journal*. It boasted completely fireproof construction, an indoor swimming pool—the first in Martinsville—lit by a vita-glass skylight, a roof garden, a spacious solarium, and tennis courts. The reverse side of this linen card resumes the decades-old debate between *sanitarium* and *sanatorium*.

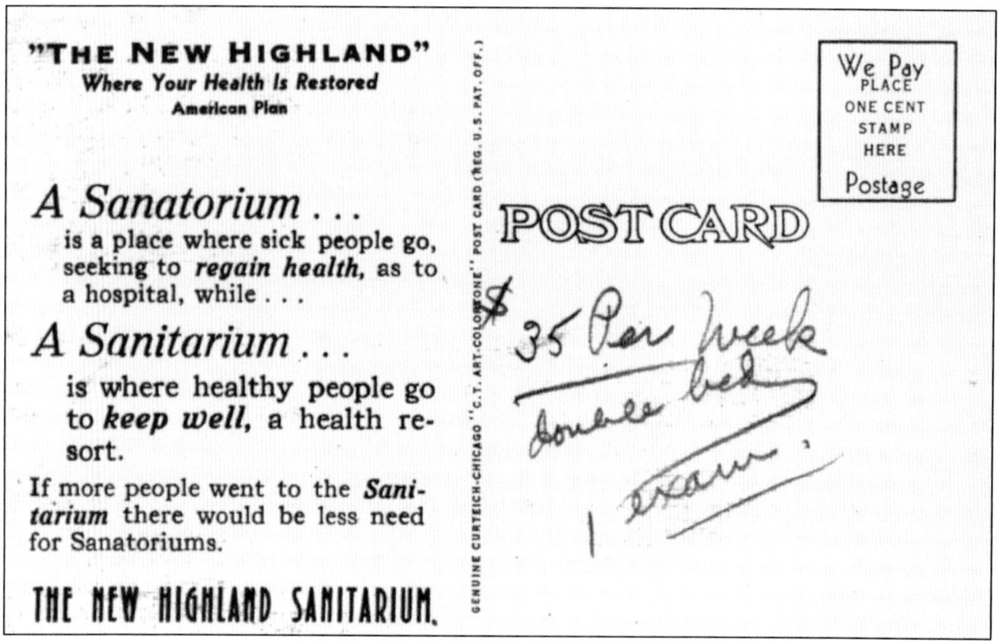

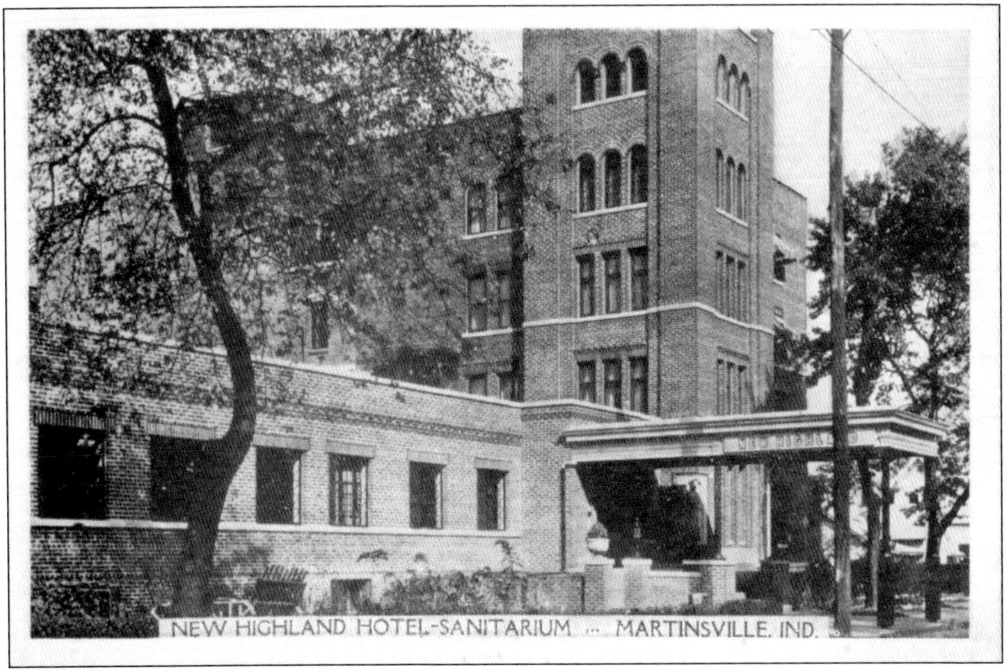

NEW HIGHLAND HOTEL-SANITARIUM, C. 1930. The one-story brick sunroom shown here replaced the portion of the original sanitarium destroyed in the March 1929 fire. At the time of its grand opening, the new five-story building was declared "fireproof in every detail—the last word in noncombustible hotel construction." Put to the supreme test, it passed with flying colors.

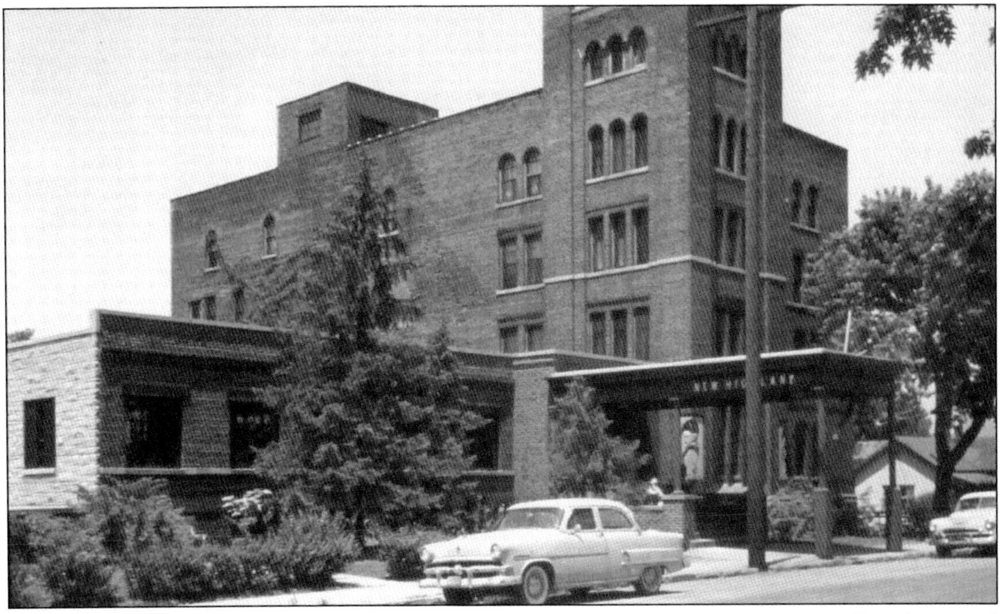

NEW HIGHLAND NEARING CLOSURE, C. 1950. On February 7, 1951, a fire destroyed Dr. Scherer's 1923 clinic. By this time, Martinsville's sanitarium industry had nearly come to an end. The New Highland was closed. Hopes to convert it into first a nursing home and then a retirement home never materialized. In 1971, following extensive renovation, the New Highland reopened as Morgan House, a federally subsidized housing project.

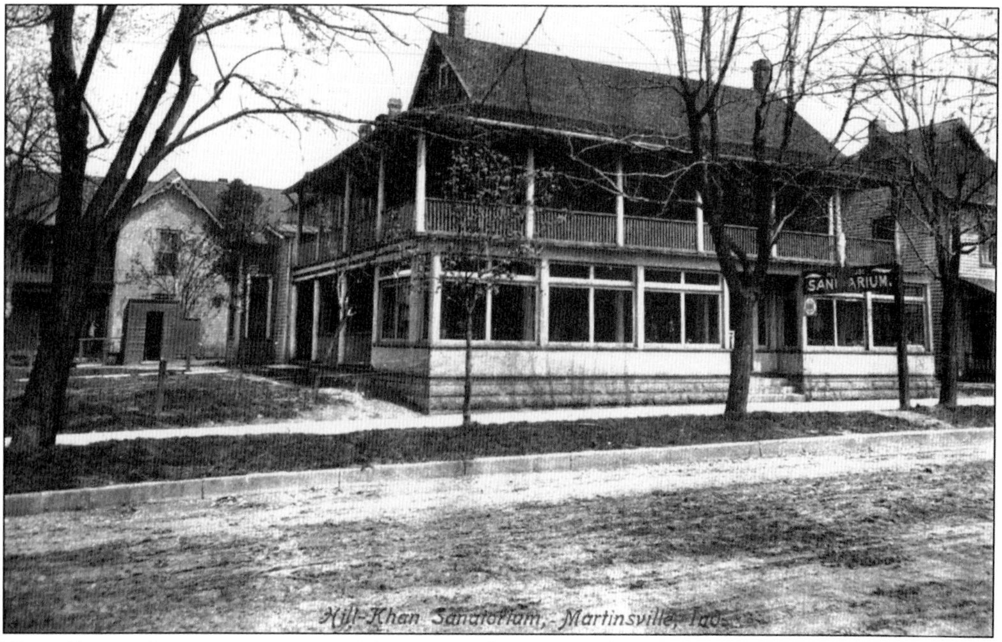

HILL-KHAN SANATORIUM, C. 1907. Variously named, this sanitarium stood at the northeast corner of Morgan and Marion Streets. It originated as several private dwellings purchased and combined in 1904 by Harrison and Mary Hill and their son-in-law David Cohn. The sign on the entrance reads "Hill House," but the caption reads "Hill-Khan." The name Cohn has been misspelled; ironically, the incorrect spelling, *khan*, is a Turkish word for inn.

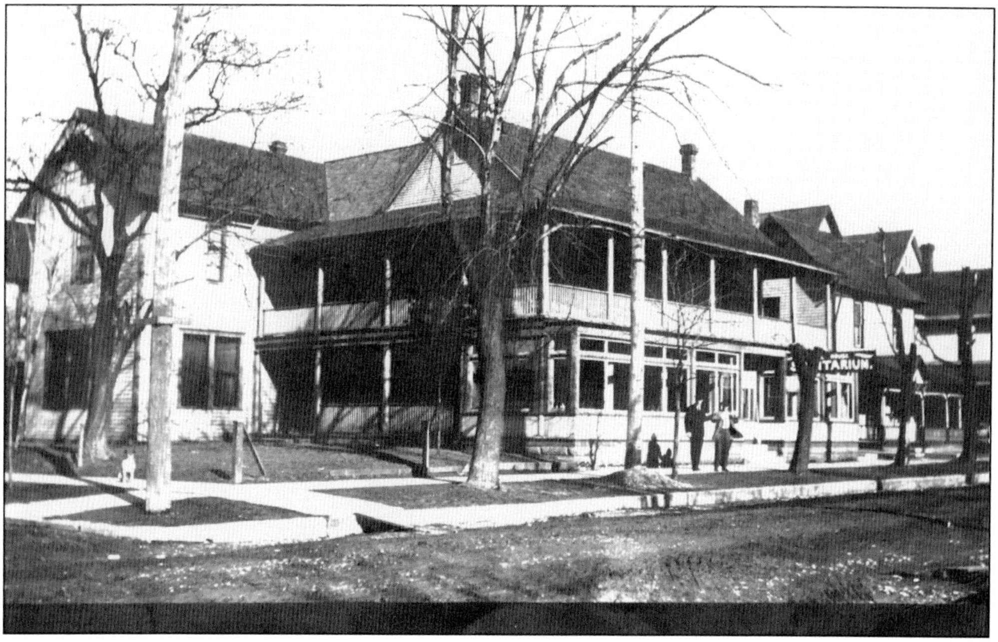

COHN SANITARIUM, C. 1910. Built at a cost of $8,000, the bathing facilities included 14 bathrooms. Ladies' rooms were on the second floor, with men's on the first. Rooming capacity was 100 guests, with overflow housed in a number of nearby boardinghouses owned and operated by the Hills and Cohns.

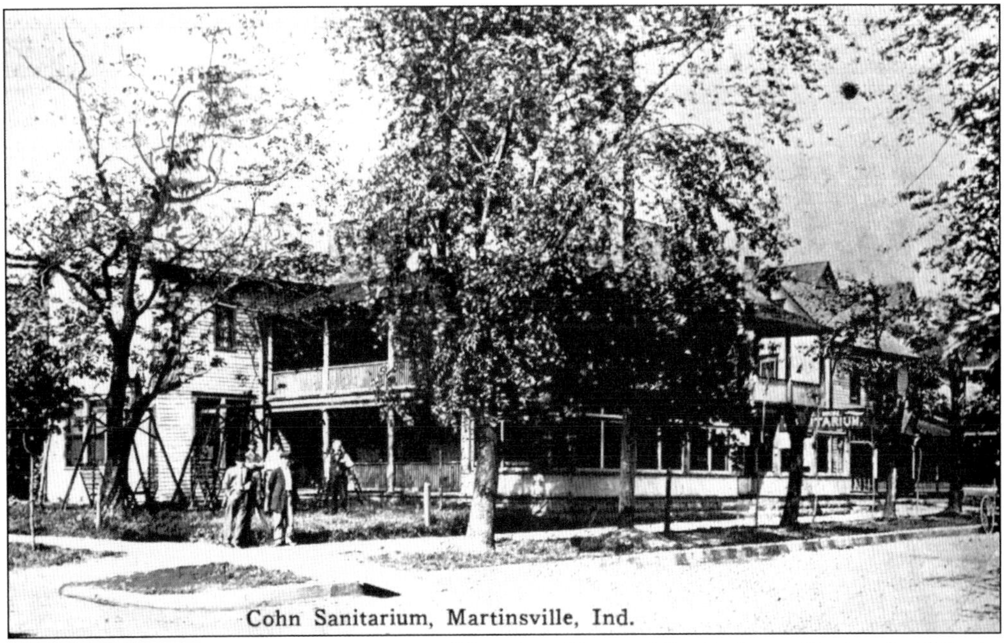

COHN SANITARIUM, 1911. "Dear Friend," writes Alta to Miss Rilla in Flat Rock, Illinois. "Ernst is better I will go home Wednesday I had to stay as along as he cannot dress himself yet. he can walk alone this is the finest place on Earth it has been a benefit to me also as the rest and the water is good for me."

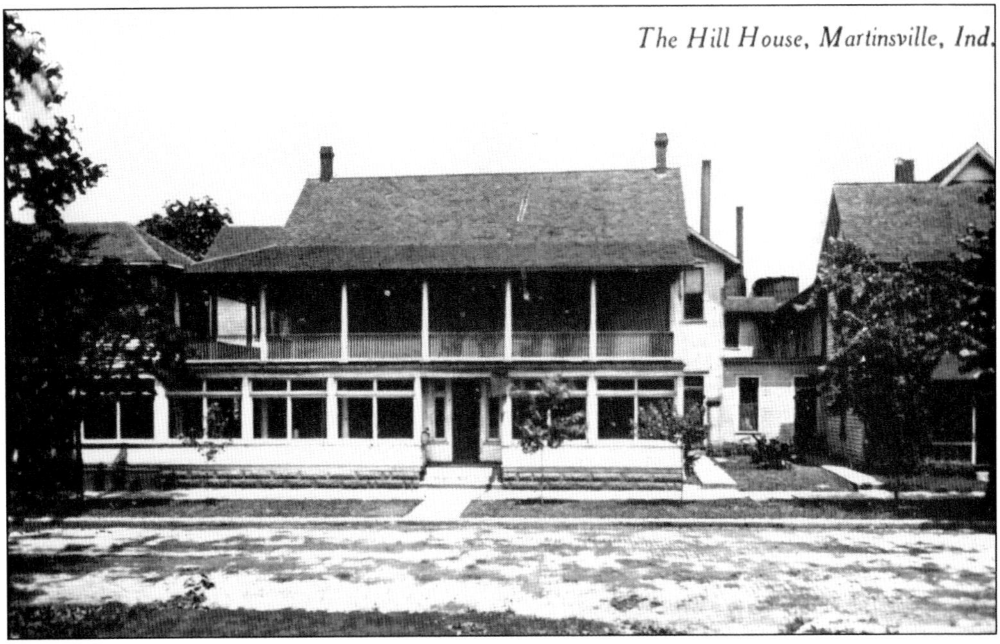

THE HILL HOUSE, C. 1915. Demand for services and accommodations led to another expansion in the spring of 1914. The dwelling on the east, shown at the far right, was connected to the sanitarium, neighboring buildings on the north were also subsumed, and an addition on the west was built. It was about this time that David Cohn bought out Mary Hill's interest and became sole owner.

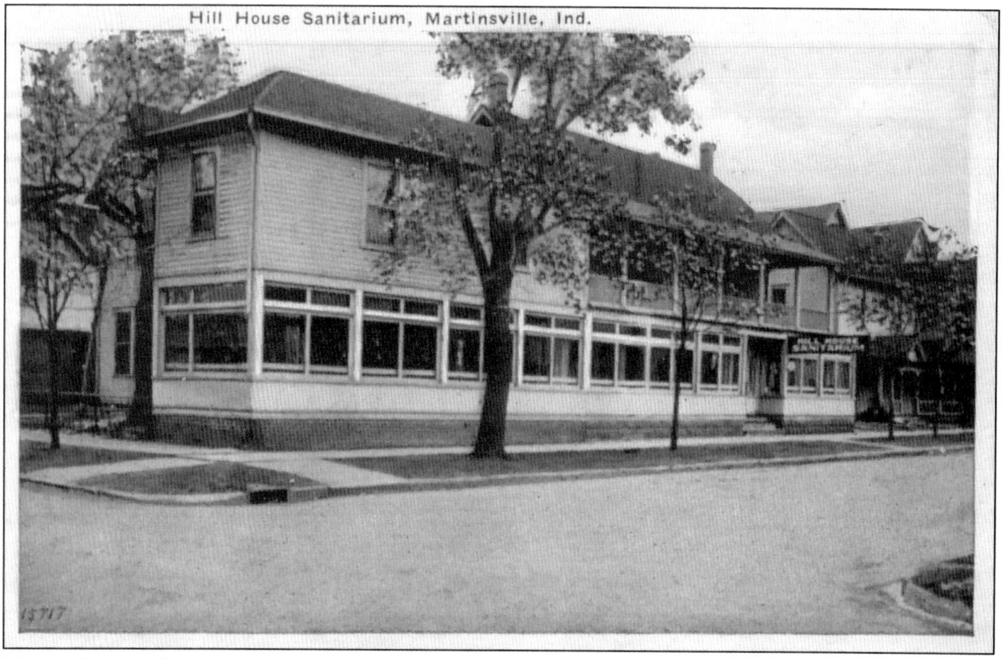

Hill House Sanitarium, Front and Back, 1926. In 1920, David Cohn sold the Hill House on contract to Dr. T. W. Longfellow, the physician at the Highland Sanitarium, and retired a year later. In 1926, the business was returned to the Cohns, who in 1925 had purchased the Colonial Sanitarium. Michael Cohn operated the Hill House until his father's death in 1933. The building was then sold to Schnaiter Lumber Company and demolished in 1934.

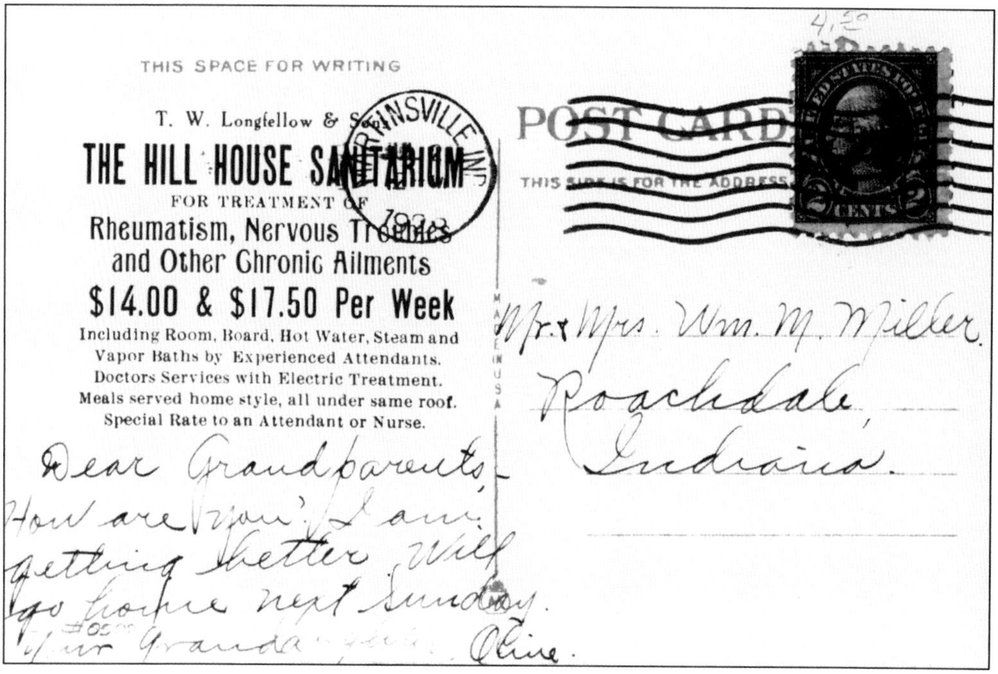

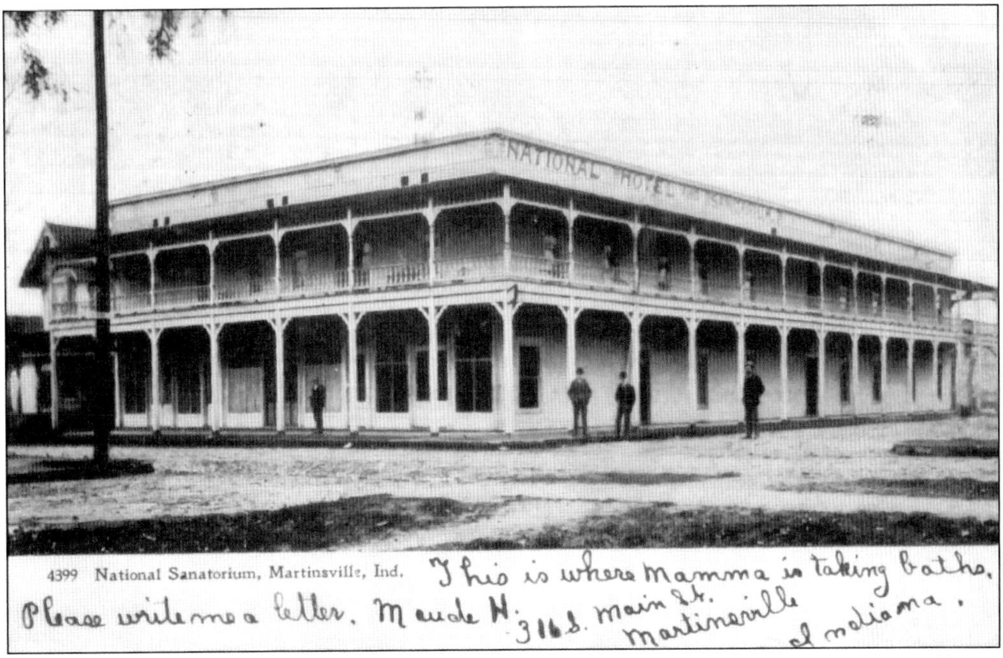

NATIONAL SANITARIUM, 1907. Located at the northwest corner of Morgan and Mulberry Streets, just east of the Hill-Cohn Sanitarium, the National originated as the Cottage Hotel, built in 1894 by Wilbur Rose. Converted into a sanitarium the following year by Dr. Edward Sweet and Isaac Nutter, the 25-room facility was popular with middle-class guests and businessmen.

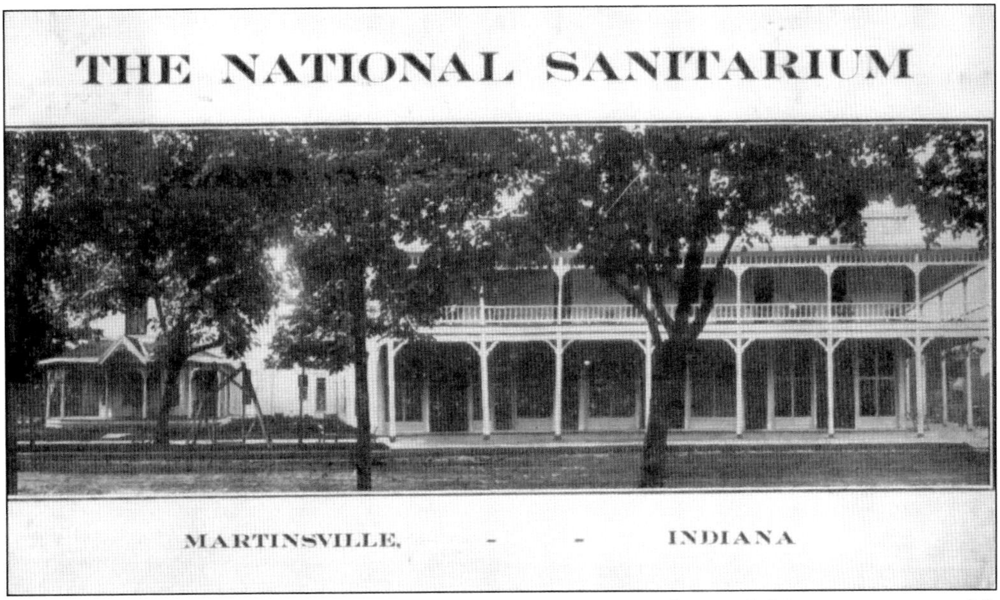

NATIONAL SANITARIUM, C. 1906. The frame sanitarium featured 25 guest rooms with 10 bathrooms, steam heat, a second-floor veranda that was popular as a promenade, and Dr. Sweet as attending physician. Rates ranged from $5 to $8 per week. By 1908, the National had expanded and absorbed the house that appears at left.

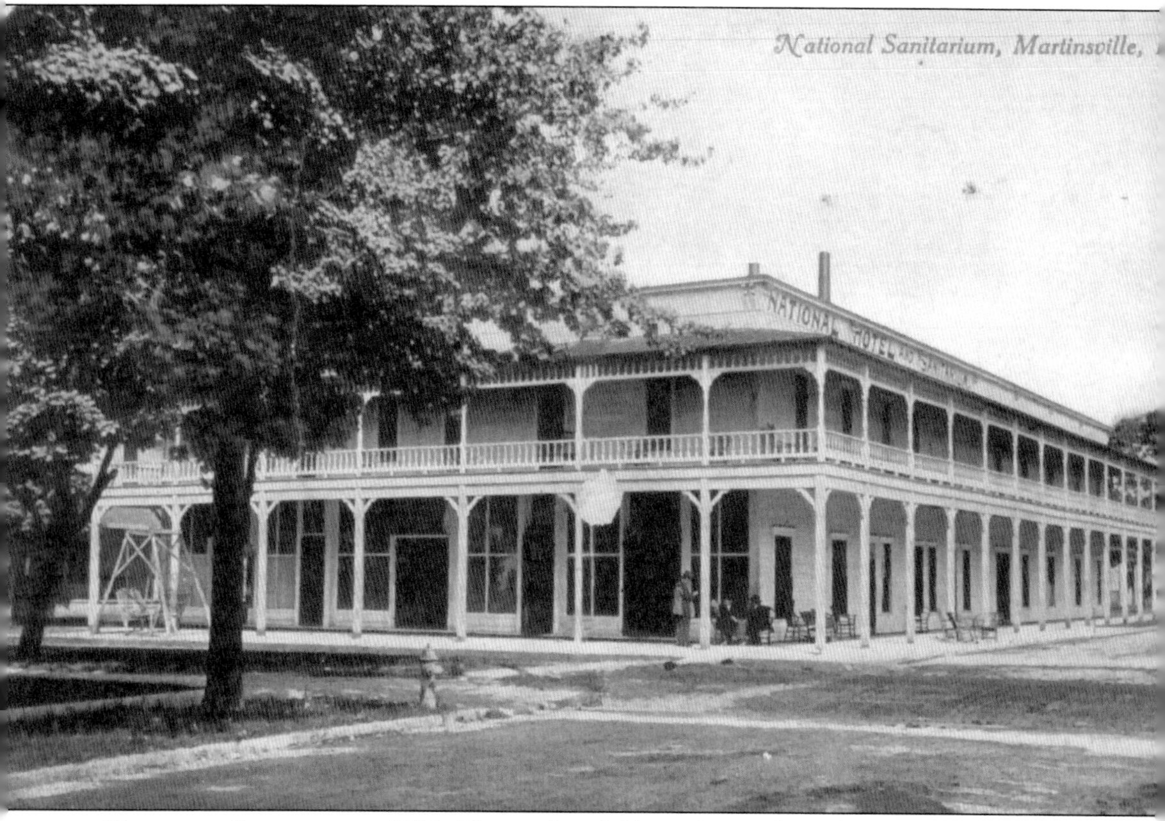

National Sanitarium, 1906. The sender of this card provides a glimpse of the treatments many years ago. She writes, "As I am down here taking the hot baths they seem to be hard for me to get use to, my heart and nerves give way, and I fainted some for them in the bath, but the Doctor is treating me for my nerves, am a little better today, but can't stand them as hot as they would like, they sweat the very juice out of a person. I take one hot water bath, one steam bath and electric treatment at noon in bath room over one half hour and then, put you to bed and sweat you an hour after the three, so you see I do keep busy undressing and dressing up there is lots of people here now We have fine meals, they are very nice to me here."

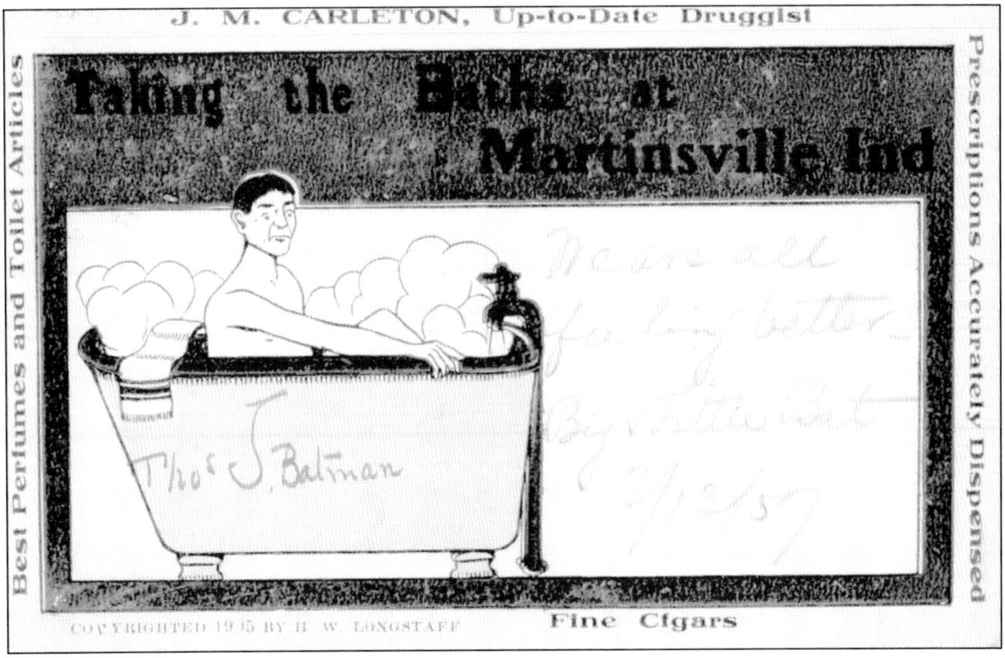

Taking the Baths at Martinsville, 1907. "We are all feeling better," writes Thos. J. Batman, nicknamed "Little Bat." John M. Carleton, the "up-to-date druggist," settled in Martinsville in 1889. His City Drug Store was located on the west side of the square immediately north of the alley. A veteran of the Civil War, Carleton resided on East Washington Street. He died in 1917.

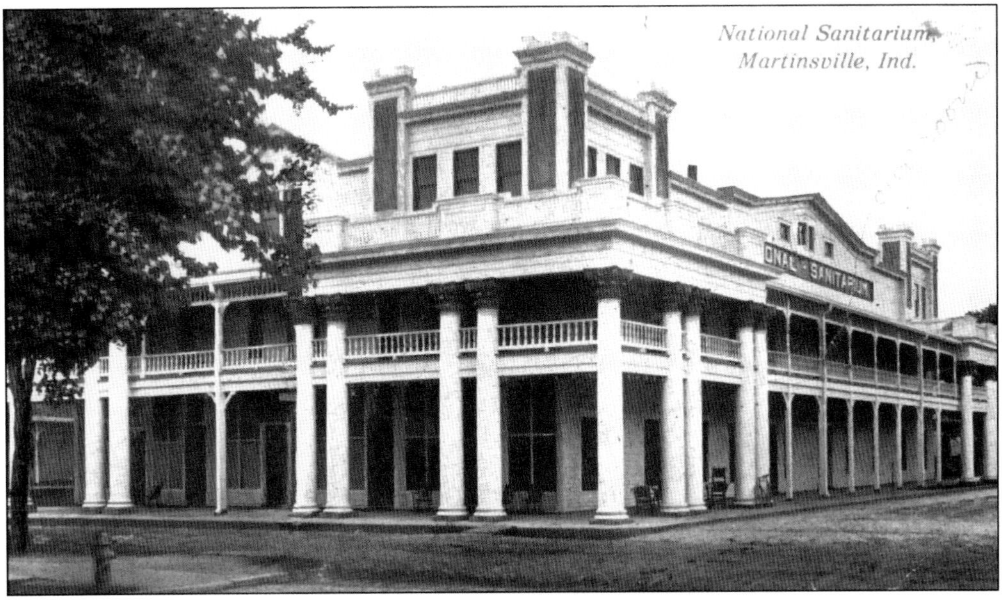

National Sanitarium After Remodeling, 1912. The sanitarium was expanded and renovated in 1907 to the appearance shown here. "Have been in Mville about two weeks," wrote Edna to Bruce Ferguson of Oxford, Ohio, on May 12, 1912. "This town has about 5 thousand people, and most of the streets are paved. Seems like everyone has an automobile. We have a dandy room facing the east."

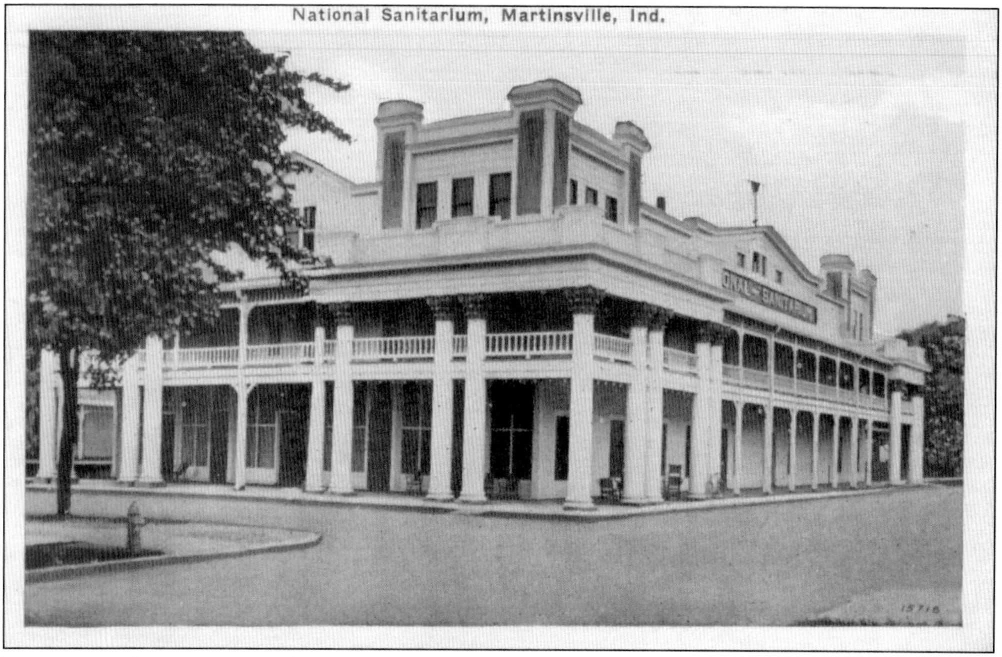

NATIONAL SANITARIUM, FRONT AND REVERSE, 1925. The year 1925 marked the National's 30th year. Remodeling occurred again in 1931. In the midst of the Depression, with a noticeable decline in out-of-town guests, the management encouraged Martinsville residents to avail themselves of the sanitarium's high-class hotel, dining room, and the mineral baths "right here at home." Dr. Edward Sweet sold the sanitarium in 1935 to several local businessmen. Two years later it was closed and sold to Schnaiter Lumber Company. On March 24, 1944, it was completely destroyed by fire. A new building of concrete block was erected as the Schnaiter Lumber Company retail store.

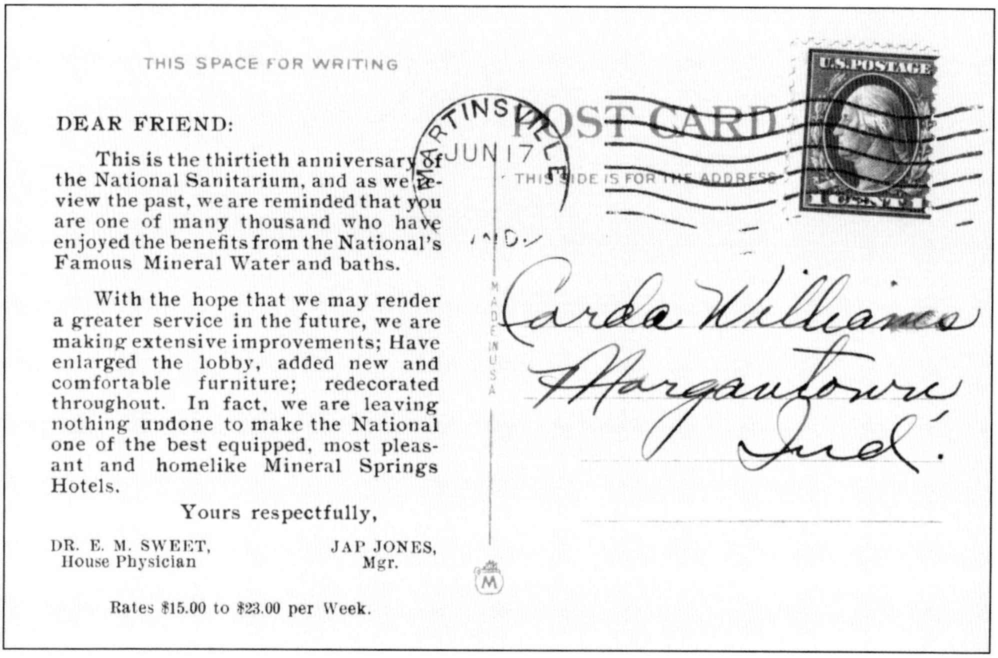
THIS SPACE FOR WRITING

DEAR FRIEND:

This is the thirtieth anniversary of the National Sanitarium, and as we review the past, we are reminded that you are one of many thousand who have enjoyed the benefits from the National's Famous Mineral Water and baths.

With the hope that we may render a greater service in the future, we are making extensive improvements; Have enlarged the lobby, added new and comfortable furniture; redecorated throughout. In fact, we are leaving nothing undone to make the National one of the best equipped, most pleasant and homelike Mineral Springs Hotels.

Yours respectfully,

DR. E. M. SWEET, House Physician

JAP JONES, Mgr.

Rates $15.00 to $23.00 per Week.

POST CARD

THIS SIDE IS FOR THE ADDRESS

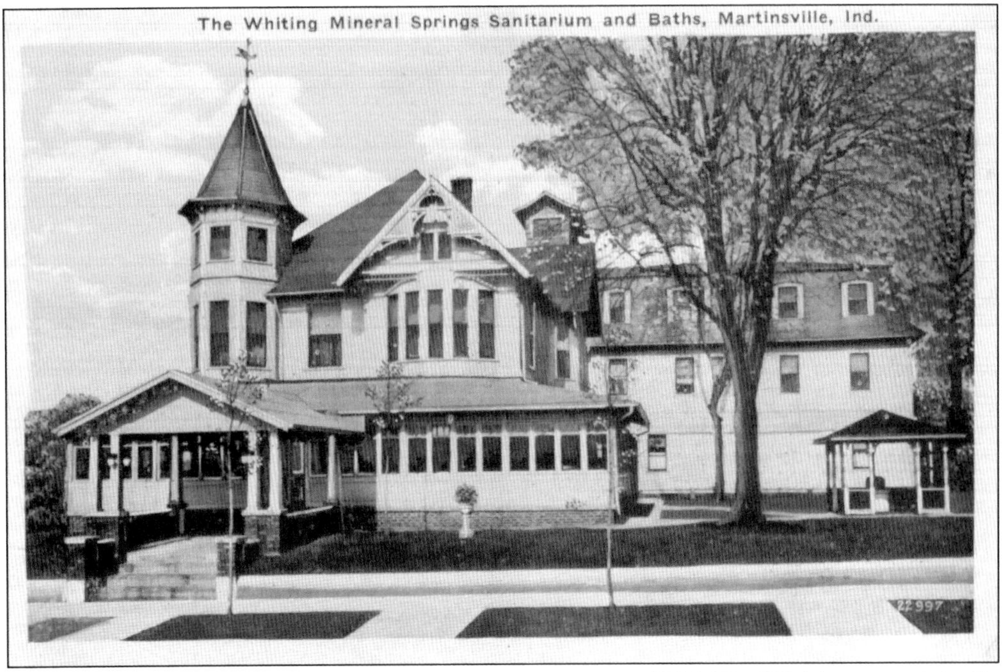

WHITING MINERAL SPRINGS SANITARIUM AND BATHS, C. 1925. The Whiting was originally a private home purchased by Dr. Ulysses G. and Lula Whiting in January 1920. A well was drilled that spring, but money soon ran out. Three years later drilling resumed, and a large addition to the Whiting house was completed. The sanitarium opened in 1924.

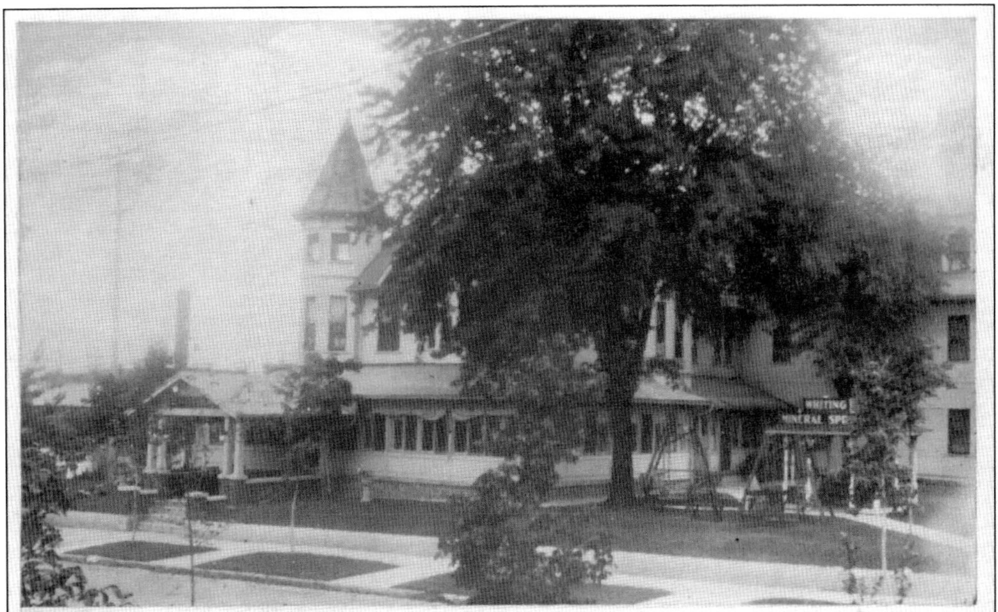

WHITING SANITARIUM, C. 1928. The 45-room Whiting offered "scientific application" of hydrotherapy in enormous bathrooms lined with white ceramic tile and equipped with cots overlaid with rubber sheets and pillows. This same view appears on sheet music for "The Whiting Sanitarium Song," written and published by Dr. Whiting in 1929.

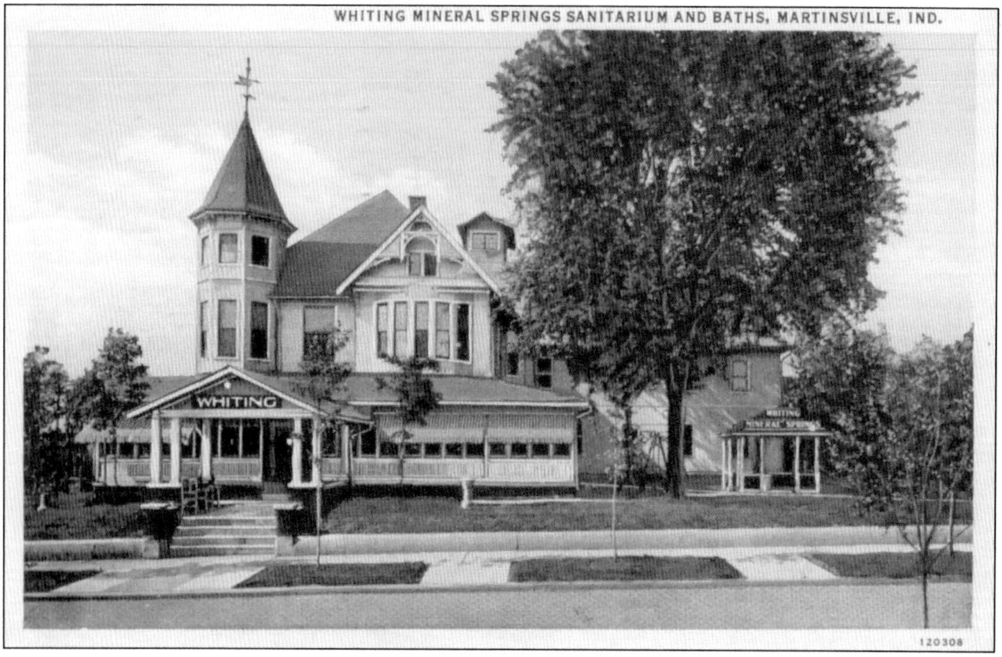

WHITING SANITARIUM AND WELL HOUSE, C. 1930. In the midst of the Depression, Dr. Whiting died. His daughter and son-in-law, Faye and Emory Smith, managed the sanitarium until 1947, when it was sold to Dr. David Eisenberg. The well house with a sign on the roof, seen at the right, was located on the east lawn.

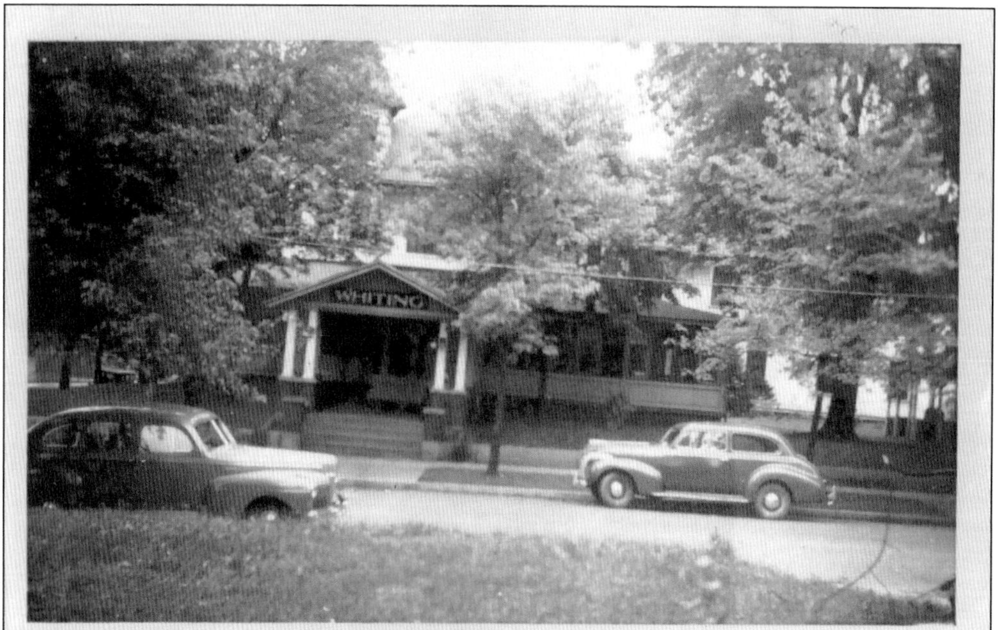

WHITING SANITARIUM IN SUMMER, C. 1945. The Whiting suffered fire damage in 1948. Dr. Eisenberg repaired and rebuilt, only to lose the sanitarium for good in a devastating fire on October 10, 1949. By the time he and his colleague, Dr. Leon Gray, could make their way from surgery in the hospital on Main Street, the Whiting was gone.

Two

Martinsville Sanitarium

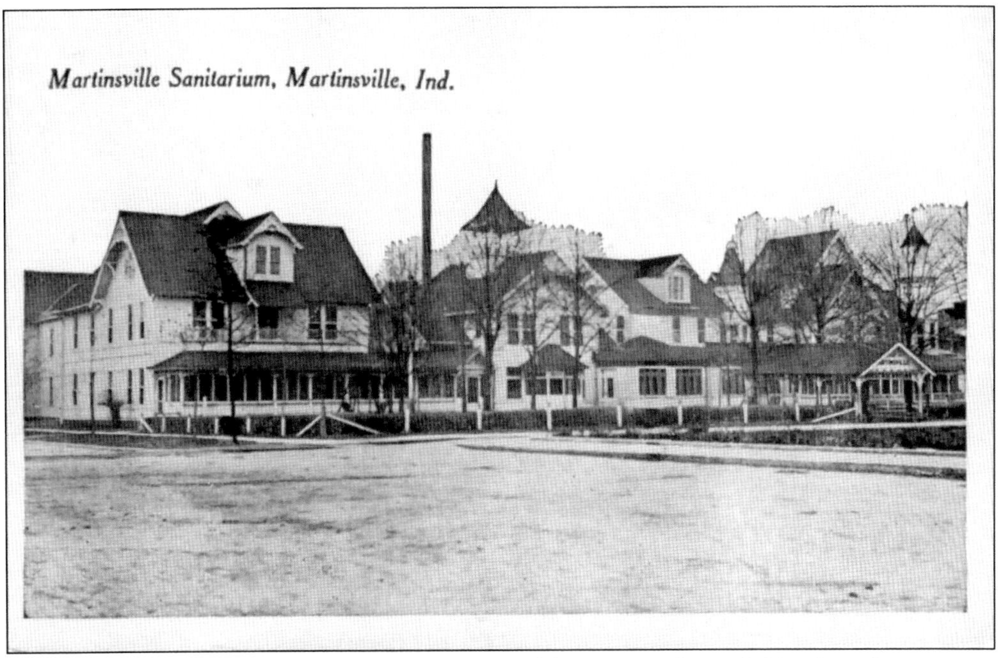

Martinsville Sanitarium, c. 1905. Located between Pike and Harrison Streets west of the Indianapolis and Vincennes Railroad (later the Vandalia Railroad), the Martinsville Sanitarium originated from two separate sanitariums: the Artesian at the far right and the original Martinsville Sanitarium at the center and left. In 1897 and 1898, William K. Bellis, an Indianapolis businessman, and other "capitalists" combined and enlarged them into one rambling structure they named Martinsville Sanitarium.

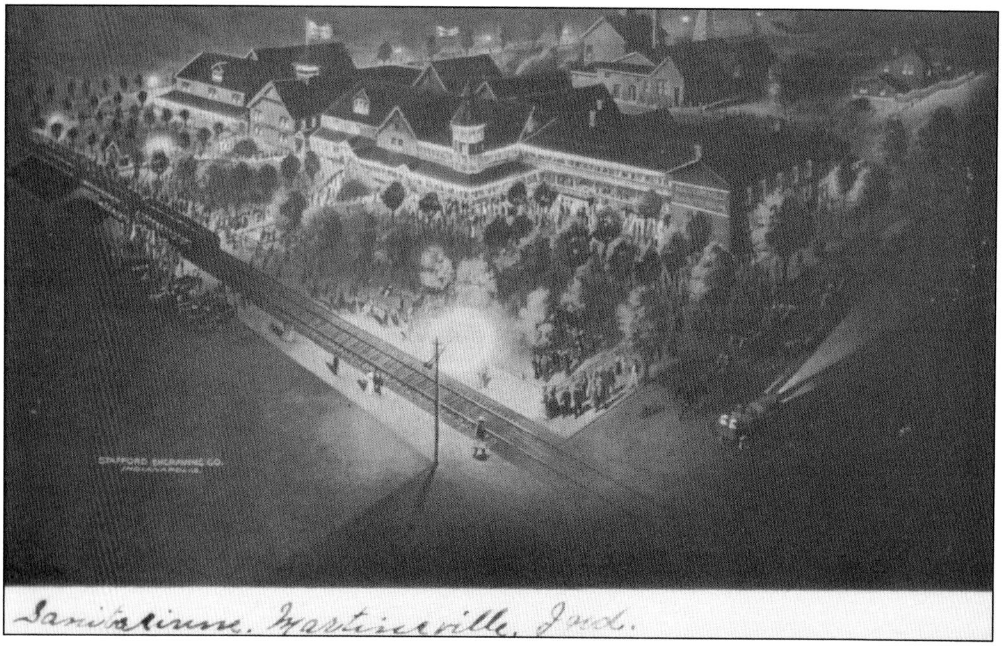

BIRD'S-EYE VIEW, C. 1906. This early panorama shows a sprawling 19th-century sanitarium anchored solidly in modern times. Gas streetlamps extend daytime into night. On Harrison Street, located along the card's right edge, a newfangled automobile shares the road with horse-drawn buggies. Guests swarm from the railcars, promenade on the sidewalks, and linger on the front lawn.

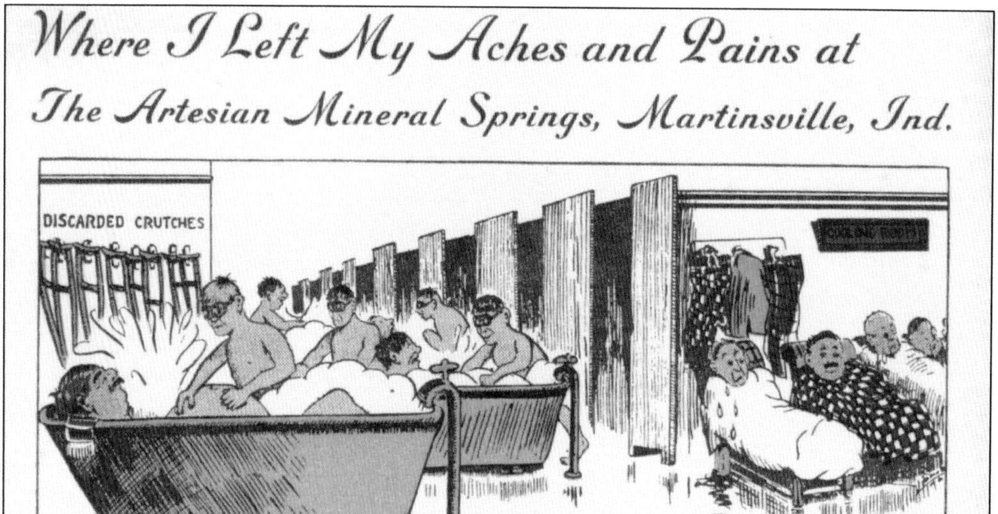

"WHERE I LEFT MY ACHES AND PAINS," C. 1906. Suffering from various infirmities, the gentlemen in this card soak in Martinsville's restorative mineral waters, cared for by goggled attendants. The crutches that carried them to the bathhouse are corralled at the upper left. After their baths, they are bundled in blankets and put to bed to sweat out their bodies' contaminants—impediments to full health—in the cooling room.

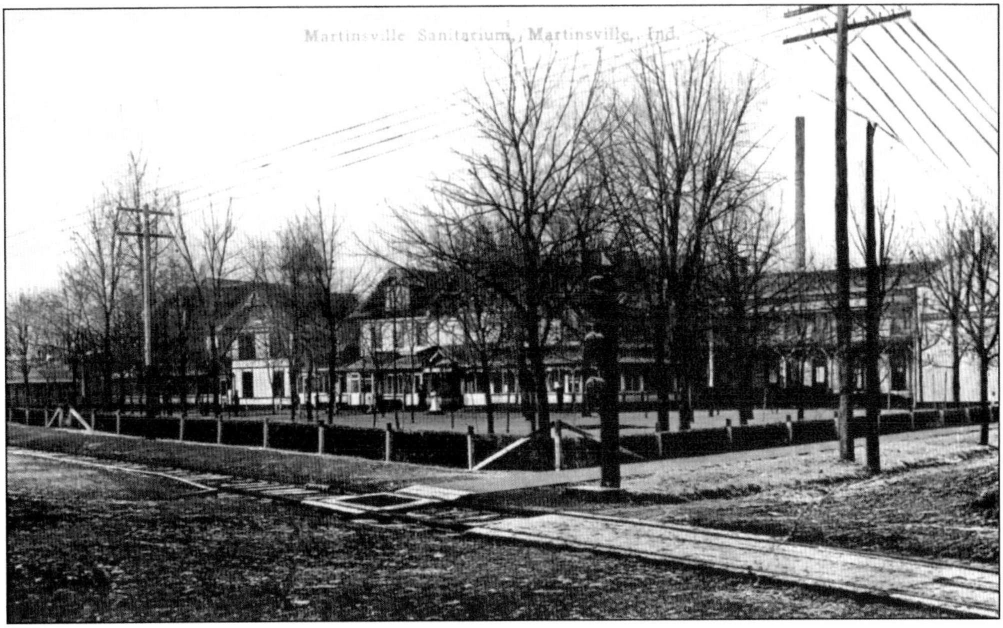

LOOKING SOUTHWEST FROM HARRISON AND MARION STREETS, 1912. From the beginning, the Martinsville's proximity to the railroad, located about 150 feet to the east alongside Marion Street, was integral to its success. Passengers disembarked at the depot and walked across the shaded front lawn to the sanitarium's main entrance or waited in a covered shelter to be transported by "wagonettes."

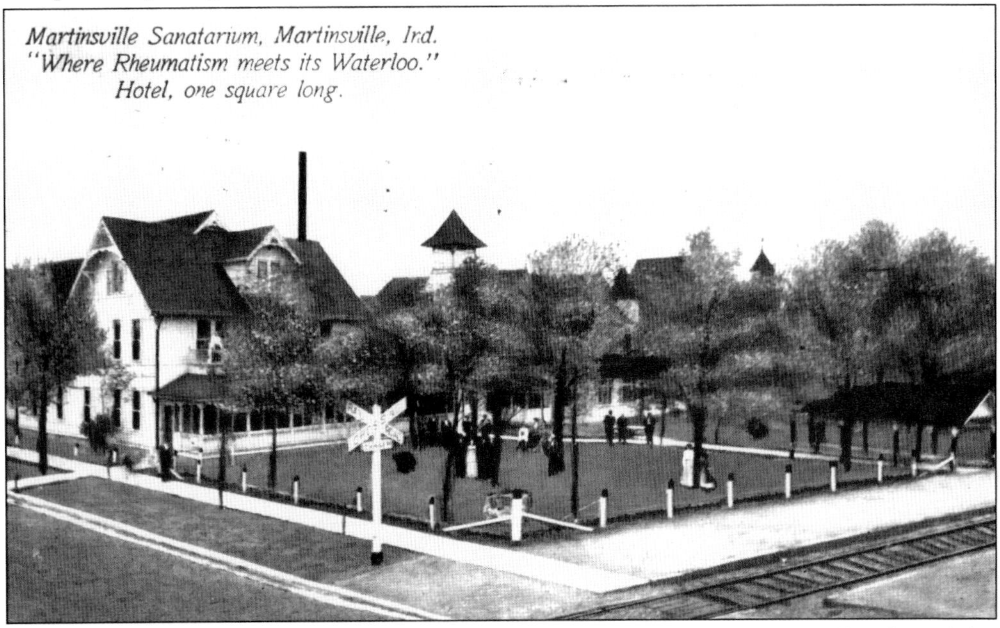

"WHERE RHEUMATISM MEETS ITS WATERLOO," 1915. Pres. William K. Bellis adopted this catchy slogan, printing it on promotional pieces as early as 1911–1912, three years before the 100th anniversary of the defeat of Napoleon Bonaparte and the French Empire at Waterloo. At Okawville, Illinois, the same slogan was attached to the Original Springs Hotel in the 1930s. Someone must have encountered it during a stay in Martinsville and taken it home.

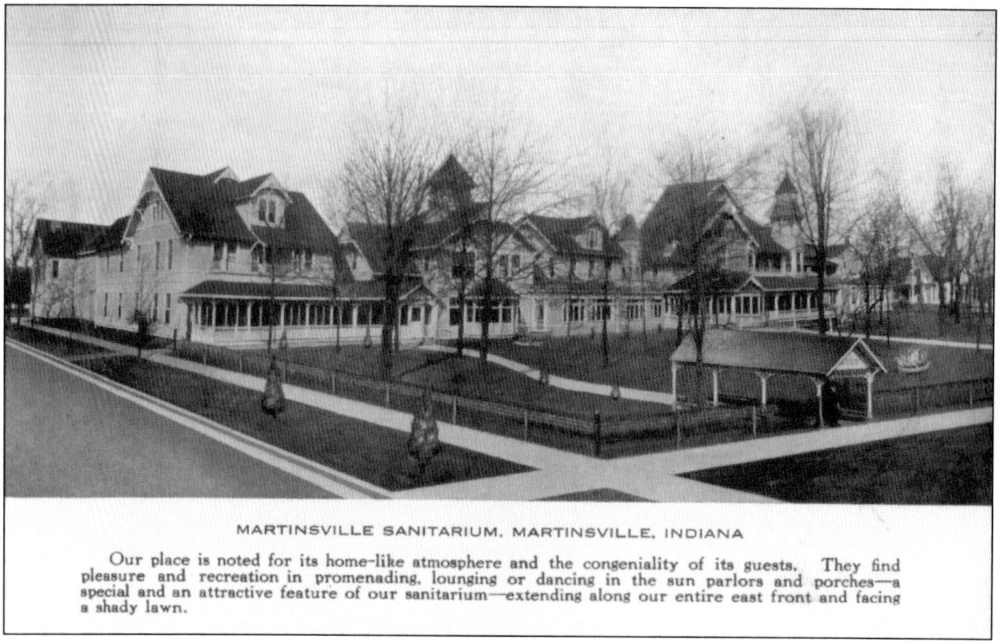

LOOKING NORTHWEST FROM PIKE AND MARION STREETS, *C.* 1915. In 1916, the Martinsville Sanitarium was purchased by Walter A. (W. A.) Kennedy, already owner of the Home Lawn Sanitarium on East Washington Street, who embarked on an ambitious expansion. A two-story brick addition on the west included a dining room, kitchen, and store room, with guest rooms on the second floor.

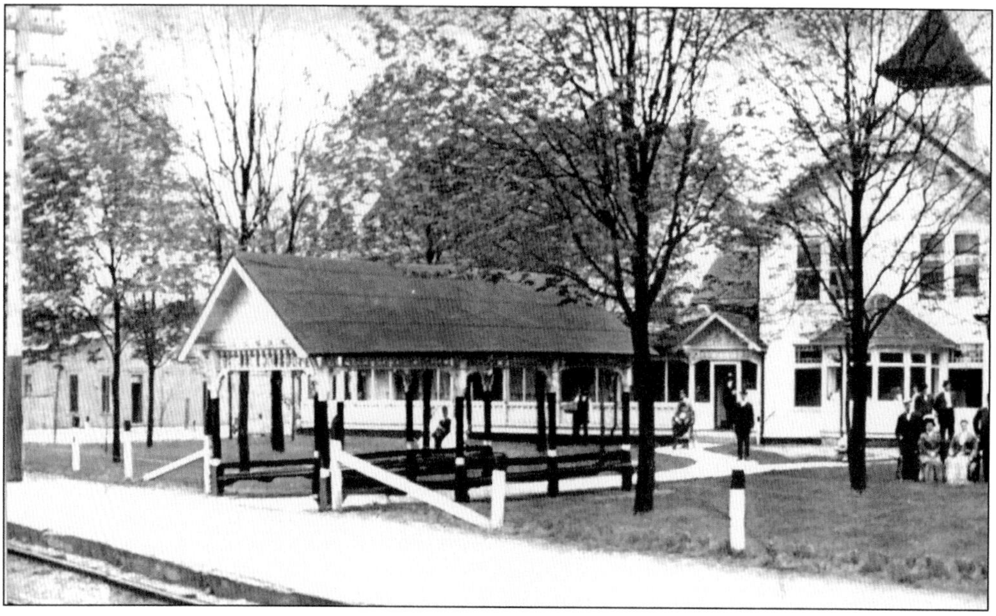

WAIT STATION AND VANDALIA RAILROAD, *C.* 1915. This and the following two views are panes of a trifold postcard. In this, the left pane, the railroad tracks and passenger wait station are clearly seen. "The lawn between the sanitarium and the railway station is spacious and well-shaded," wrote W. S. Blatchley, geologist for the State of Indiana, in a 1901 report. Martinsville's restorative rural setting was the antithesis of the large, dirty, and crowded city.

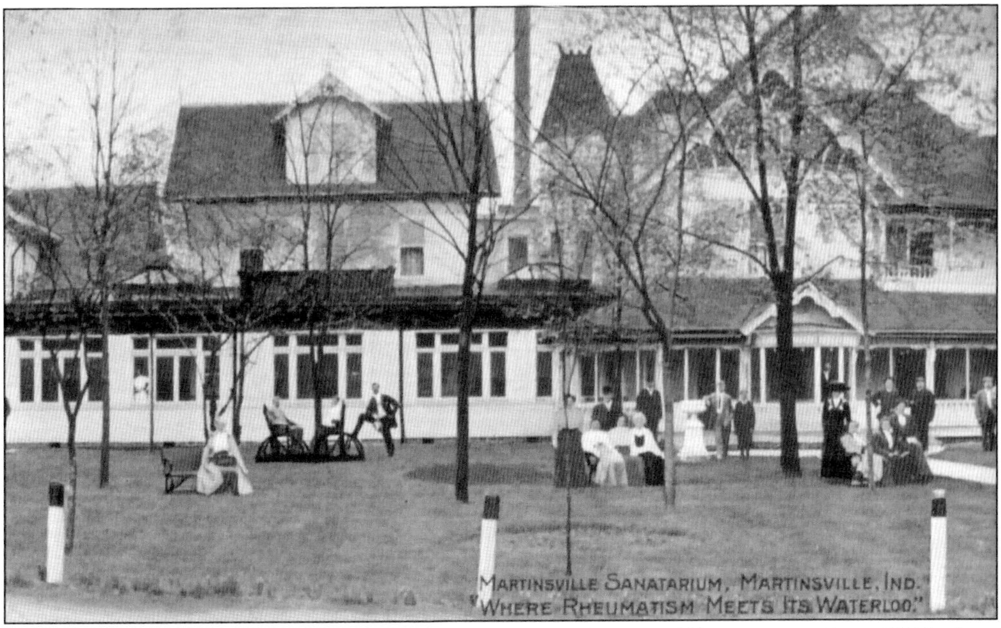

MIDDLE FRONT LAWN, *c.* 1915. This is the second, or middle, pane in the trifold view. Mother writes, "Good Morning My dear—Have just had breakfast 9 a.m. was up at 5:30 for bath took first a vapor bath—thru hot water—then to bed to 'sweat it out,' don't feel very spry after these baths, but they say that is expected. . . . Martinsville isn't much of a town—have wide streets and any number of saloons."

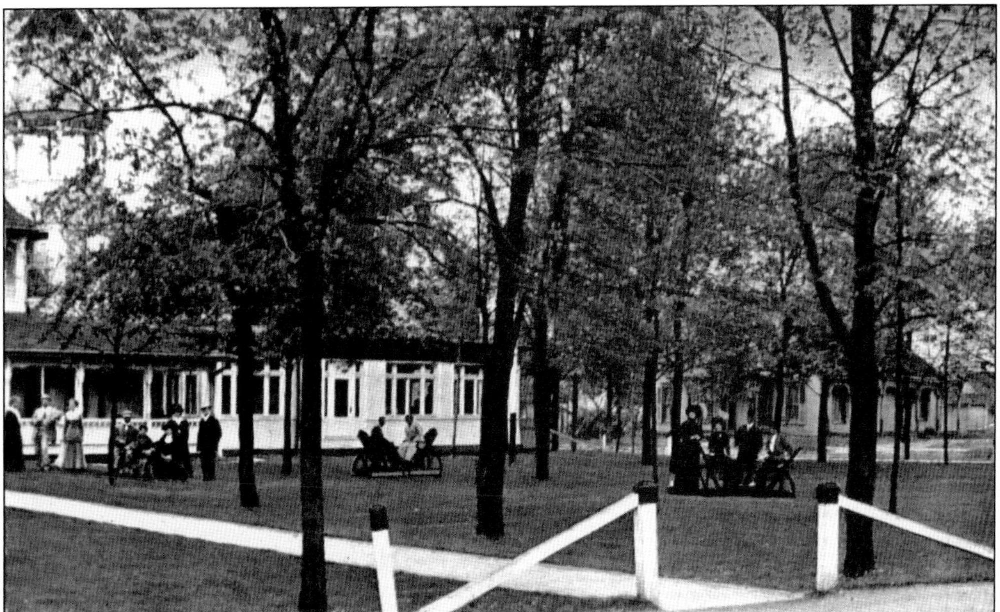

NORTH FRONT LAWN, *c.* 1915. This is the third, or right, pane of the trifold view. Mother's message continues, "[my] room is called 'the Blue hen' a big blue hen is painted in the window. Several went to movies last evening saw John Barrymore in an American Citizen again. They keep this Sanitarium so warm it is very uncomfortable."

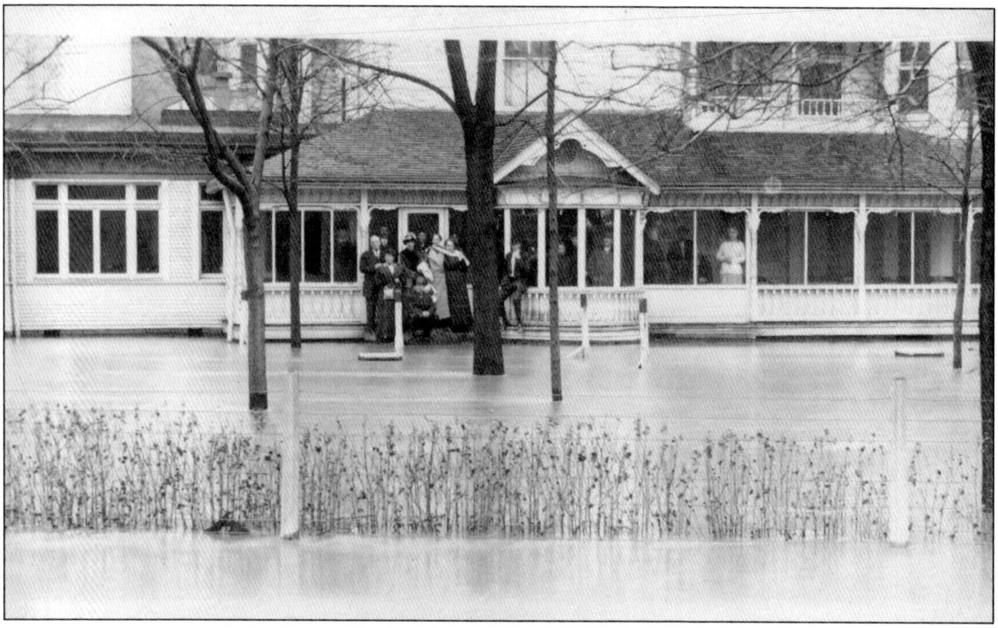

CLOSE-UP VIEW OF FLOODED SANITARIUM, 1913. Stranded on the front porch by the great White River flood of March 1913, these guests pose for the camera and ponder their choices. Should they wait for receding water in the relative luxury of the sanitarium or take a chance by accepting the offer of refuge in a local home? For additional views of the flood, see chapter 9.

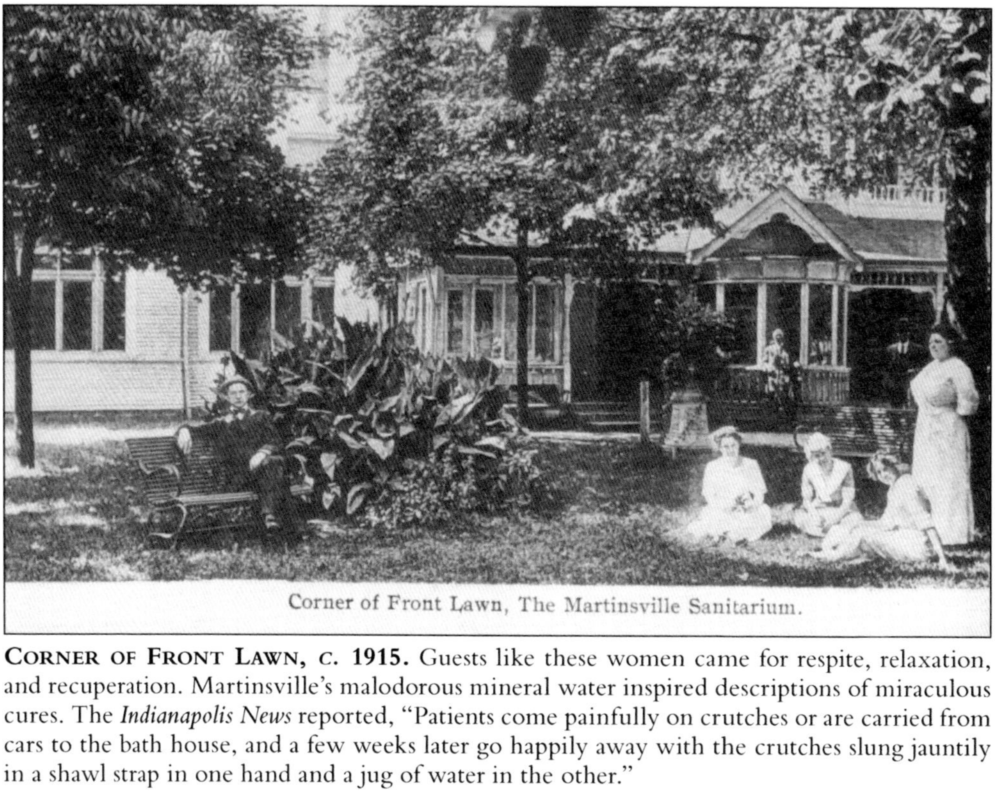

CORNER OF FRONT LAWN, C. 1915. Guests like these women came for respite, relaxation, and recuperation. Martinsville's malodorous mineral water inspired descriptions of miraculous cures. The *Indianapolis News* reported, "Patients come painfully on crutches or are carried from cars to the bath house, and a few weeks later go happily away with the crutches slung jauntily in a shawl strap in one hand and a jug of water in the other."

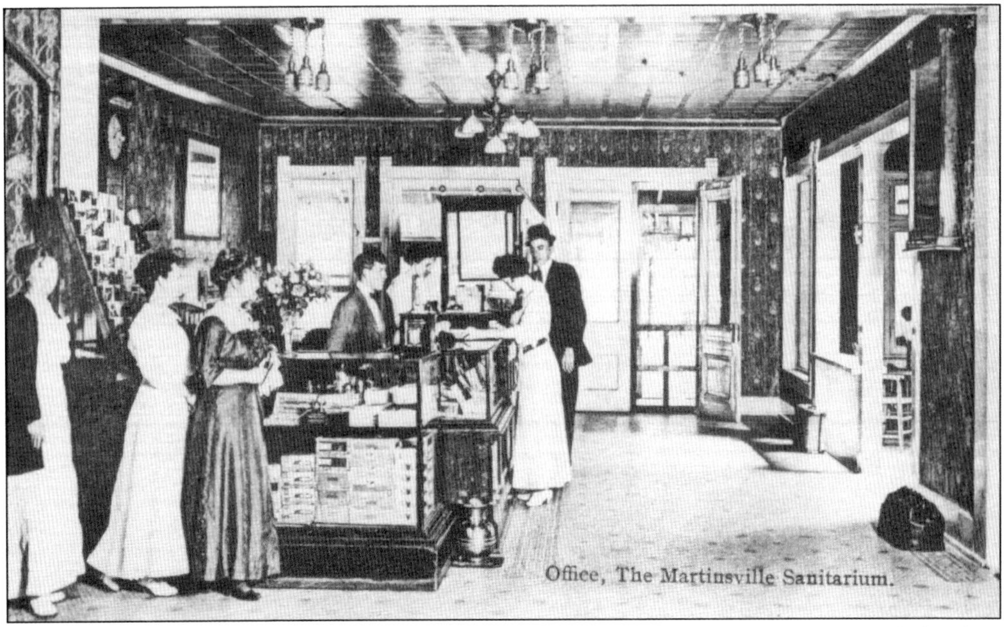

OFFICE, 1914. Guests checked in and out of their rooms at this desk. They could also buy "postals"—or postcards—seen on the rack behind the clerk. "Generally I'm much better," writes the sender of this card, "but I don't know when I'll be able to walk as the soreness seems to be awfully slow in leaving my ankles, but I hope another ten days or two weeks will see me well again."

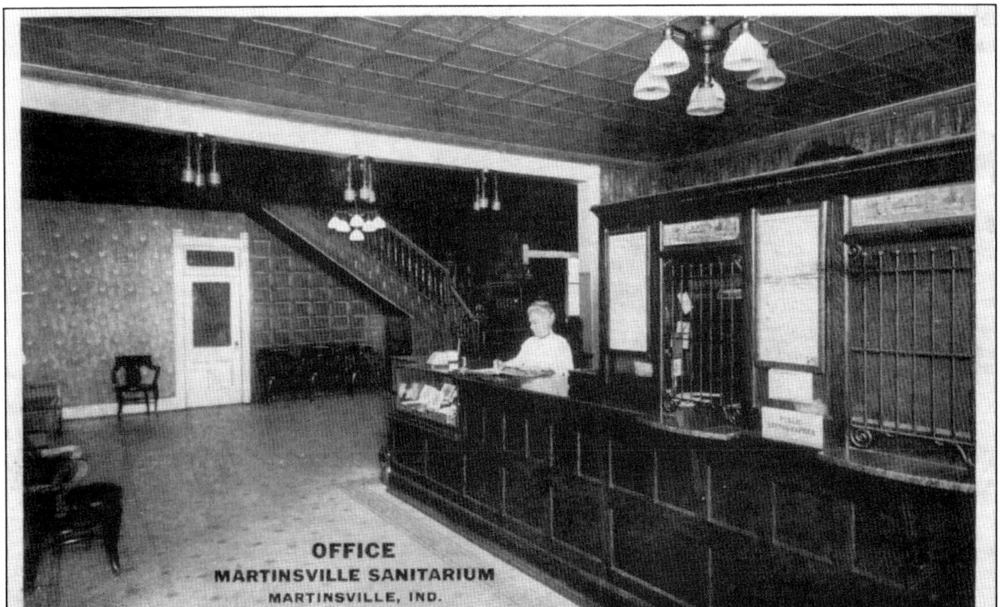

OFFICE AND FRONT DESK, C. 1920. Here is a different view of the desk and lobby, plus the stairs leading to the upstairs guest rooms.

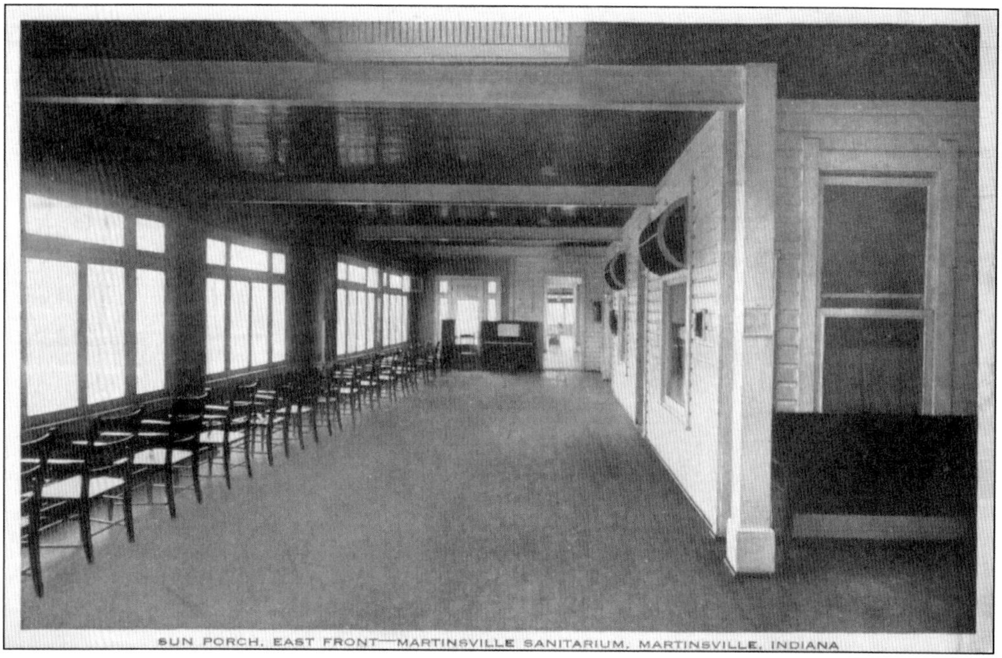

SUNPORCH, C. 1920. A 1901 description remains apt: "The front, facing the shady lawn, is a delightful promenade . . . its entire length being brilliantly lighted by electric light, and in the winter season a space of 275 feet of it is enclosed in glass, thus permitting [guests] to experience the sensations of the warmth of summer in the midst of winter's inclement weather."

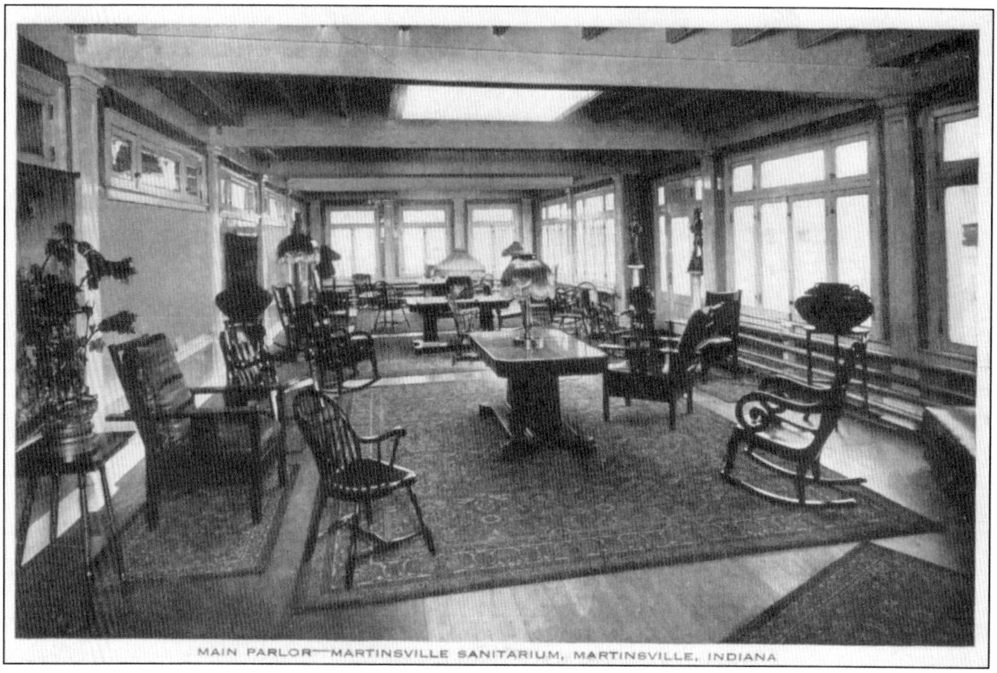

MAIN PARLOR, C. 1920. A guest's typical day was one of leisure. Rising early, one might enjoy breakfast, a bath, a massage, and a nap before dressing for dinner. Afternoons and evenings might be spent reading or conversing or playing a game with fellow guests in the tastefully appointed parlor.

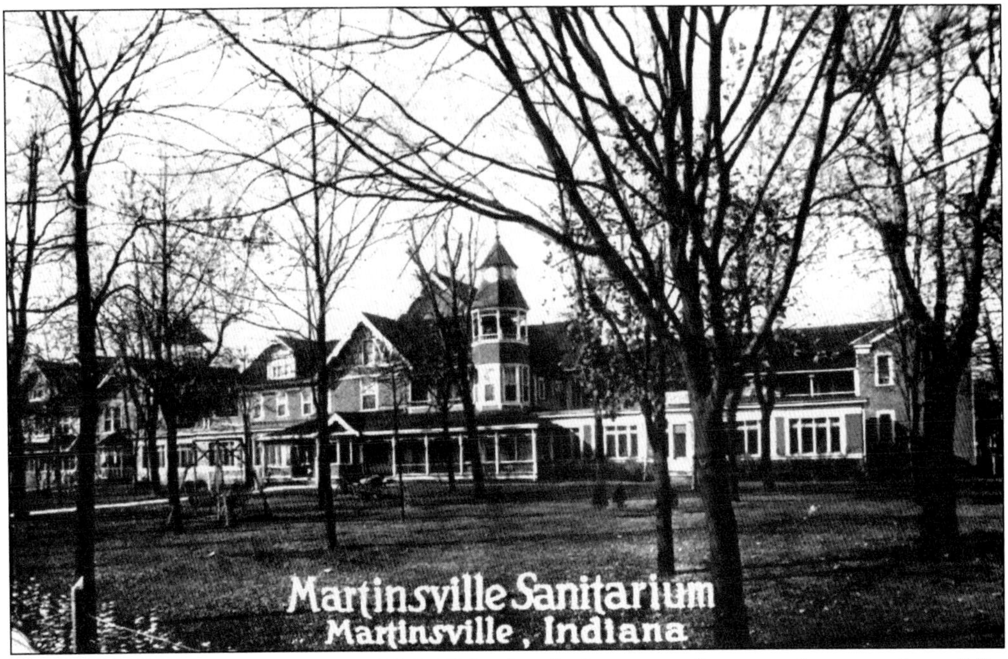

MARTINSVILLE SANITARIUM, C. 1920. This view is the cover of a souvenir postcard portfolio that boasts, "Great care has been taken to make the Martinsville an attractive place for folks out of health. Buildings are uniformly heated with a new noiseless vacuum system. All the rooms have outside exposure. The rooms are well ventilated, quiet and have splendid sanitary condition."

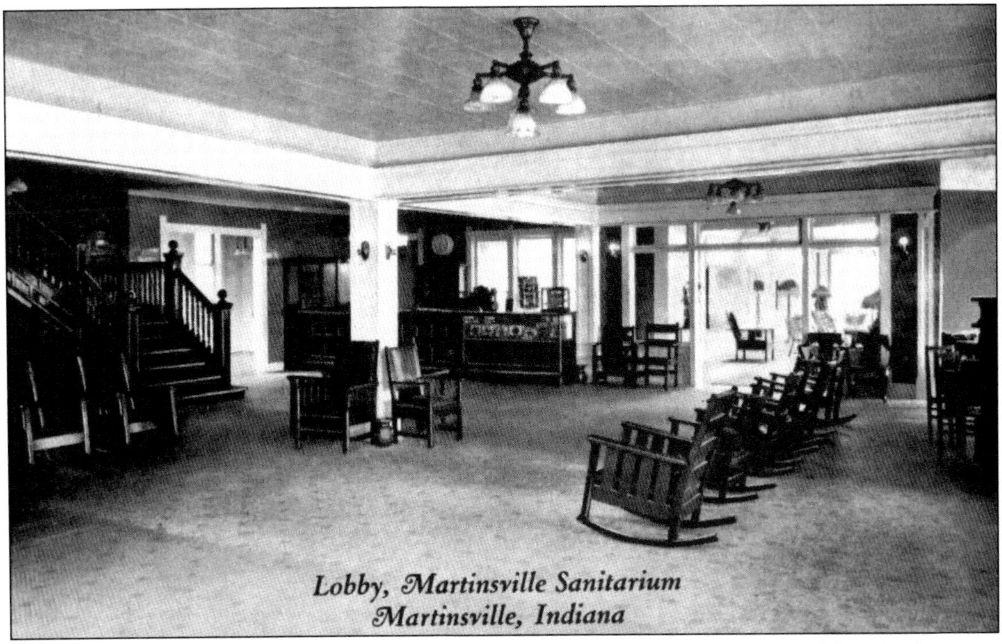

LOBBY, C. 1920. This view and the one that follows are from the same portfolio. "When you enter the Martinsville lobby you are at once impressed with the quiet dignity, simplicity and homelike atmosphere that prevails everywhere. The whole environment appeals to those who enjoy wholesome and well-ordered surroundings."

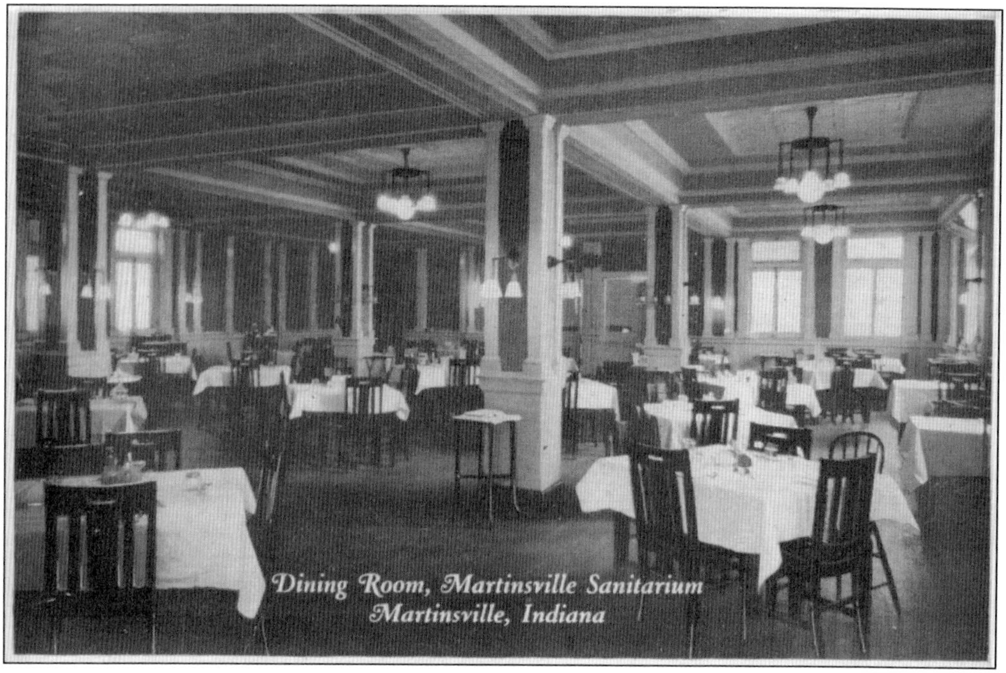

DINING ROOM, *c.* 1920. In messages penned on postcards, guests raved about the finely prepared foods. Menus reflected the social status and culinary experiences of the majority of guests (and puzzled and amazed the staff of locals). Multiple-course dinners were known to blend French cuisine—for example, barigoule, vol-au-vents, remoulade—with traditional American favorites such as venison, beef, turkey, trout, ice cream, and pie.

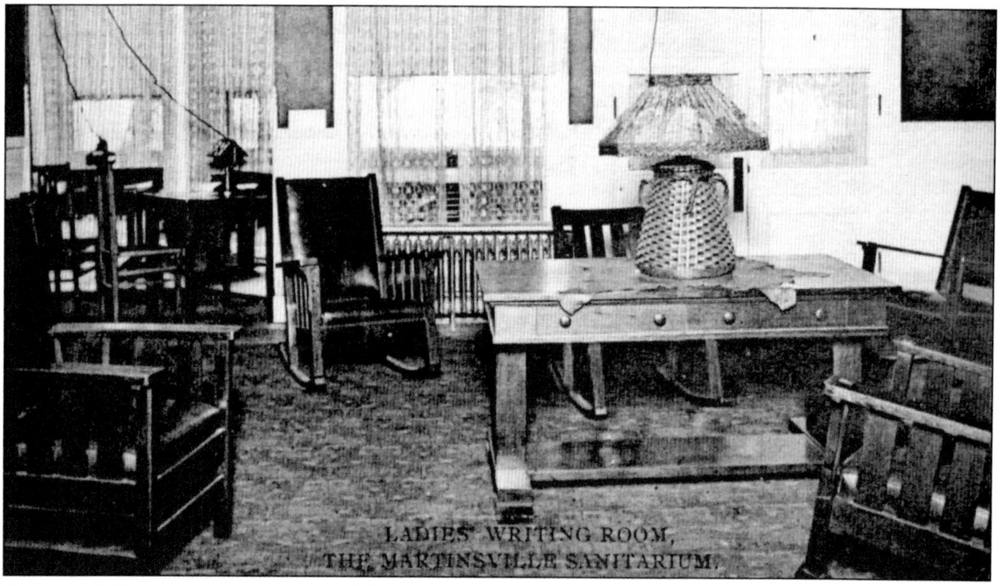

LADIES' WRITING ROOM, *c.* 1920. Having purchased a postal from the clerk at the front desk, a woman could retire to this well-furnished nook to write about her bath regimen and daily ambles around the square. Perhaps she bought chocolates from Jimmy Zapapas at the Martinsville Candy Kitchen or stopped for a soda at Phelps's Drugstore, or she may have bought stockings or a dress at Toner's new store on Jefferson Street.

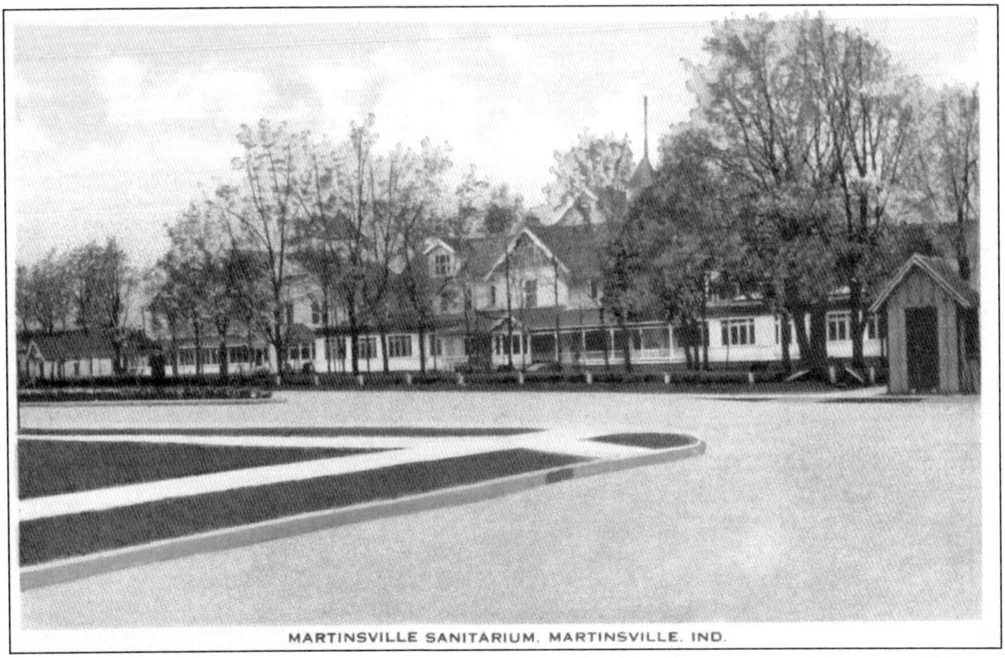

VIEW FROM HARRISON STREET, C. 1920. "Seeking health often means taking a rest," boasts a souvenir portfolio, "hence a vacation while taking Mineral Baths in a quiet country town, with electric lighted and paved streets, and a good sewer system, furnishes all the protection and convenience of a large city and an environment which makes it possible for us to obtain results that could not be accomplished in one's own home, or by the use of drugs alone."

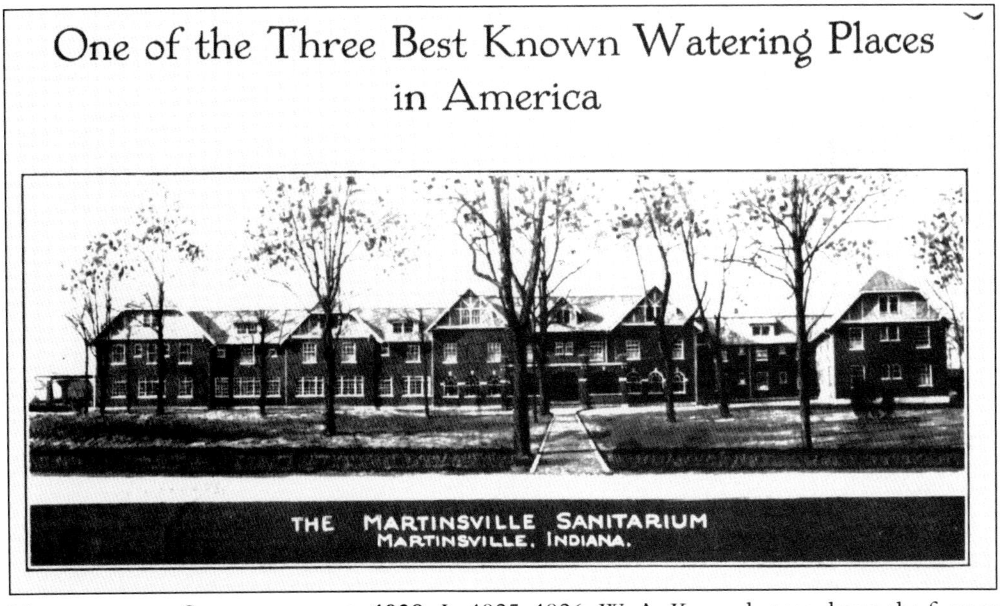

MARTINSVILLE SANITARIUM, C. 1928. In 1925–1926, W. A. Kennedy tore down the former Artesian Sanitarium and replaced it with a new brick building containing 30 guest rooms, two bathhouses, and physicians' offices. In 1927, the original Martinsville Sanitarium was replaced by a south unit. The popular slogan on this card seems to refer to the city of Martinsville itself. The identity of the other two "best known watering places" remains a mystery.

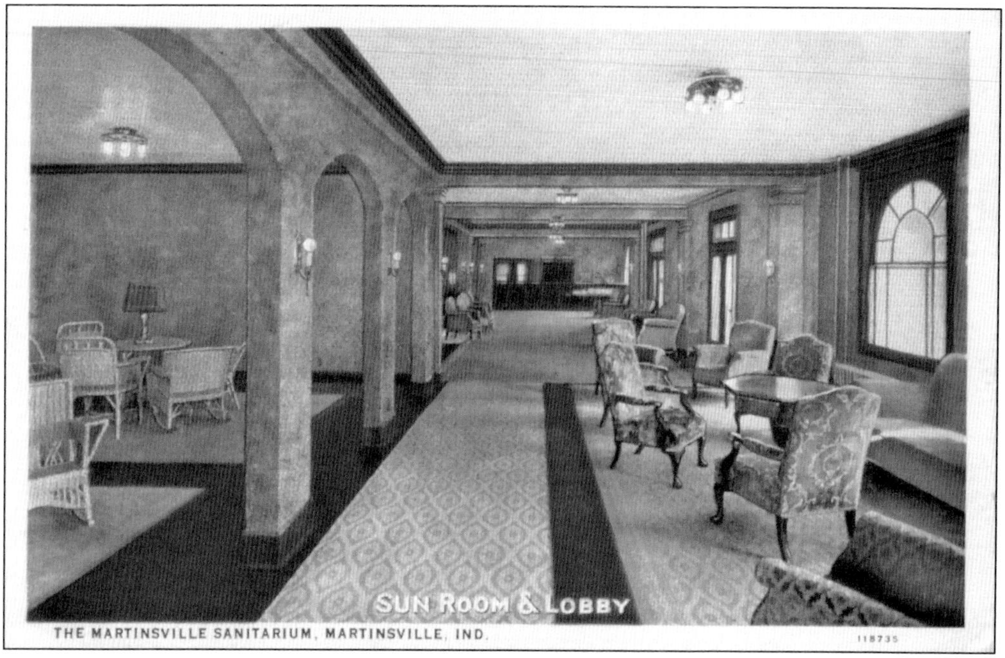

SUNROOM AND LOBBY, C. 1928. An open porch framed the front entrance, which led into the formal lobby decorated in cool shades of Prussian blue. Patterned wool velvet carpet covered hardwood floors. Woodwork was Louisiana gum and birch stained a rich mahogany. Wicker and upholstered furniture was in keeping with current fashions of the period.

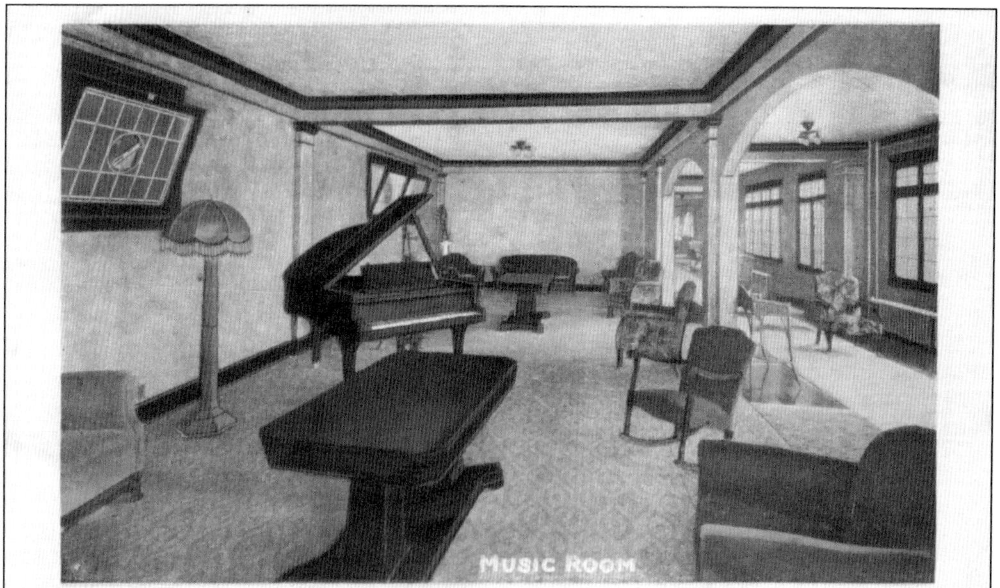

MUSIC ROOM, C. 1928. Anse Hendricks, the son of W. E. Hendricks, remembered in 1961, "The sick would come here on cots, wheel-in cases, and in two weeks they would be up and at 'em, enjoying their meals, enjoying their friends, and the music put out by musical artists. Some of whom still reside [in Martinsville.]" The music room was located south of the main lobby.

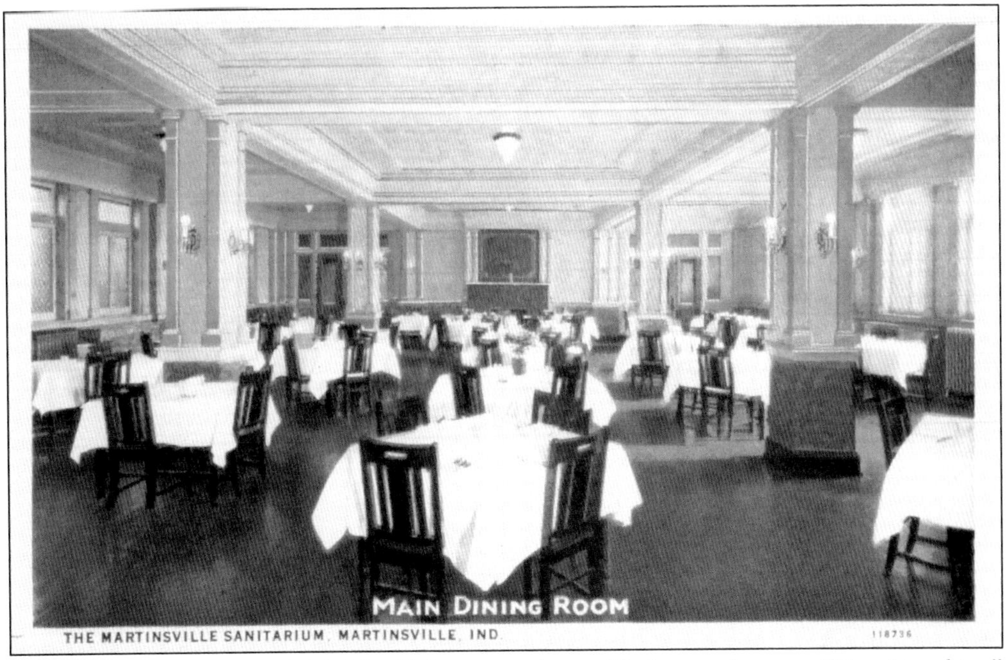

MAIN DINING ROOM, *C.* 1929. The dining room changed little over the years. "Dear Daughter," writes Mother. "How are you and the [indecipherable] making it? The hotel is kept like a hot house—so we do not suffer from the cold. There is nothing to write for nothing happens. We just eat and bathe—and take treatments and rest in bed. How would you like that program?"

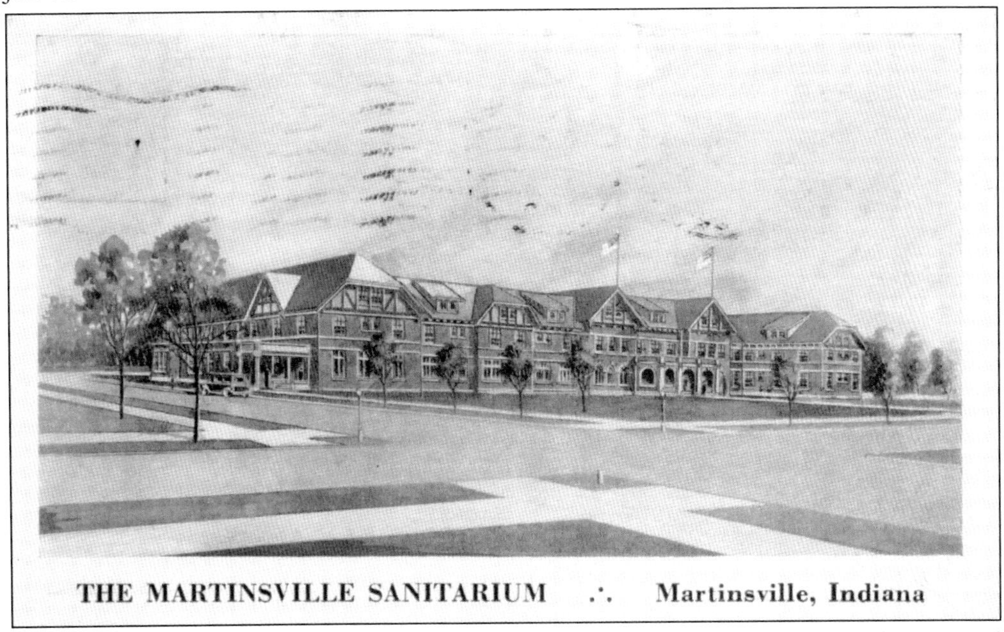

VIEW NORTHWEST FROM MARION AND PIKE STREETS, 1936. The publisher of this postcard has enhanced the scene by omitting the depot. "Thank you so much for the nice birthday greetings. It will be nice to be home again, next Thursday, I hope. The treatments are quite weakening but am told I will feel the benefit after I'm home a while and rested," writes Margaret to friends in Westfield, New Jersey.

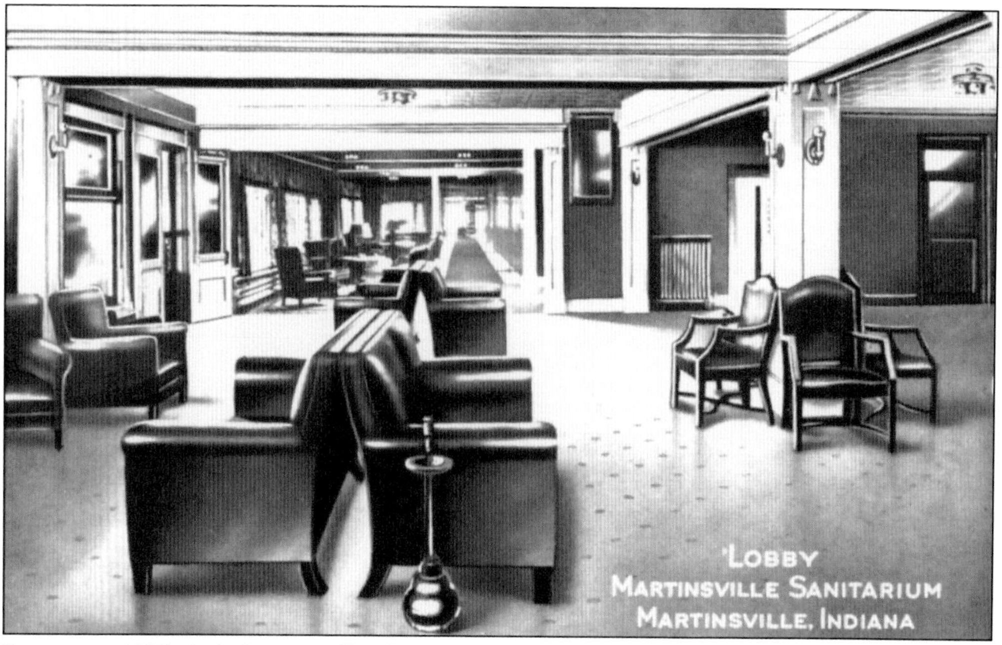

LOBBY, C. 1935. A sleek, streamlined appearance and the efficient use of space are hallmarks of the art moderne style, well-represented in this view of the lobby. The carpet has been removed and replaced with a white ceramic tile floor, and the upholstered easy chairs have been replaced by leather couches and armchairs. No longer homelike, the updated lobby is reminiscent of a public train or bus station.

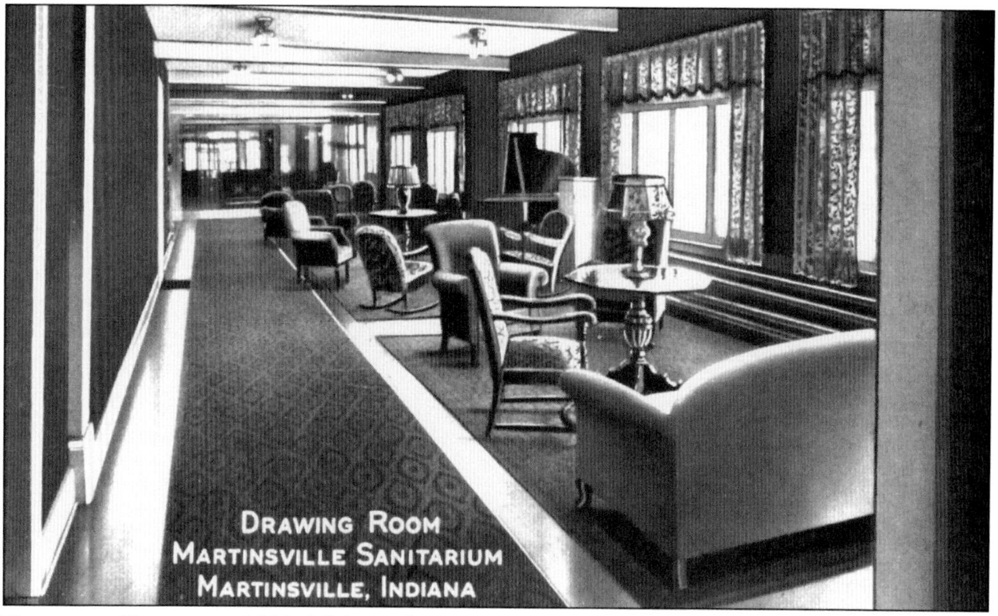

DRAWING ROOM, C. 1935. This card is a contemporary to the previous card, yet it reveals decor and furnishings that changed very little since W. A. Kennedy's rebuilding of the Martinsville Sanitarium in the mid-1920s. Providing an area for relaxation, entertainment, and social interaction, the drawing room ran the length of the east wall of the south wing shown in the top card on the following page. The lobby appears in the distance.

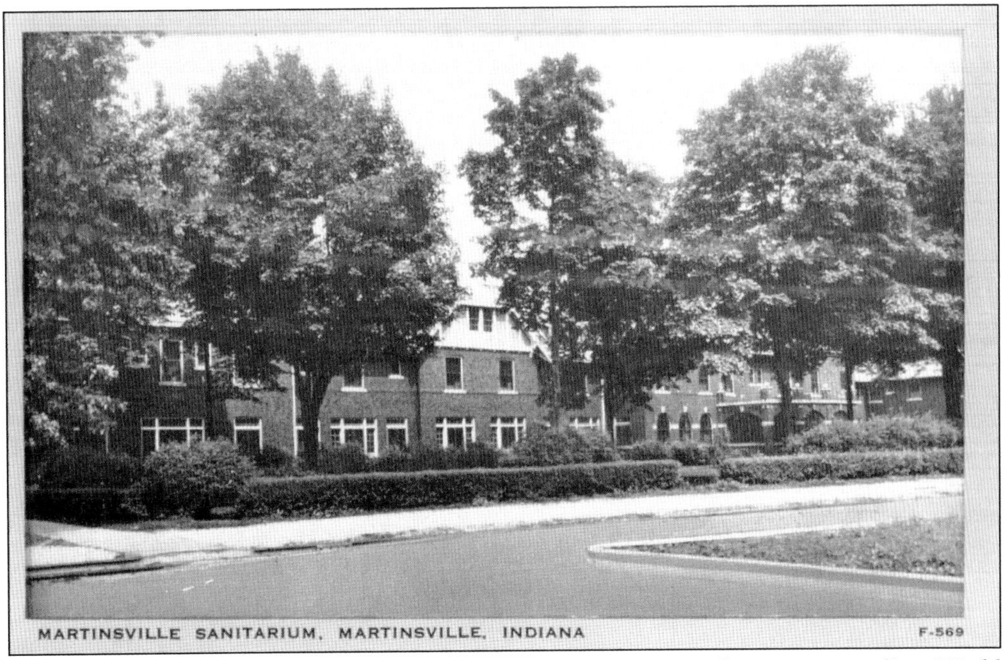

View from Pike and Marion Streets, c. 1940. During the years preceding World War II, Martinsville's sanitarium industry declined dramatically. This was due to a number of factors: the development of vaccines and wonder drugs that revolutionized medical treatment, the discontinuation of the interurban and passenger rail service, and Americans' changing recreational habits. This is an unusual view in that the main entrance is not the focus.

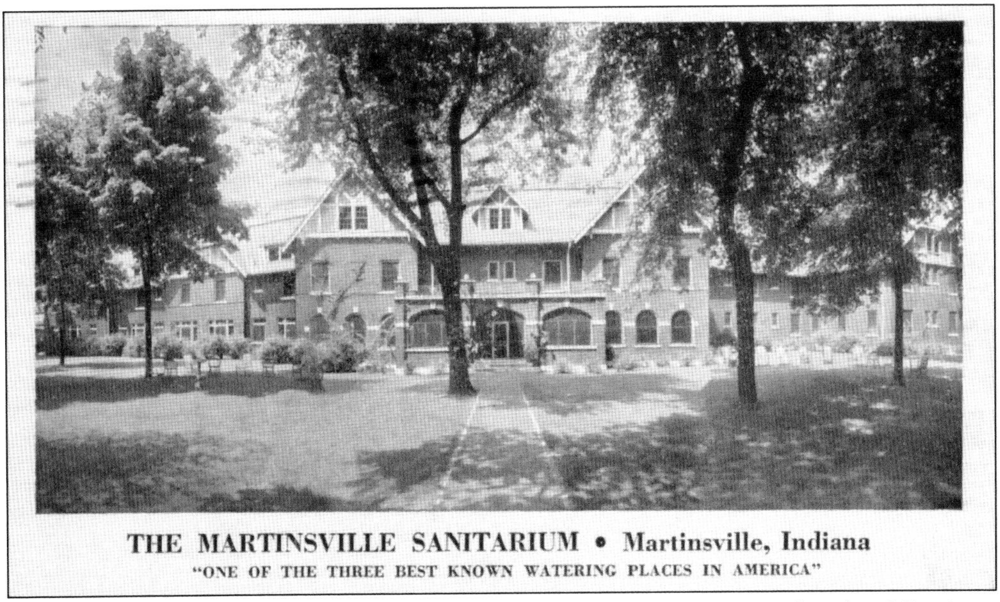

Front Entrance, 1947. "I arrived here Saturday having a nice time," writes Minnie to friends in Hoopeston, Illinois. "Thanks for telling me about this place. It sure is grand. Every thing so nice and every body so friendly. Hope Hoopeston gets along okay with out me." The caption on reverse reads, "Under same management and ownership as the Home Lawn Mineral Springs Company."

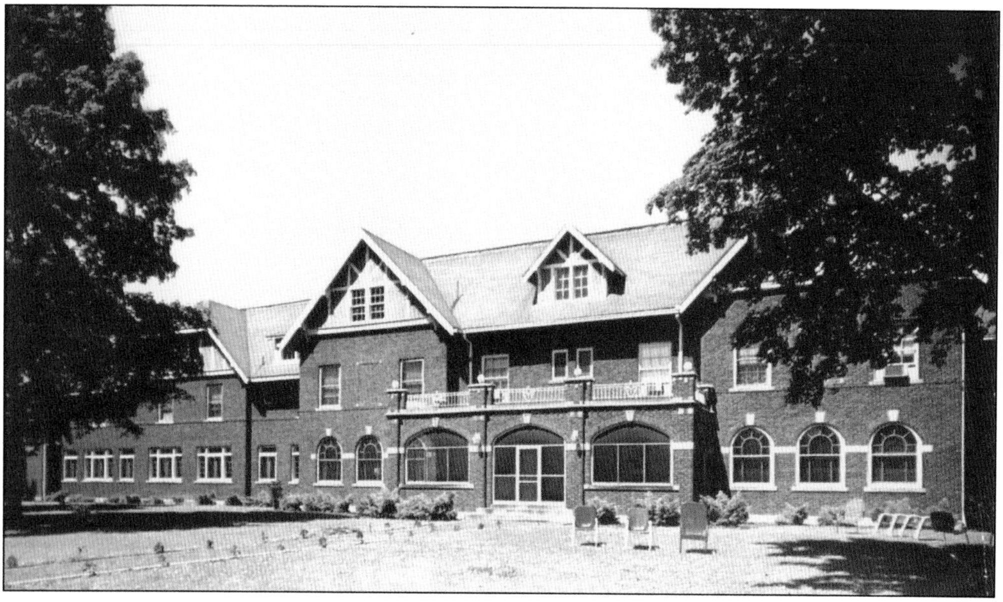

MARTINSVILLE SANITARIUM BECOMES KENNEDY HOME, C. 1960. With a dwindling guest list, increasing maintenance costs, and an eye on retirement, W. A. Kennedy placed the Martinsville Sanitarium on the market. Offers were not forthcoming. Kennedy refused to sacrifice the property for less than his $250,000 asking price, so he donated it in the memory of his deceased son, Charles, for use as a residential care facility for the aged.

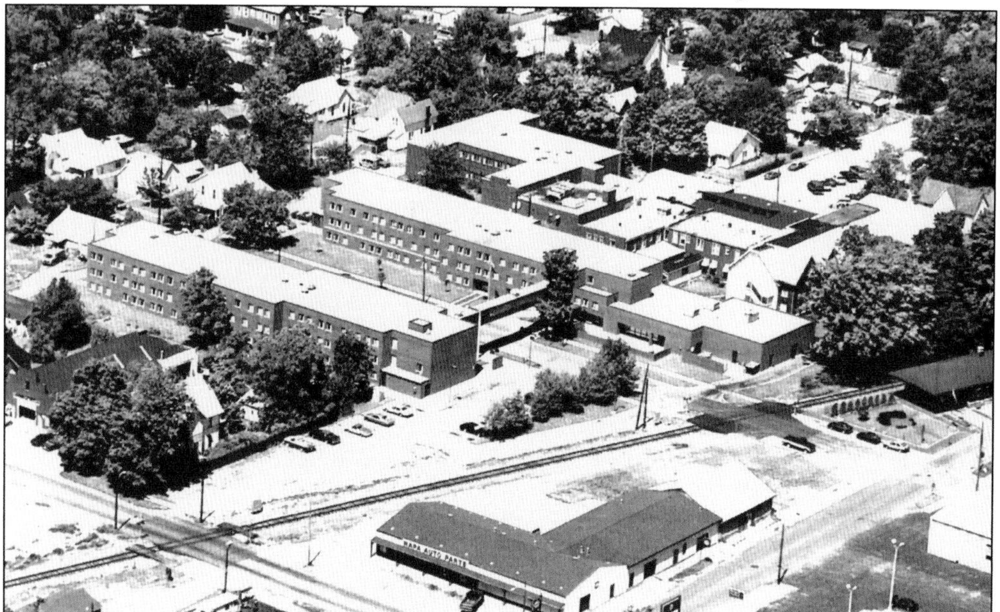

KENMAR APARTMENTS AND KENNEDY LIVING CENTER, C. 1982. Between 1967 and 1984, approximately two-thirds of the Martinsville Sanitarium was torn down for construction of the KenMar Apartments on the north side of Pike Street and expansion of the Kennedy Living Center, which closed in 2002. Now owned by Wellspring Center of Morgan County, the surviving 1925–1926 portion of the Martinsville Sanitarium is listed on the National Register of Historic Places.

Three

HOME LAWN SANITARIUM

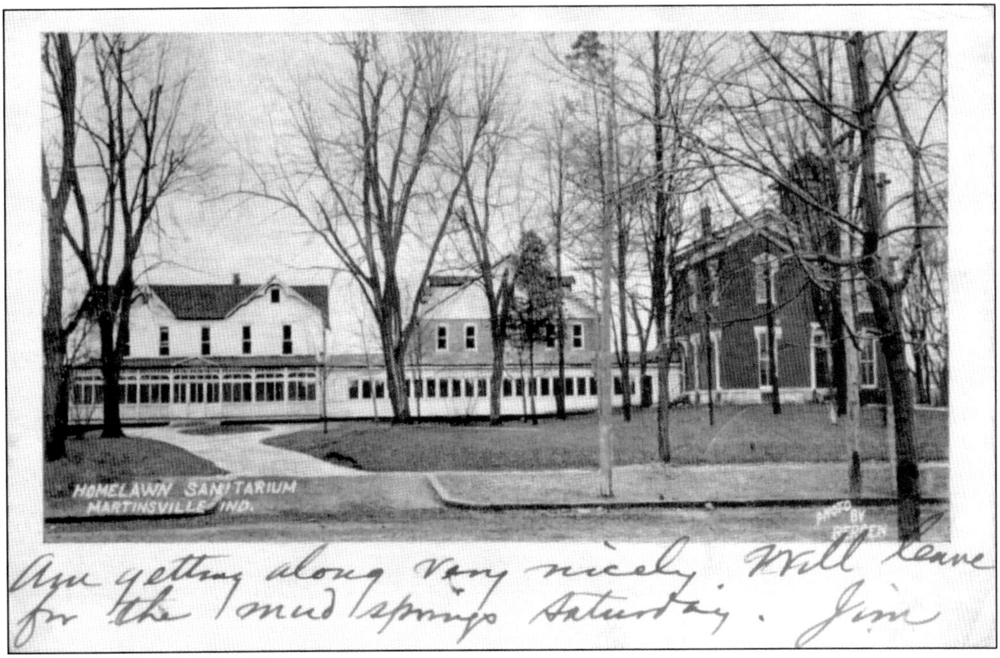

HOME LAWN SANITARIUM, 1906. Martinsville's grandest sanitarium had humble beginnings. Inspired by the success of Sylvanus Barnard's sanitarium, Ebenezer Henderson and his son-in-law and neighbor, Willard E. Parks, drilled for water on Henderson's East Washington Street property in August 1889. A frame bathhouse and engine house were erected adjacent to his fine two-story brick house, shown at the right. Henderson's plan for a two-and-a-half-acre lake was never realized.

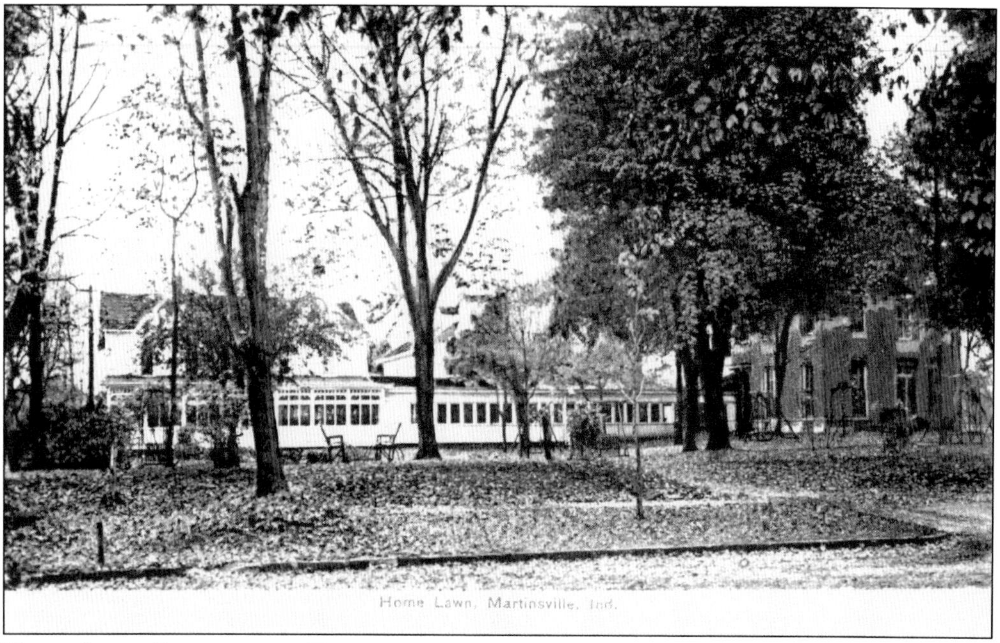

HOME LAWN BATHHOUSE, HOTEL, AND HENDERSON HOUSE, C. 1907. Success was quick to come. In 1892, Henderson dug a second well and added a second story to the bathhouse for guest lodging. Prior to the erection of the hotel, guests stayed in the Henderson home, "surrounded by the family circle and presided over by his good wife, [who provided a] table bountifully supplied with wholesome and toothsome home cooking."

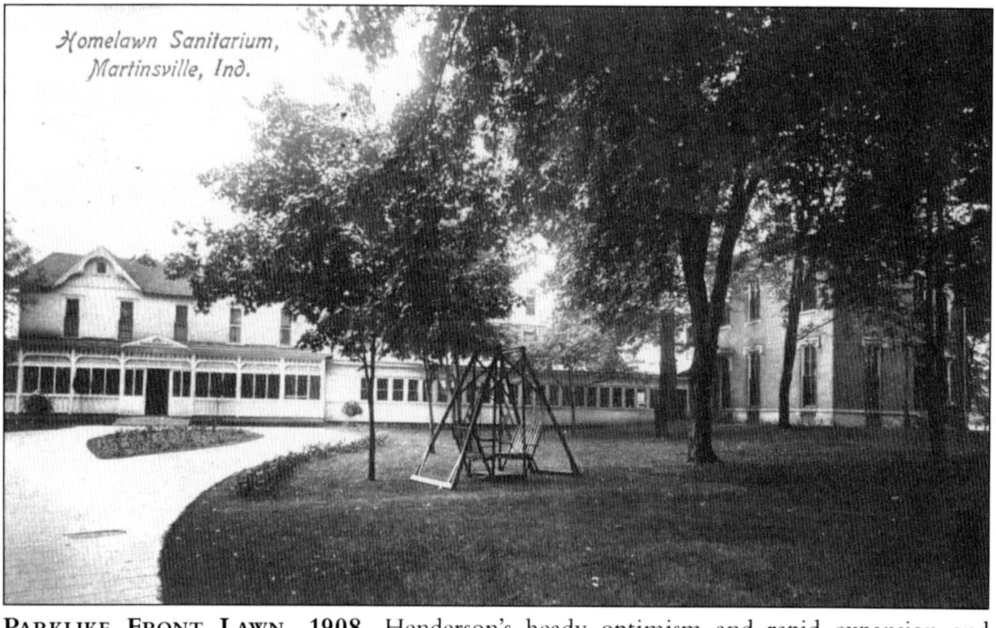

PARKLIKE FRONT LAWN, 1908. Henderson's heady optimism and rapid expansion and improvements, combined with mismanagement and the nationwide economic panic of 1893, led to bankruptcy. Henderson lost the Home Lawn—and his own house—at a sheriff's sale in 1898. The Home Lawn's new owners were Dr. Charles A. Kessinger and Dr. Walter E. (W. E.) Hendricks and investor John A. Burbank of Richmond, Indiana.

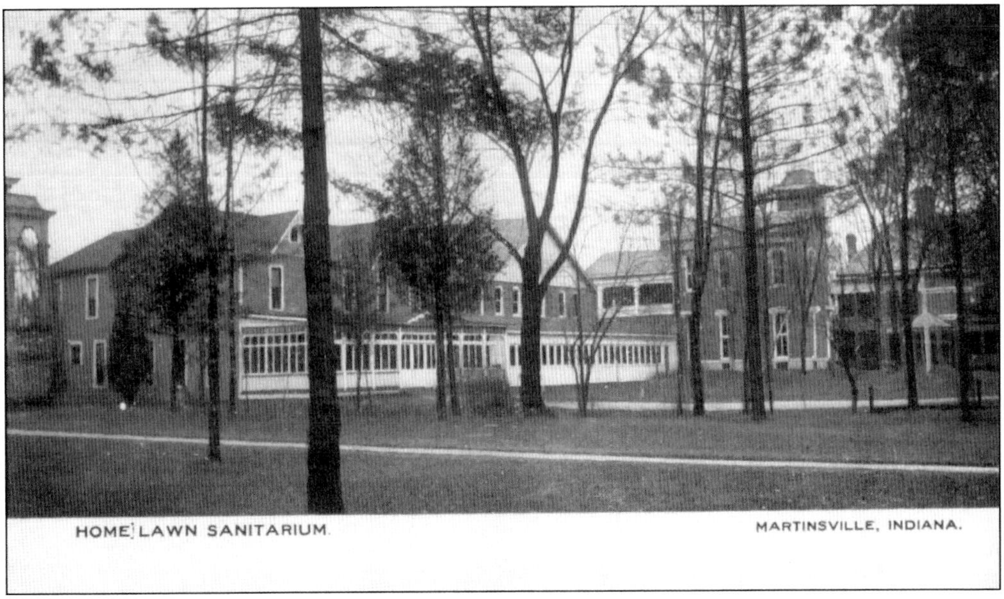

Home Lawn, Henderson House, and Parks House, c. 1906. In 1899, the new partners expanded the sanitarium, building a two-story hotel and updating the bathhouse. "The house on left where you see just corner is where Hazel takes her music lessons," writes the sender of this card. To the right of the Henderson house is the Willard E. and Fannie (Henderson) Parks house, which Hendricks would buy for a hotel annex.

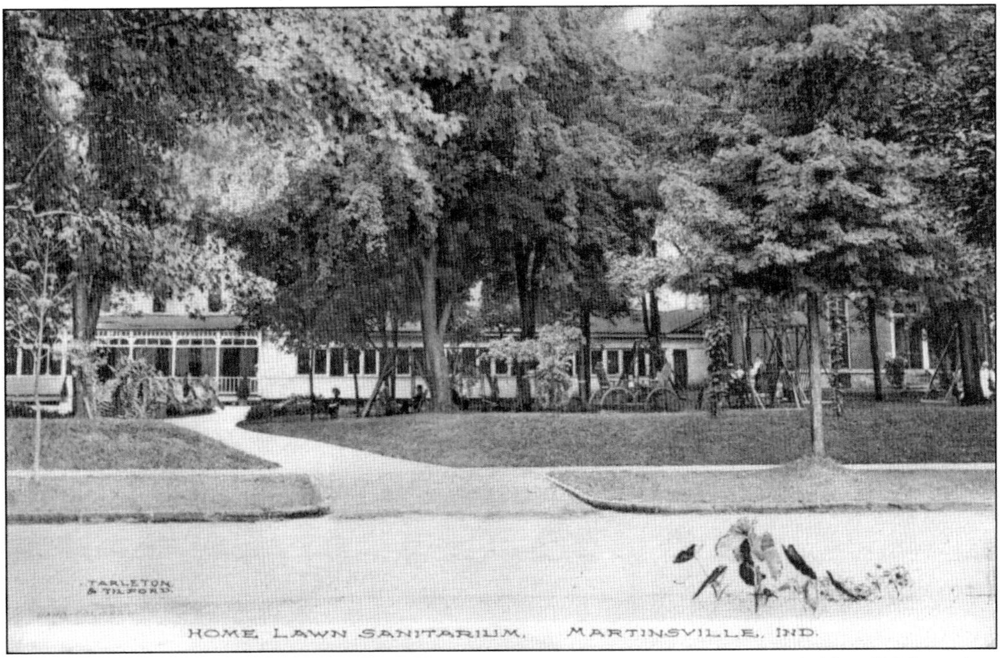

View from North Side of Washington Street, c. 1908. "Dear Neighbor," Ida writes to her neighbor in Washington, Pennsylvania, "Allie took his first treatment in afternoon, slept pretty well last night. Dr. Hendricks thinks he can help him he will have a bath a day but I don't think they will sweat him like they did at Mt. Clemens. They are giving me best of everything."

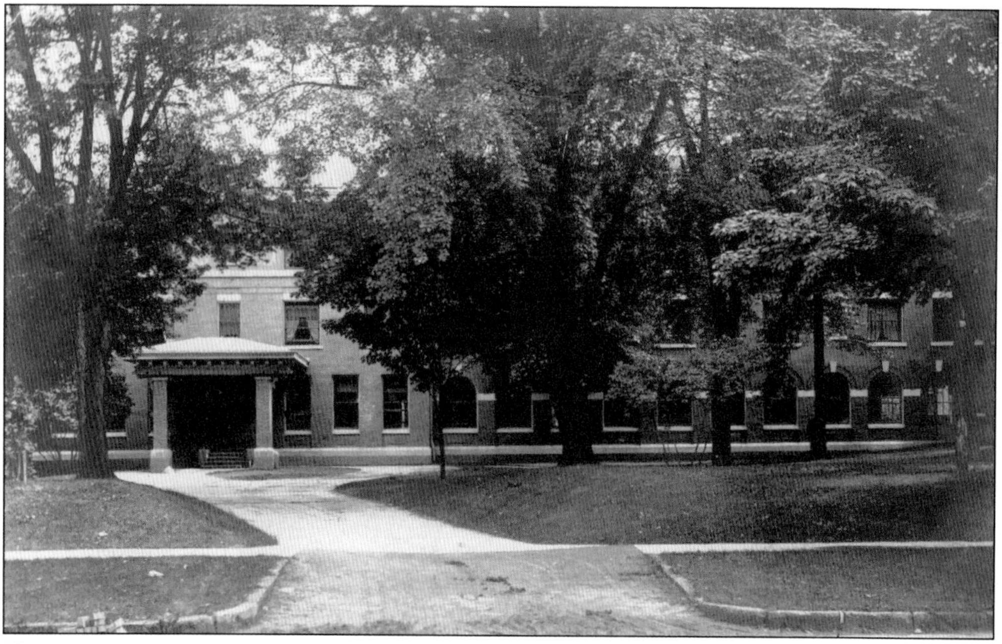

HOME LAWN SANITARIUM, 1909. In 1904, W. E. Hendricks became the Home Lawn's sole owner. Within a few years, the old frame structures were entirely replaced by the three-story brick building shown here. "This is a picture of the new Home Lawn Mineral Springs. Mama wants you to see," writes Rosa. "She has improved and gained 3½ pounds."

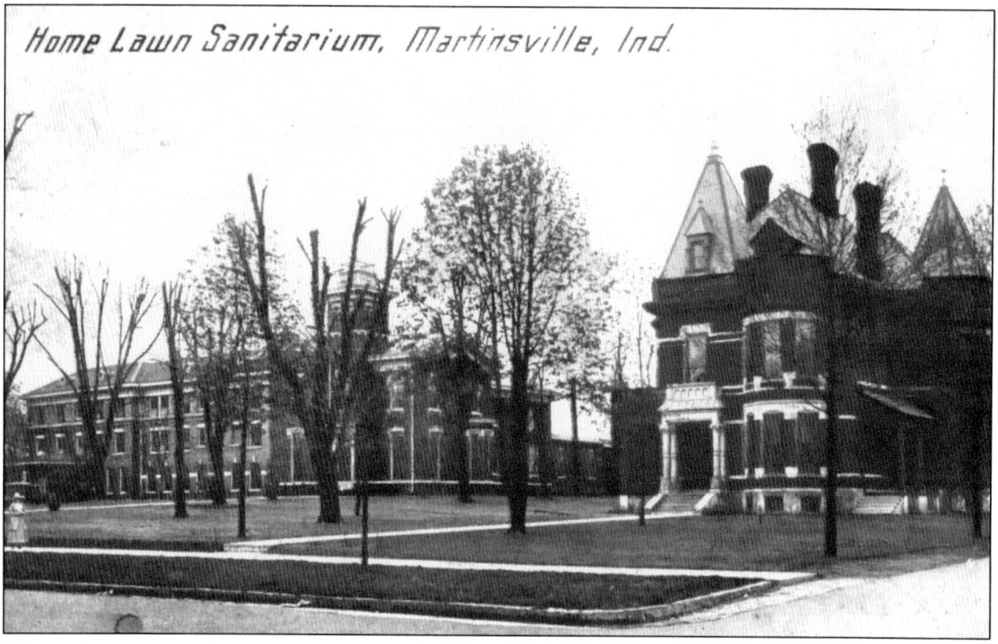

HOME LAWN AND PARKS HOUSE, 1912. In 1911, W. E. Hendricks bought the Parks house for use as a hotel annex. Instead, it became the home of his daughter and son-in-law, Mary Eloise and W. A. Kennedy. The sender of this card writes, "I'm spending my spring vacation at this place taking hot sweats, baths, and drinking water till I feel as if I'd burst, trying to boil that old rheumatism out of me."

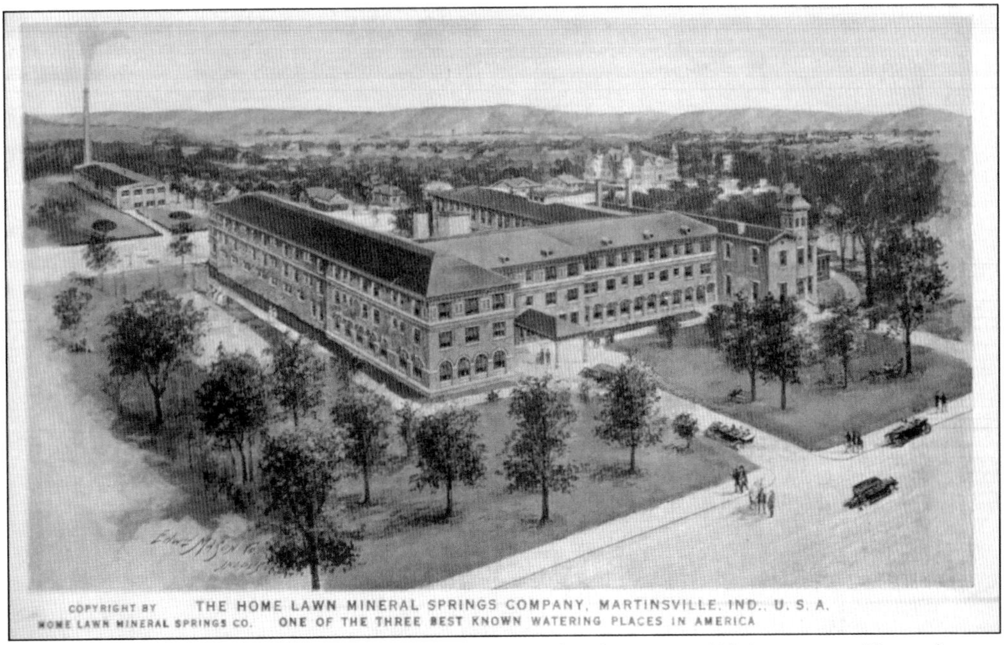

BIRD'S-EYE VIEW, c. 1918. W. A. Kennedy made his fortune in life insurance. He took over the Home Lawn in 1911. In a period of rapidly changing technologies, Kennedy saw the future. Between 1915 and 1917, he added a huge east wing; heating, ice, and cold storage plants; and on the south side of Jackson Street, a laundry to handle the piles of linens dirtied daily by guests.

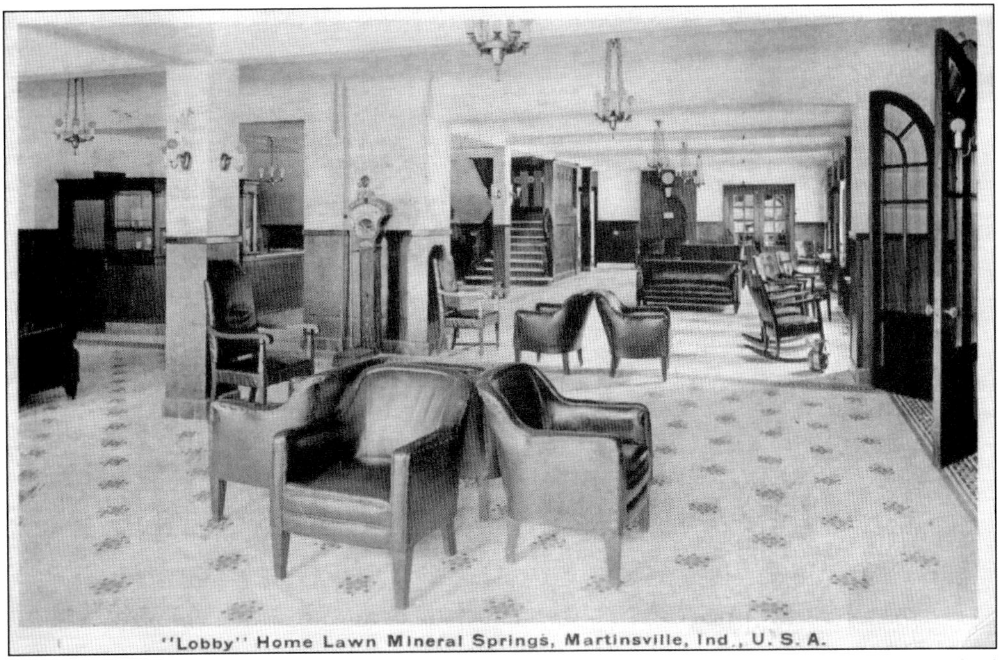

LOBBY, c. 1920. The Home Lawn faced Washington Street. Upon passing through the arched doors, guests entered the grand lobby. With its tile floor, leather chairs, mohair-seated rockers, and elegant chandeliers, it was a popular place for socializing, card playing, waiting for the dinner bell, or merely to see and be seen by one's fellow guests.

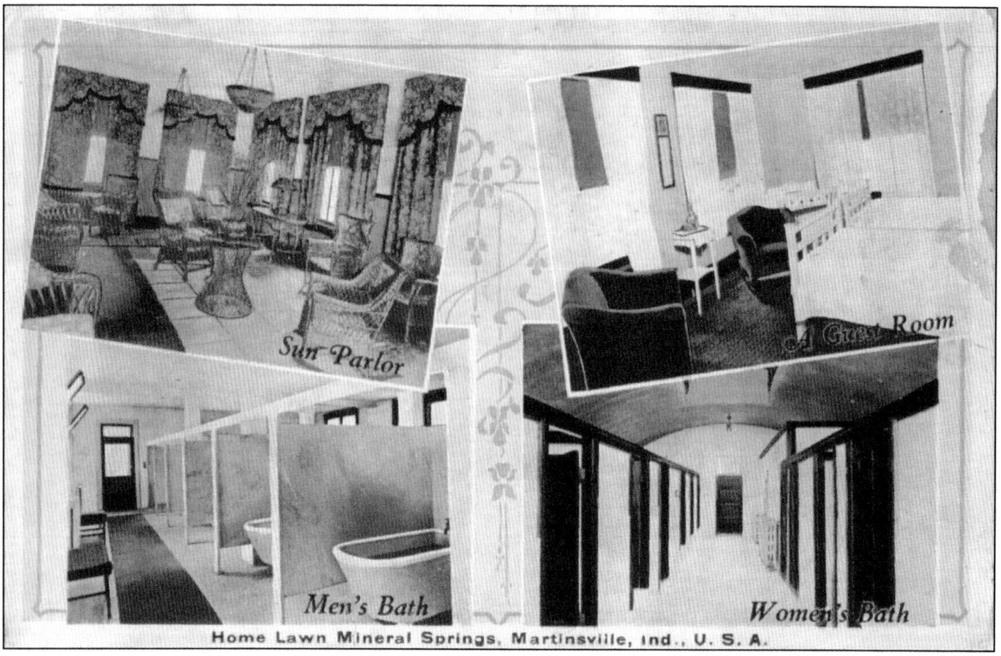

MULTIPLE INTERIOR VIEWS, C. 1920. The sun parlor shown at the upper left was appointed with wicker furniture. Guest rooms, shown at the upper right, had private telephones and twin beds of a hospital-like style. The men's and women's bathhouses, shown below, featured porcelain tubs, tile floors, marble dividers, and trained attendants. Only the women's had doors for privacy.

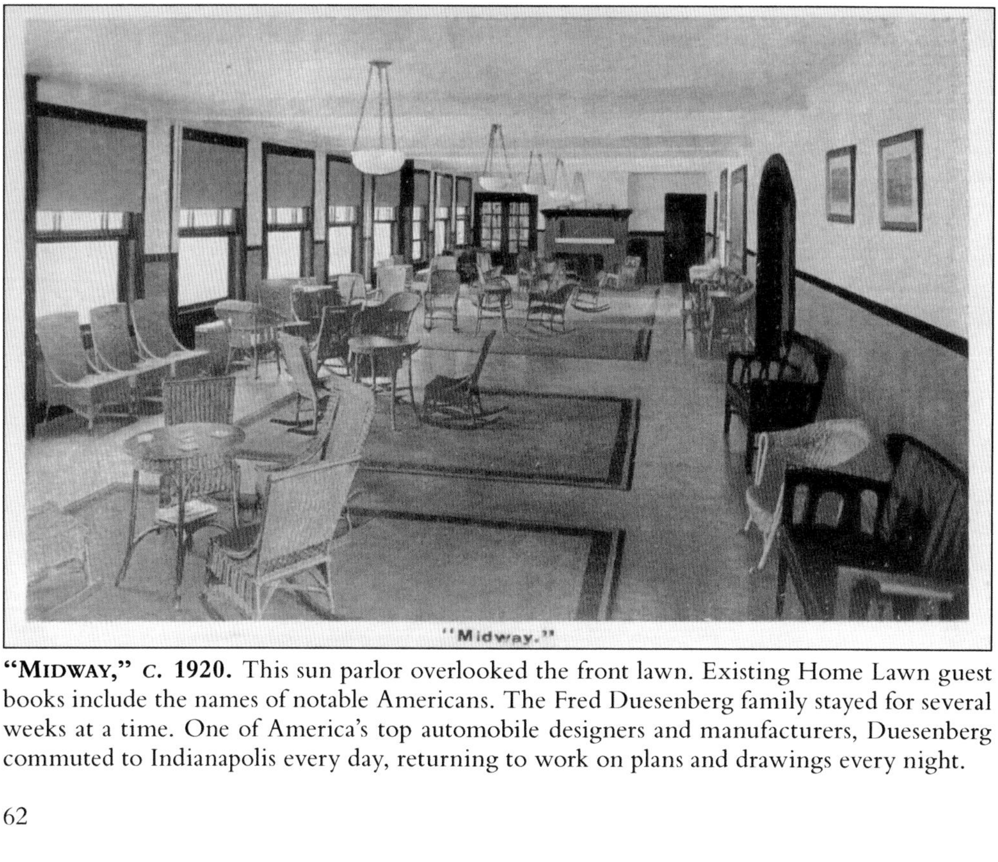

"MIDWAY," C. 1920. This sun parlor overlooked the front lawn. Existing Home Lawn guest books include the names of notable Americans. The Fred Duesenberg family stayed for several weeks at a time. One of America's top automobile designers and manufacturers, Duesenberg commuted to Indianapolis every day, returning to work on plans and drawings every night.

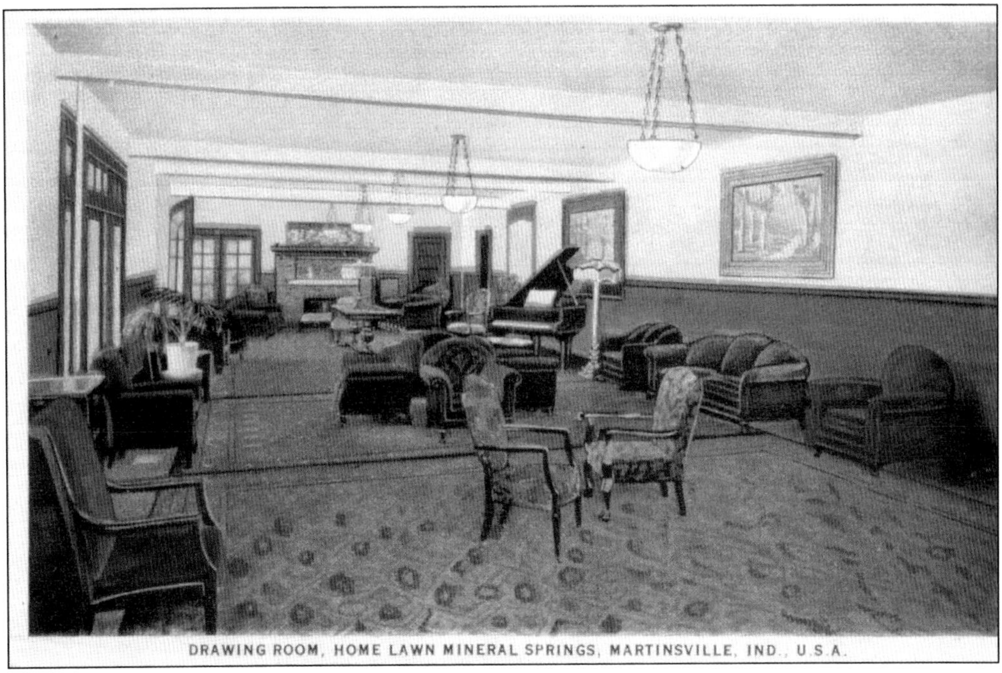

DRAWING ROOM, c. 1923. Here is the same room after the 1922 addition of a north-facing solarium. Other noteworthy guests during the 1920s and 1930s were magician Harry Blackstone and entertainer Al Jolson, who was amused that the local Cure and Hensley funeral home would have "cure" as part of its name.

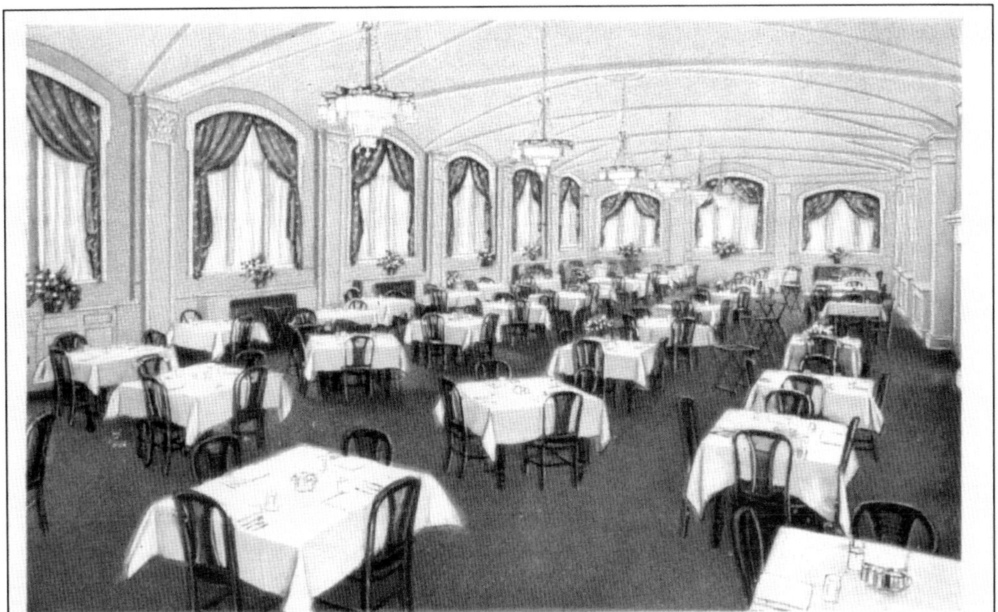

MAIN DINING ROOM, c. 1923. Many guests were Jewish. Kosher foods were purchased in Indianapolis and served in the beautiful dining room. Nearly as deep as a city block, it featured a coffered ceiling, Italian marble wainscoting, hardwood floors with velvet carpet, tiered crystal chandeliers, and windows draped with seasonal silk or velvet panels.

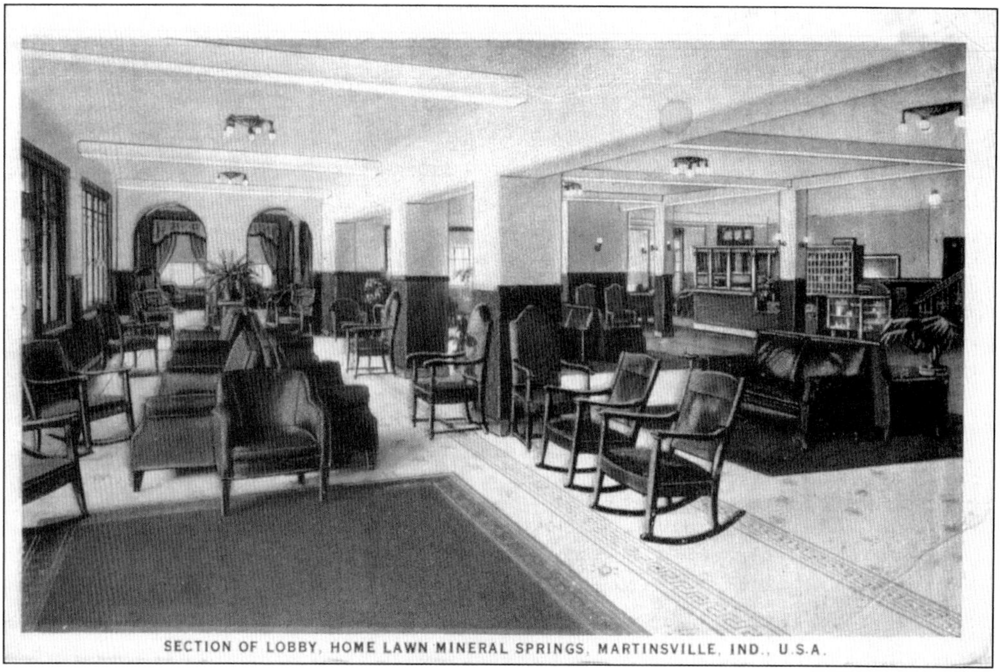

SECTION OF LOBBY WITH VIEW OF MAIN DESK, C. 1923. With frequent redecorating, the Home Lawn always appeared in vogue. Many guests stayed for weeks, even months, and returned year after year. Of course, they would notice if the drapes were a bit faded or the wallpaper in their room five years out of date. Compare this view of the lobby to those on pages 61, 67, 72, and 75.

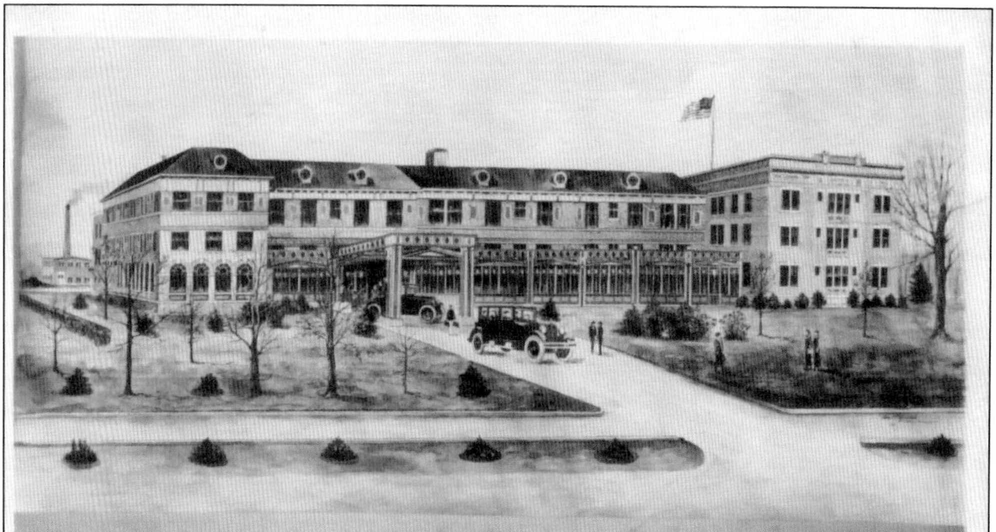

HOME LAWN AT MATURITY, C. 1925. The Henderson house was demolished in 1921 and replaced by a three-story wing, seen at the right, containing 90 guest rooms, one public and two private dining rooms, a fully modern kitchen, lounges, game rooms, a billiard room, and other recreational rooms. Constructed by Charles F. Duncan, the fireproof wing expanded the Home Lawn's capacity to 225 guests. The north solarium, seen here, was completed in 1922.

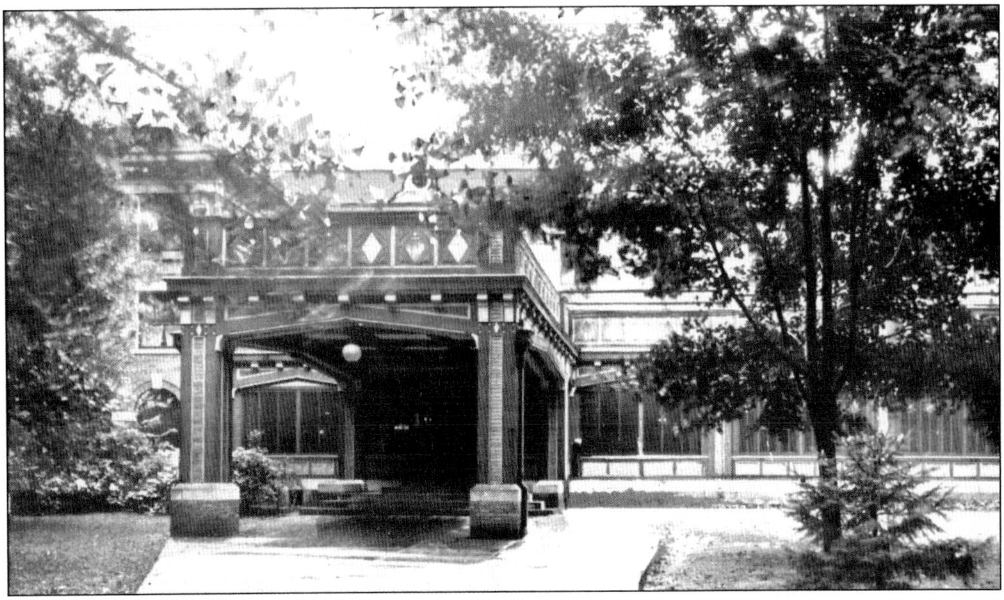

PORTE COCHERE, C. 1930. The art deco–inspired porte cochere allowed guests to arrive and depart under protection from sun, rain, and snow. The porte cochere and the expansive solarium, built in 1922, on which the geometrical decoration continued above expansive windows, were the most distinguishing feature of the sanitarium's front facade. This view is the left side of a bifold card; the right side is shown below.

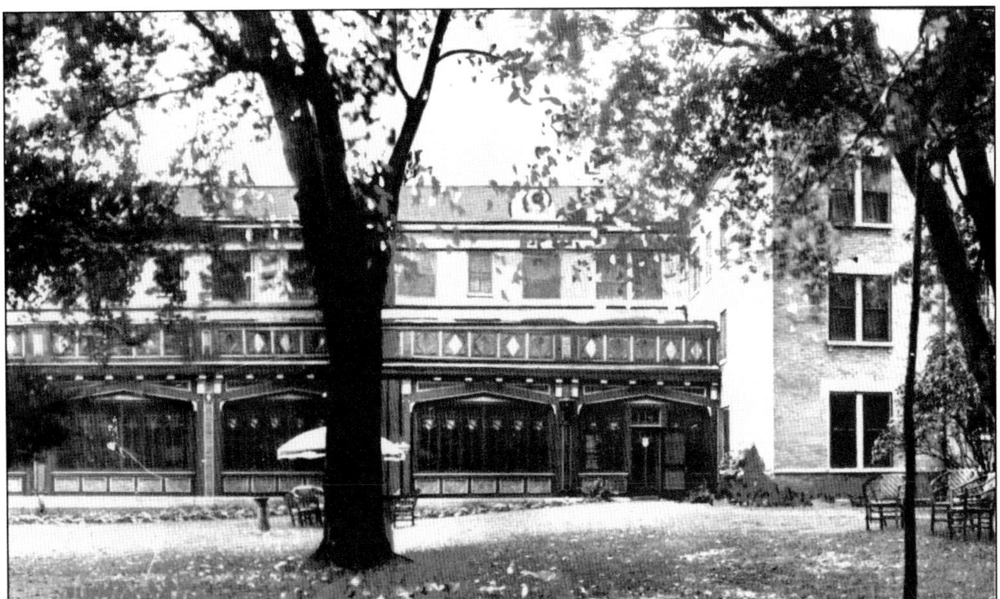

SOLARIUM AND WEST WING, C. 1930. In 1925, Don Kennedy returned from California to assist his father with the Home Lawn's management. His brother, Bud, and sister-in-law, Marion, a former silent film star, came a year later. "This is where we are staying. I never saw such a marvelous place," writes the sender of this card.

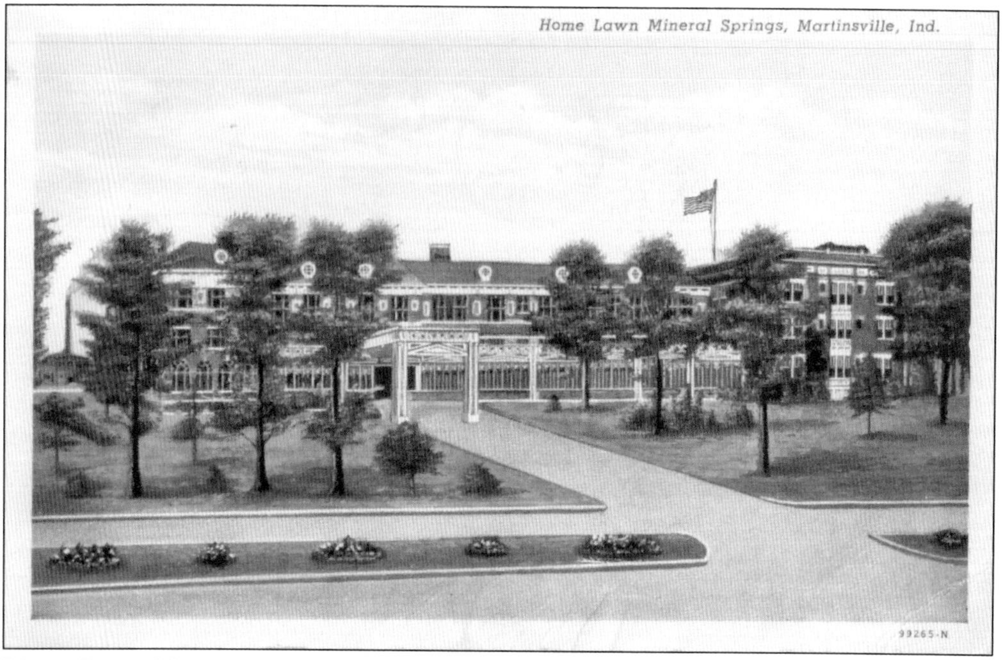

HOME LAWN MINERAL SPRINGS, C. 1928. At full maturity and the height of its popularity, the Home Lawn was one of the city's major employers. A laundry worker could earn up to $8 per week. With the addition of tips of up to several dollars per service, bellhops, waitresses, and other employees in direct contact with guests took home significantly more.

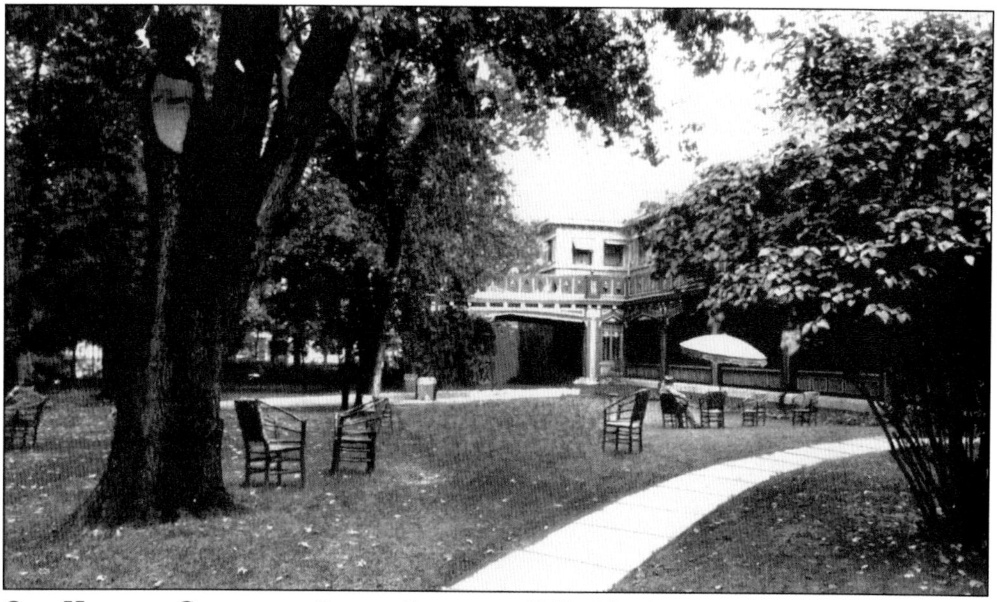

OLD HICKORY CHAIRS ON FRONT LAWN, C. 1930. The Depression greatly impacted the sanitarium industry. In 1933, a *Martinsville Democrat* headline lamented, "City should have artesian drinking fountain on the square or state highway here. Famed waters of Martinsville should be advertised to everyone who passes through. Our own county needs to drink the water. We have one of the three best watering places in America and do the least talking about it."

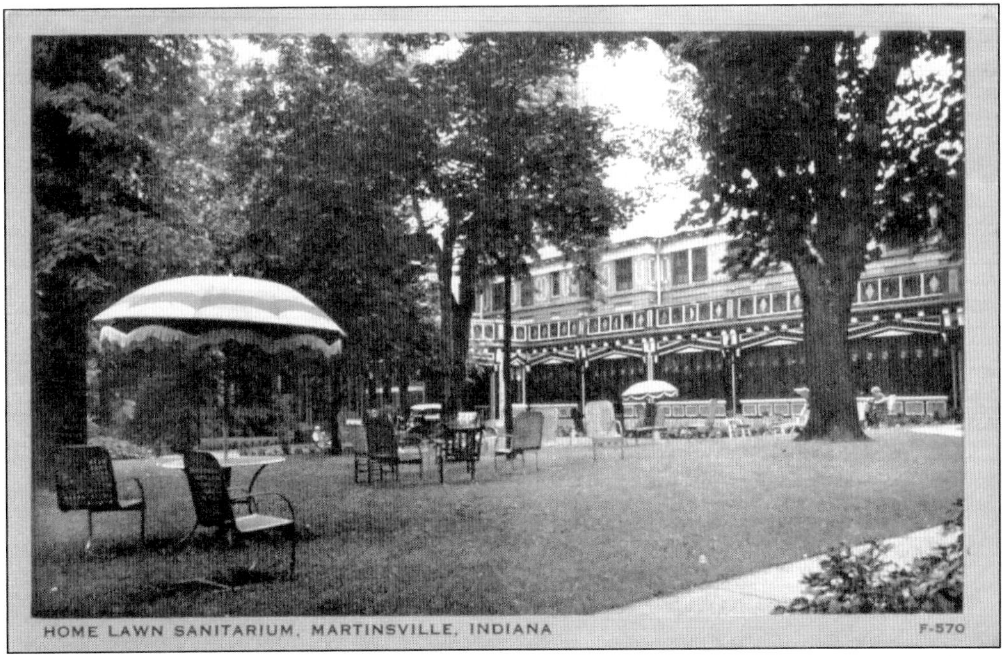

FRONT LAWN WITH VIEW OF SOLARIUM, *c.* 1942. This somewhat later view is similar to that of the previous card. Although many wealthy Home Lawn patrons continued their pattern of extended stays during the Depression, an unoccupied front lawn became an increasingly common sight. Still, W. A. Kennedy kept the doors open, refusing to lay off employees and often making up the shortage out of his own pocket.

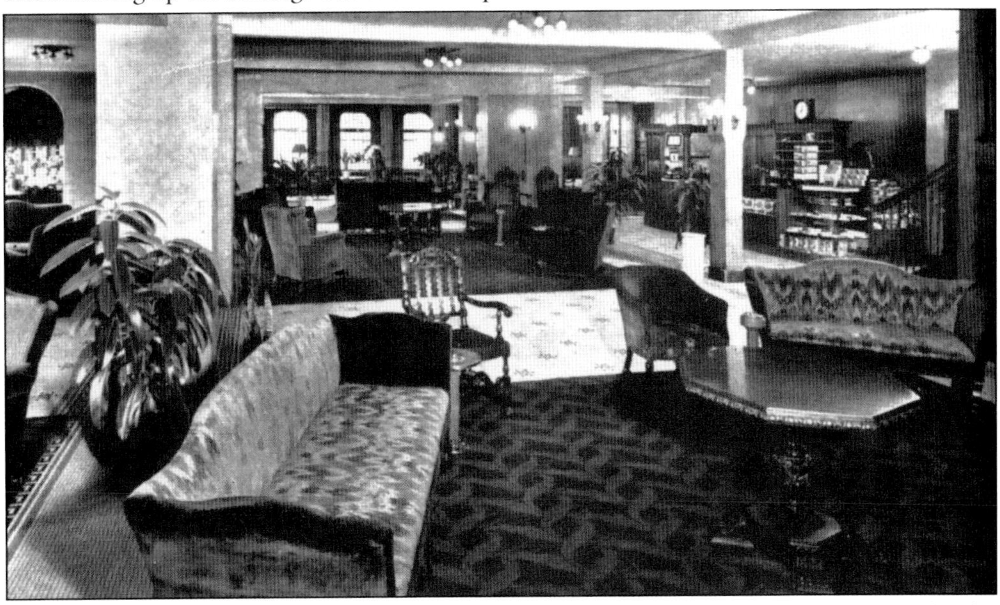

LOBBY AND MAIN DESK, *c.* 1944. This view and the nine that follow may have been taken by noted Brown County photographer Frank Hohenberger, who took promotional photographs during the early 1940s. "This is our first visit to this place, and we like it a lot," writes Ruth. "Service, food, everything fine and the hotel are turning people away every day so guess we are not the only ones spending our vacation here."

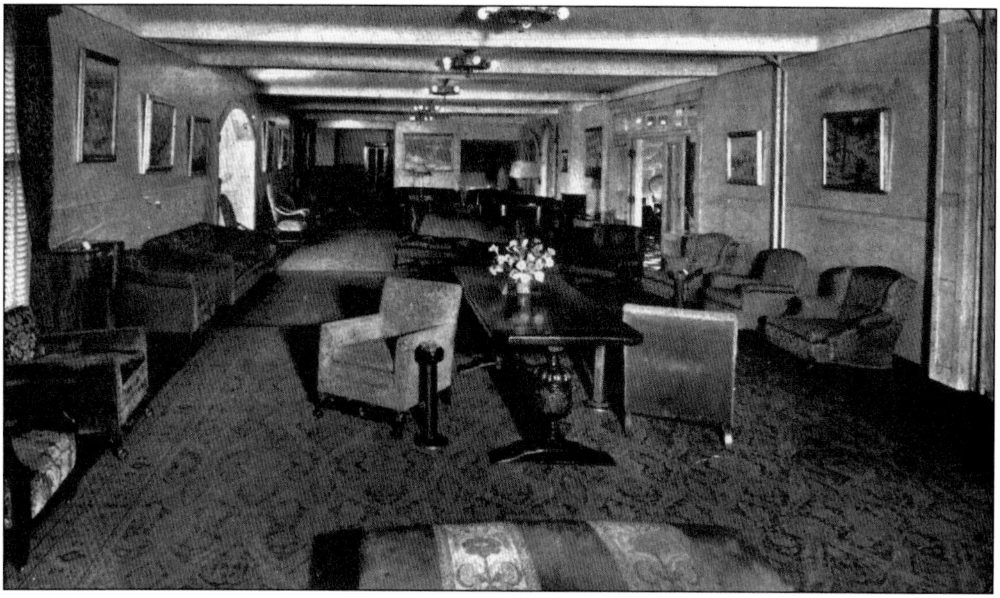

LOUNGE, 1950. Hoosier artists Carl and Wood Woolsey, who had achieved success as landscape artists in Taos, New Mexico, lived in Martinsville during the Depression, due largely to W. A. Kennedy's support. The Home Lawn lounge doubled as a gallery where guests could admire and select paintings for purchase. The paintings seen here appear to be those of the Woolsey brothers, whose frames were made by the youngest brother, Jean.

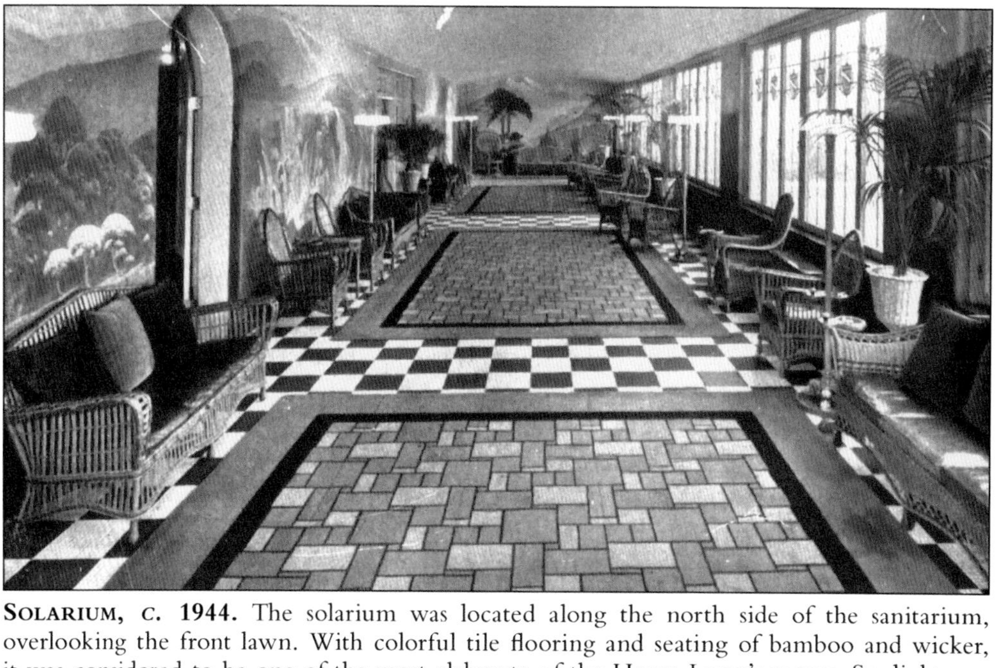

SOLARIUM, C. 1944. The solarium was located along the north side of the sanitarium, overlooking the front lawn. With colorful tile flooring and seating of bamboo and wicker, it was considered to be one of the most elaborate of the Home Lawn's rooms. Sunlight was believed to have special recuperative and restorative qualities. The mural is attributed to noted artist John Coggeshall of Massachusetts.

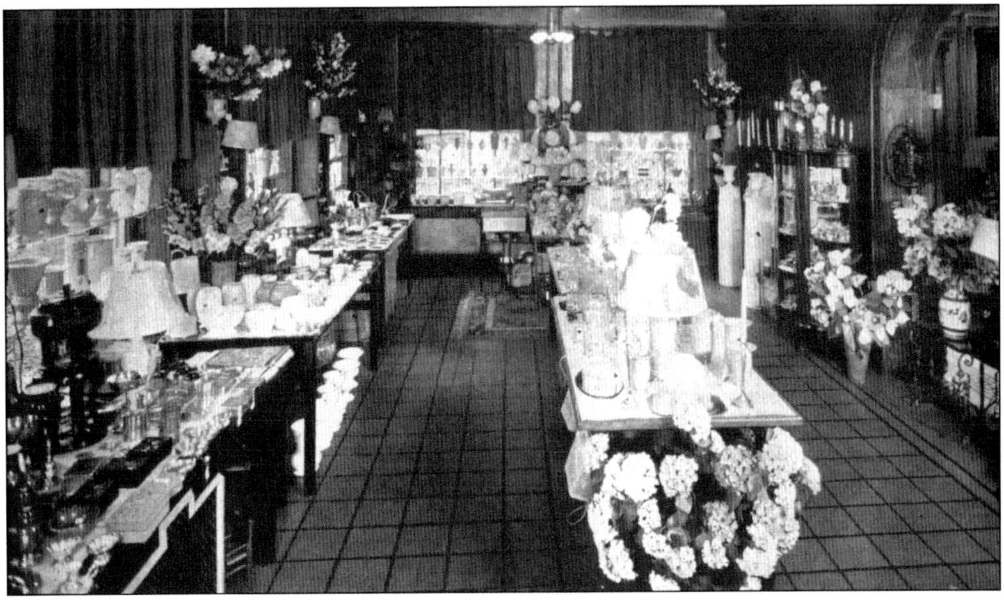

Gift Shop, 1947. "Offer[ing] exquisite merchandise for the convenience of the fastidious purchaser," the gift shop was managed by W. A. Kennedy's daughter, Mary Kay, who made regular buying trips to New York and Chicago. Guests also enjoyed shopping in downtown Martinsville. During World War II, they bought out rationed goods such as coffee and silk stockings so that the locals were often out of luck.

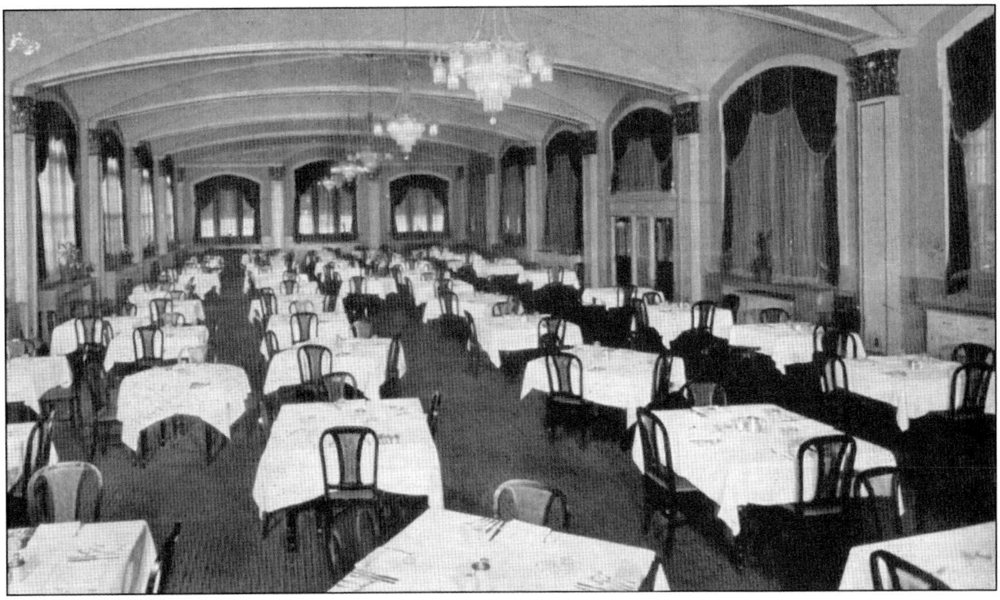

Dining Room, 1941. The Home Lawn had a reputation for painstakingly prepared choice foods. A former busboy remembers, "The food was so different from what I was used to that I didn't like it, but after I got used to it, nothing could beat it. . . . They had the most wonderful food you ever got into. I was from 128 pounds right off to about 140 just in no time."

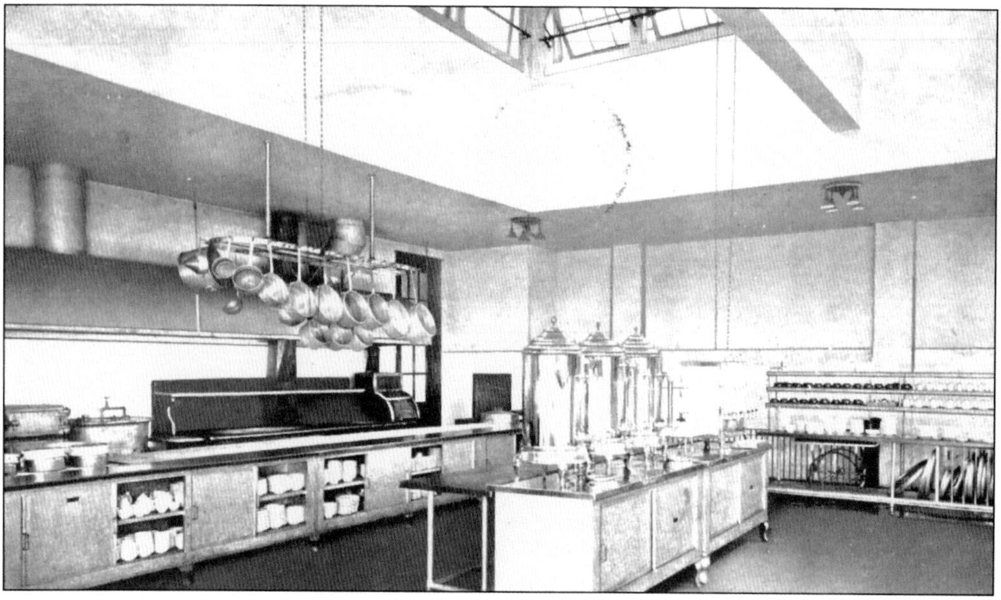

KITCHEN, C. 1940. Directing the Home Lawn kitchen for more than 60 years combined were head chefs Louis and Albert Francesconi and their successor, Alva Moss. Located at the rear of the west wing, the sanitary kitchen boasted the finest, most up-to-date arrangement, glazed floor and wall surfaces, porcelain-coated cabinets and work stations, pots and pans of both copper and spun aluminum, and silver coffee urns. Natural light streamed through a vented skylight.

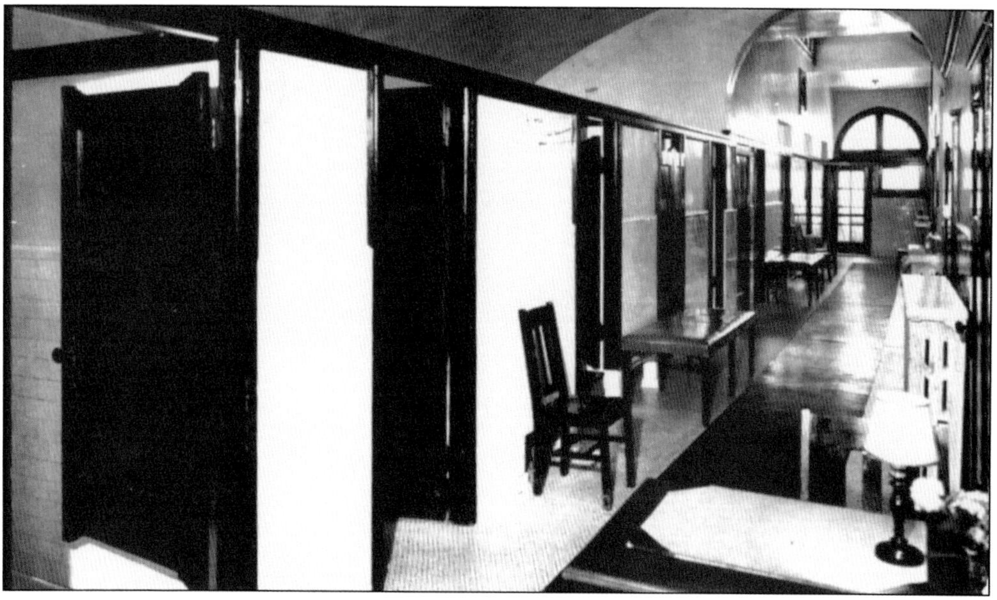

WOMEN'S BATHS, 1951. Considering that the mineral water bath was the heart of Martinsville's sanitarium industry, there is a remarkable dearth of postcards showing interior bathhouse views. If cleanliness is next to godliness, then health must not be far behind. Gleaming white tile on both floors and walls assured both. "Having a 3 day rest. Got 'jittery,'" writes the sender of this card.

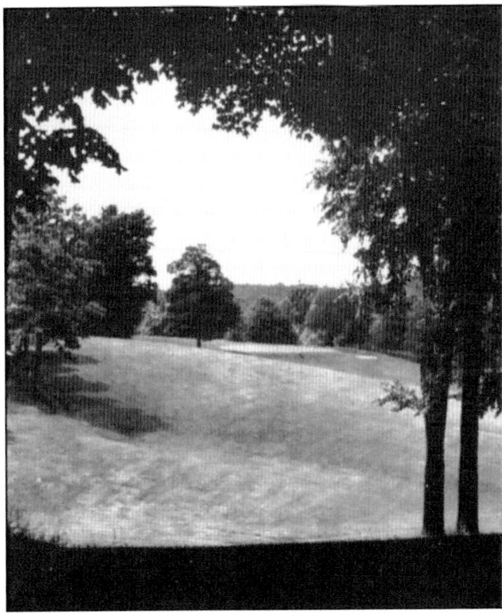
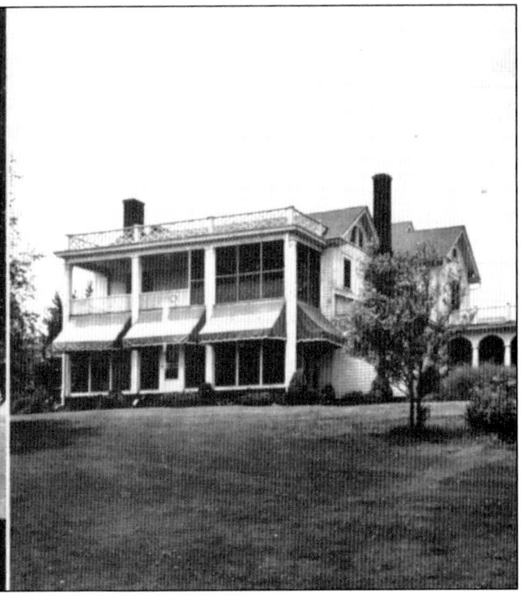

MARTINSVILLE COUNTRY CLUB, *c.* 1930. As part of the Home Lawn's 1925–1927 expansion, W. A. Kennedy established a "sporty" nine-hole golf course north of Martinsville. The clubhouse was the former Dyer farmhouse. About the Home Lawn guests waiting for a lift to the links, a Martinsville native recalls, "I was surprised that men would spend the whole afternoon playing a game when most of the men I knew worked hard all week."

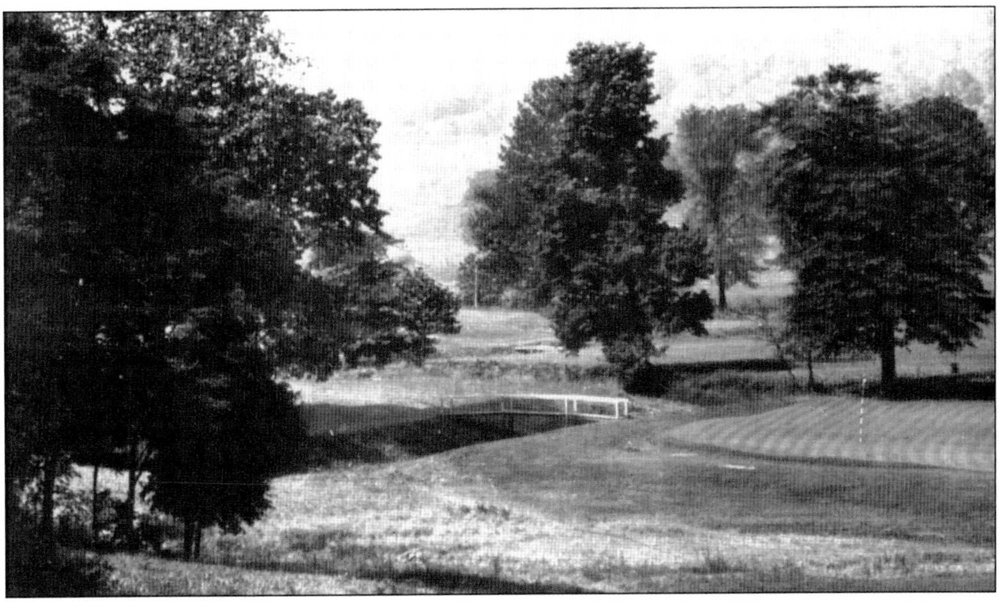

"BACK NINE," 1928. "We drove out to the country club . . . but did not get out of the car. They have a very pretty golf course," writes Katherine. Designed by Bill Diddle, the original course is today's back nine. In 1933, Kennedy hired Don and Agnes Carmichael as operators; they were succeeded by their sons, Sam and Ron. Today Sam and his wife, Sue, own and operate the country club.

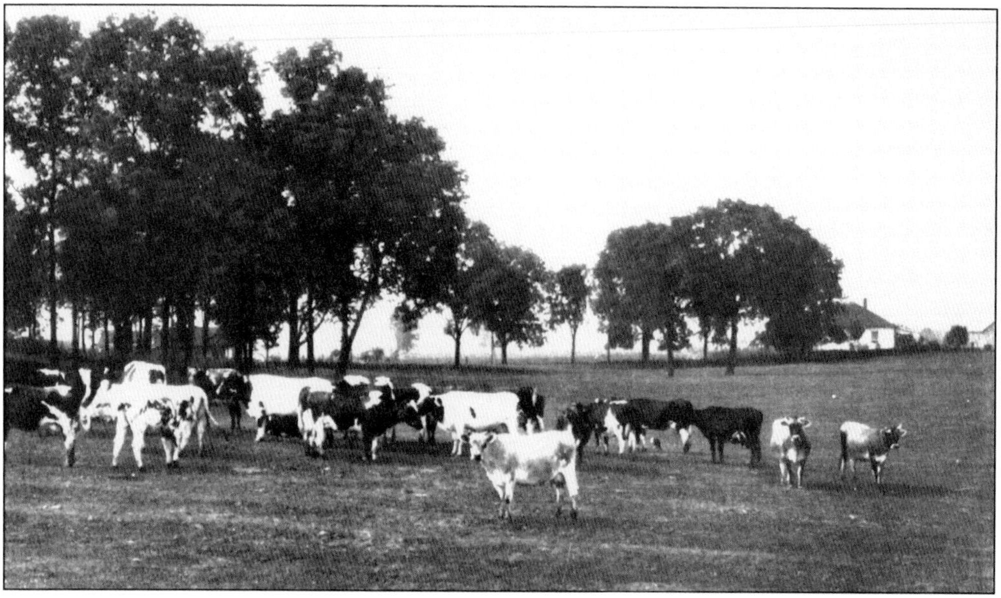

NORTH FARM, C. 1944. Located on Blue Bluff Road, North Farm provided dairy products for the kitchens of the Home Lawn and Martinsville sanitariums. Fresh vegetables were grown on South Farm, whose large barn remains near the Martinsville airport. Established by W. E. Hendricks, North Farm was later home to Bud and Marion Kennedy, who renamed it Budmar Farm.

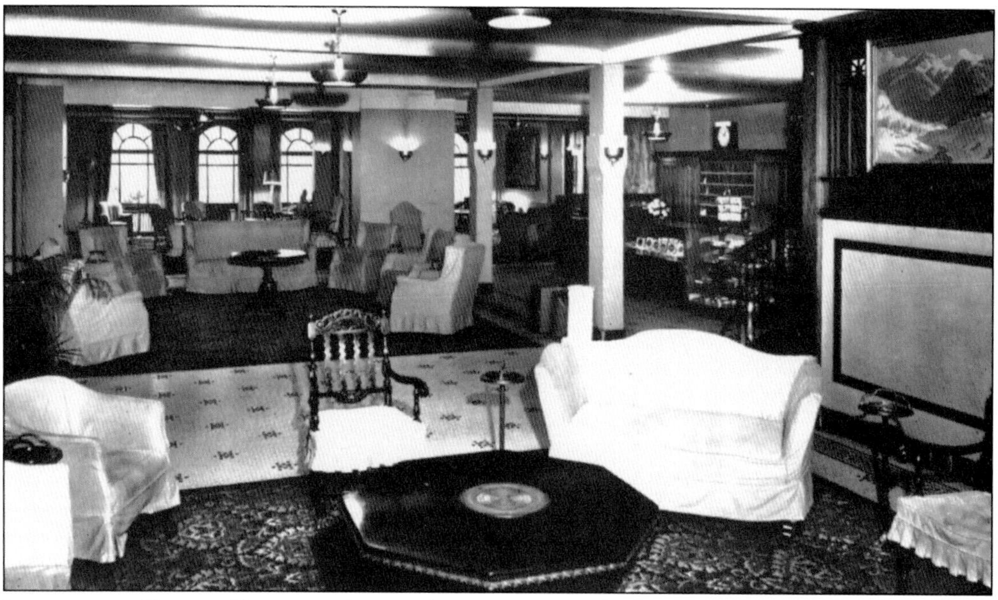

LOBBY AND FRONT DESK, C. 1950. The Home Lawn retained a large clientele throughout the 1950s and 1960s but was rarely filled to capacity. For the first time in its history, advertising became necessary. "Perk up! A few days at the Home Lawn, taking the mineral baths and revitalization treatments will make a new person out of you. . . . We are looking forward to having you at the Home Lawn for your annual tune-up."

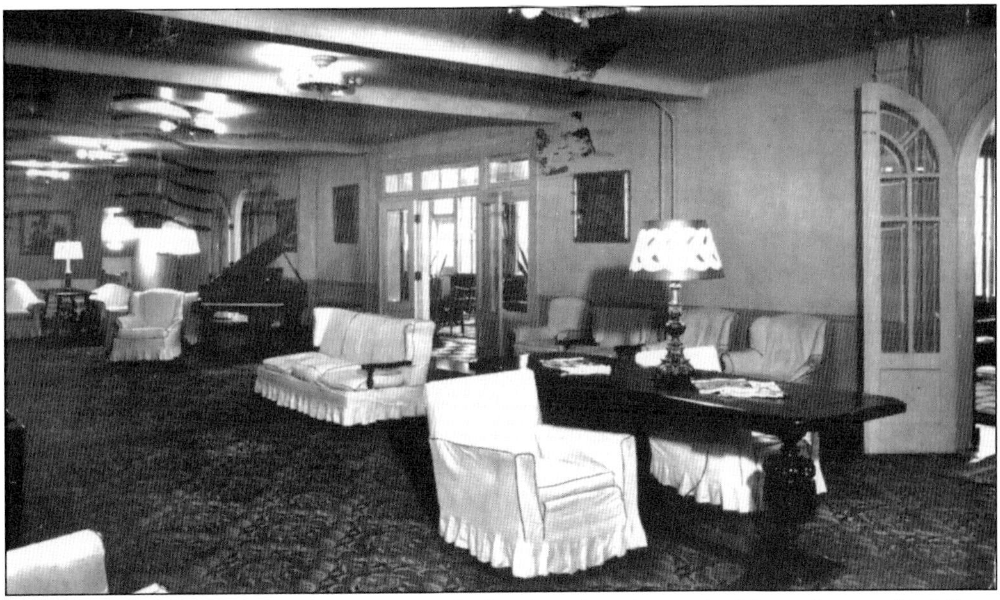

Lounge, 1955. In order to keep pace with the changing times, the Home Lawn added "one of the finest weight reduction programs in the country." Exercise bikes and rowing machines, ladies' machines for slimming the figure and improving circulation, and a men's high-humidity steam room reflected a growing interest in physical appearance and fitness. Compare this view of the lounge to those on pages 62 and 63 (drawing room) and 68.

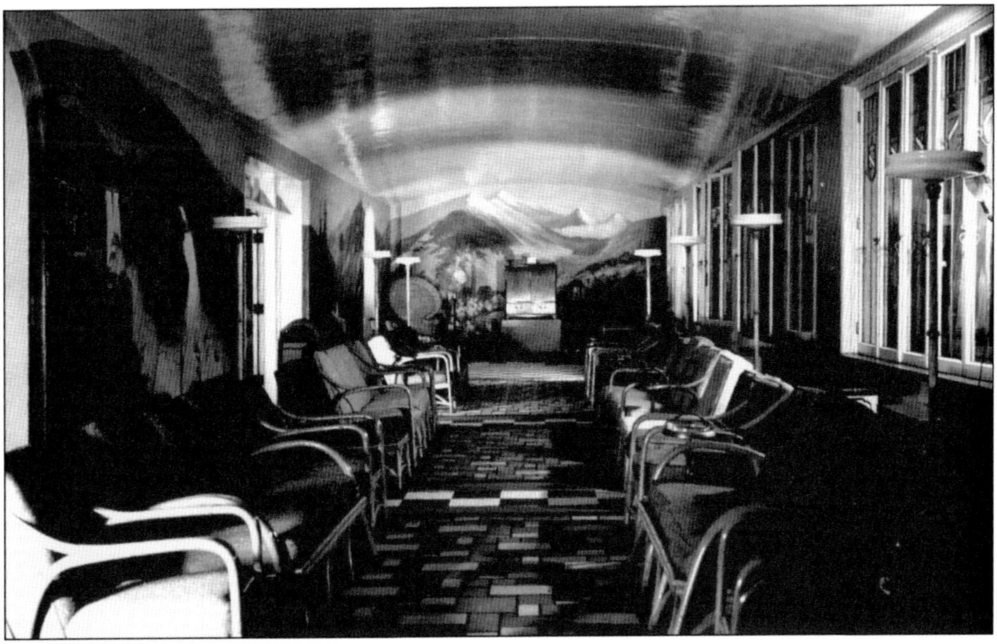

Solarium, c. 1957. Redecoration occurred only once during the mid-1950s, an indicator of the Home Lawn's decline attributed to lack of modern entertainment such as a swimming pool or cocktail lounge, lack of nightlife in the surrounding area, and the Kennedys' failure to add services while continuing to raise room prices.

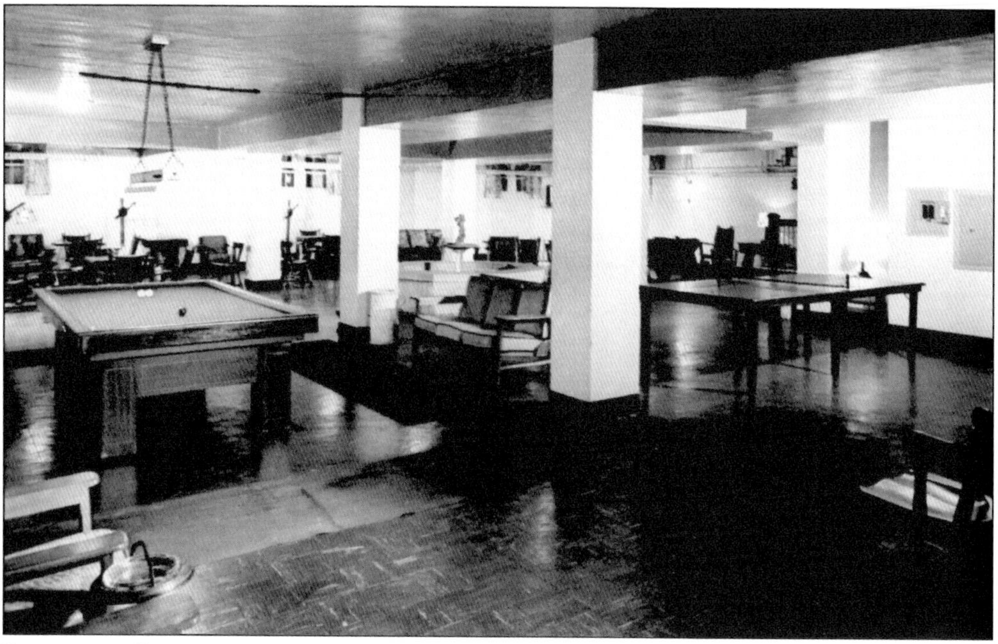

BASEMENT RECREATION ROOM, C. 1957. As his father did during the Depression, Don Kennedy attempted to keep the Home Lawn afloat with his own money. Faced with the reality of an aging facility and withering business, he finally put the sanitarium up for sale. In March 1971, the Home Lawn was sold on contract with $25,000 down to Arthur Widgery of Indianapolis. It then became Diamondhead Health Resort.

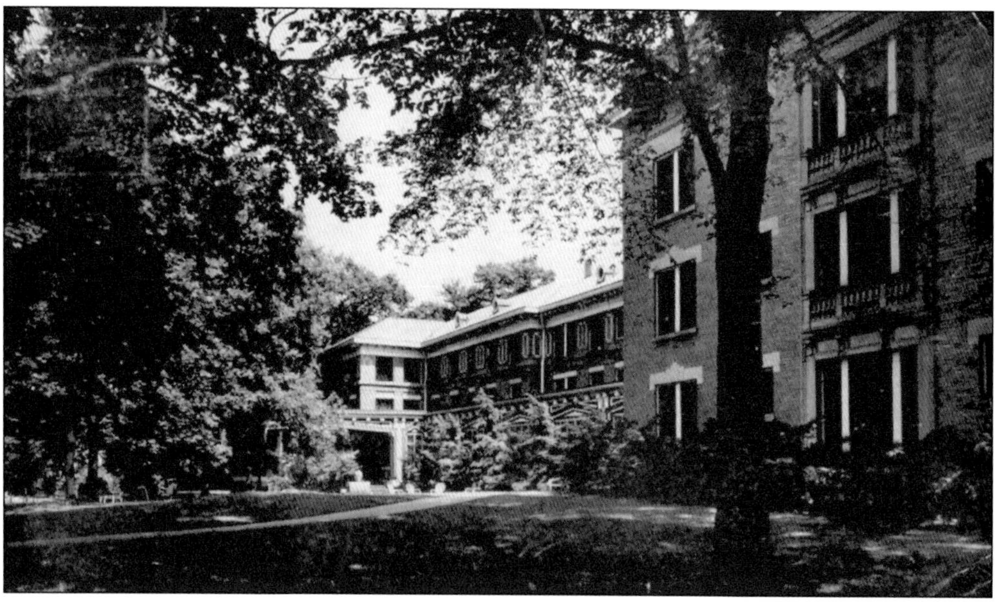

FRONT ELEVATION, C. 1960. As owner-operator of Diamondhead, Widgery had many plans for the Home Lawn's improvement, including the addition of a swimming pool. Other changes—a cocktail lounge and sale of alcohol in the dining room—offended many longtime guests and employees. Within two years, Widgery's mounting debts led to foreclosure.

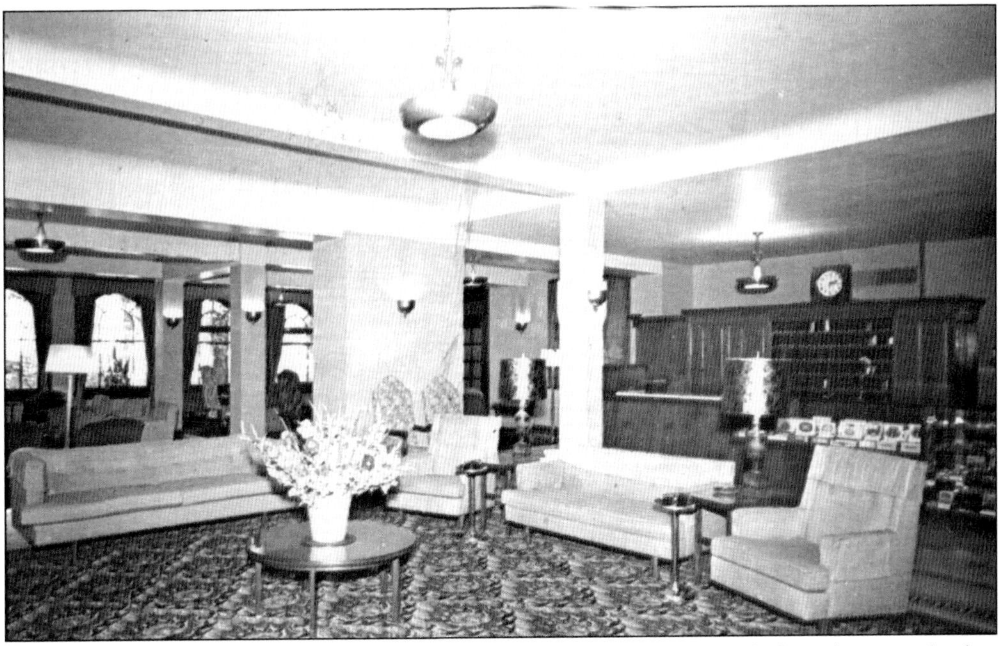

Main Lobby and Front Desk, c. 1960. A sale of the Home Lawn's furnishings and other removable items was held in 1973. Local residents report paying as little as $60 for four pickup loads of merchandise. "The once glamorous interior of the Home Lawn, which had been so carefully purchased and cared for, was effectively disassembled and sold for a pittance in a glorified yard sale," wrote Kimberly Bright, author of a history of the Home Lawn.

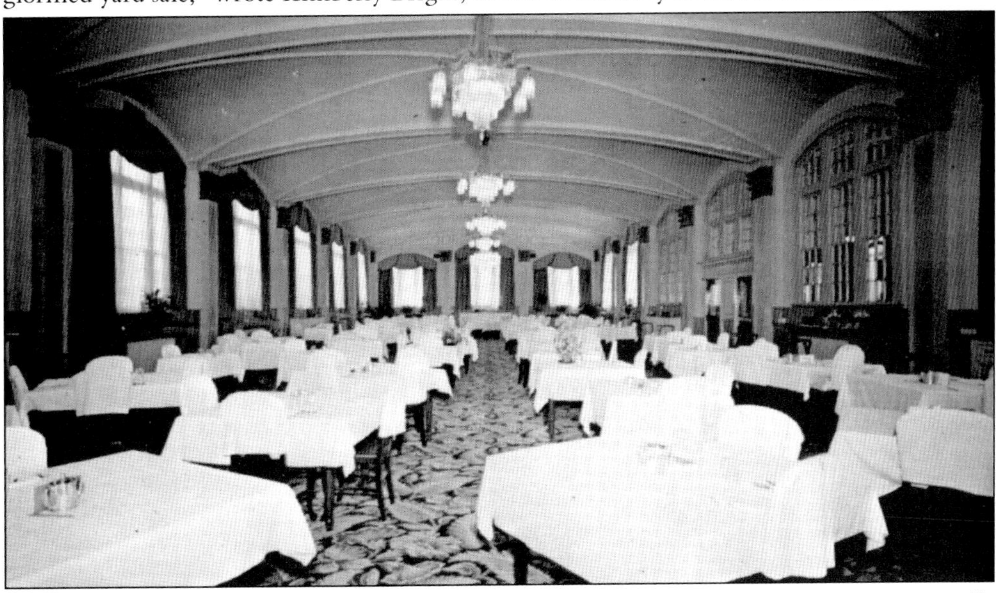

Dining Room, c. 1960. The final incarnation of the Home Lawn was as Martinsville Ministry Center, operated by Daystar Ministries (1975–1989). Residents, who pooled their resources and lived communally, "expressed the life of Christ through counseling, prayer, and practical demonstrations of love." Daystar—and the historic Home Lawn—came to an end in a devastating fire on September 10, 1989. The site has been occupied since 1996 by Costin Funeral Chapel.

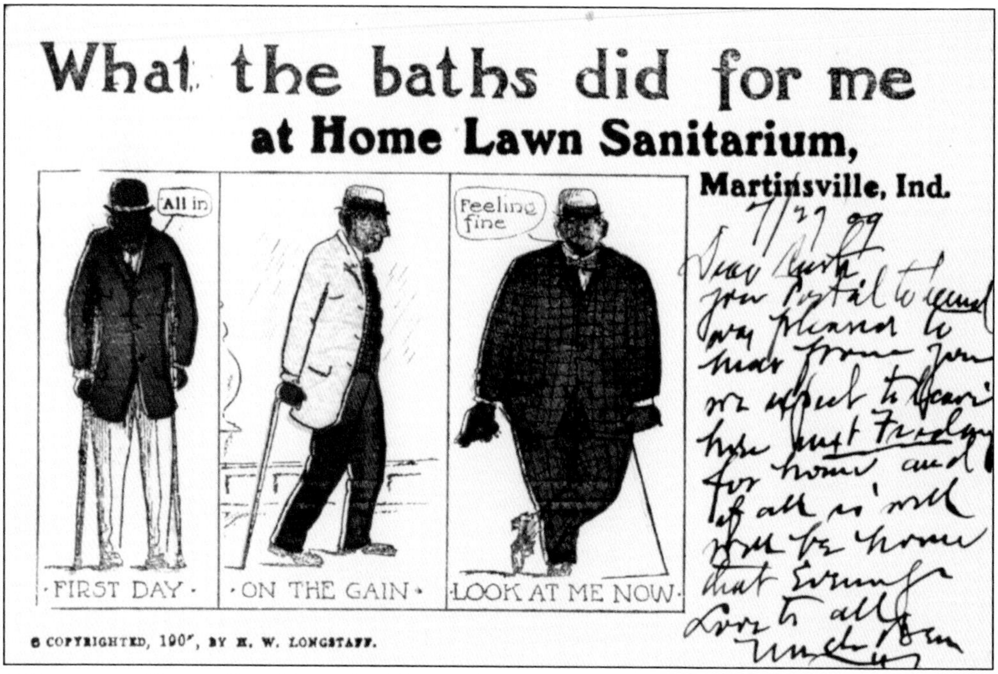

"WHAT THE BATHS DID FOR ME" COMIC ILLUSTRATION, 1909. This early card depicts the healing qualities of Martinsville's potent mineral water. A male guest arrives crippled and on a cane. With a few days of treatment, he is walking more upright. After a week or two, his cane has become a dapper accessory. He is now fit and fat and feeling fine.

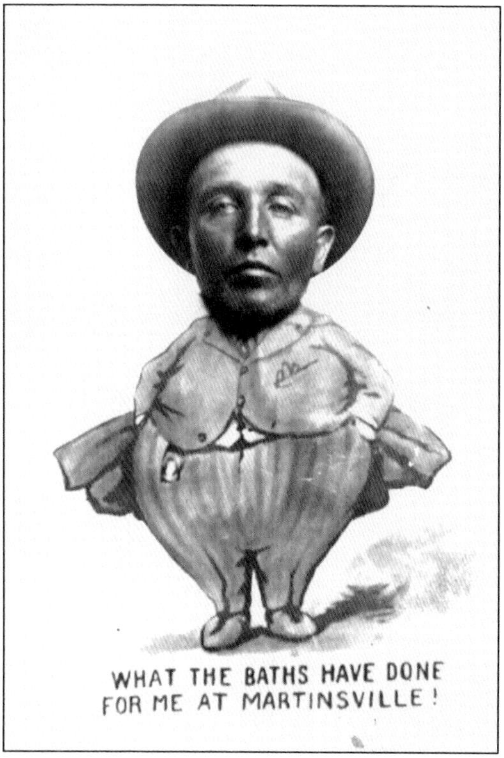

"WHAT THE BATHS HAVE DONE FOR ME" COMIC PHOTOGRAPH, *c.* 1910. Here is another fellow brought back to health by the city's sanitariums. Created by Michael Cohn—whose advertisement read, "The Comic Postcard Man—I make, finish and deliver Post Cards in ten minutes"—this postcard combines the head shot of an actual person with a caricature of a body. Michael was the son of David Cohn, cofounder of the Hill House/Hill-Cohn Sanitarium.

Four

Courthouse Square

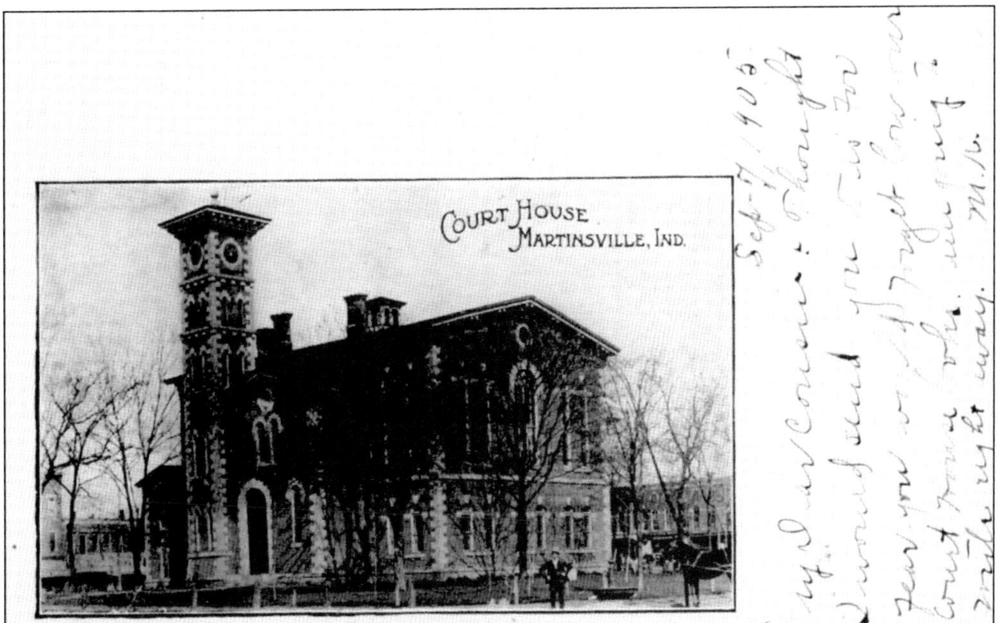

Courthouse Looking Northwest, 1905. The anchor of downtown Martinsville, the courthouse was designed by Isaac Hodgson and built by Perry M. Blankenship between 1857 and 1859 at a cost of $30,000. It has a near-twin in the Jennings County Courthouse in Vernon. Note the hitching post and water trough near the horse. At the far left is the Grand Hotel, whose third story was destroyed by fire in 1904.

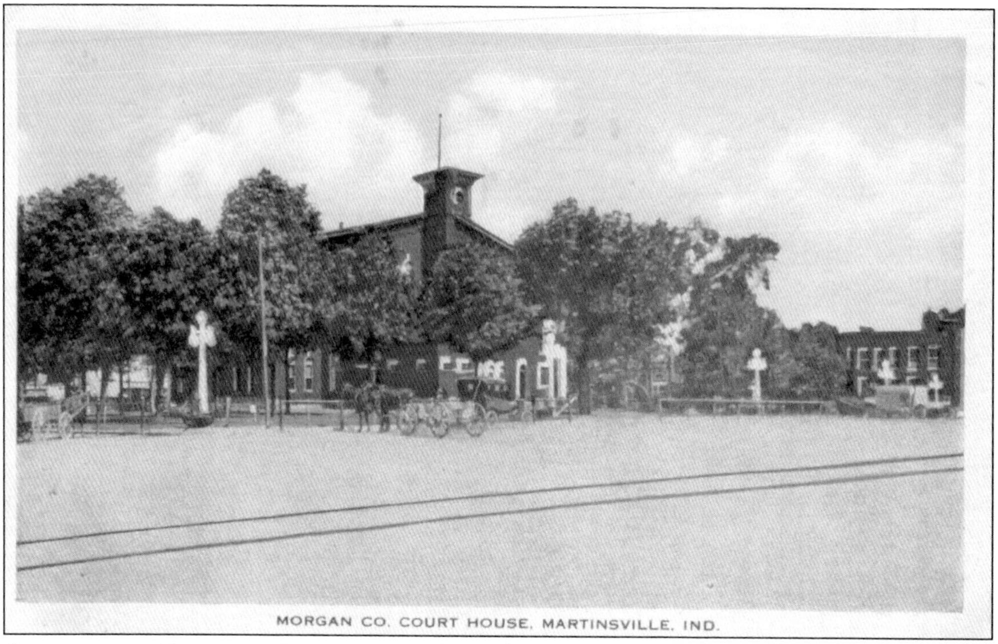

COURTHOUSE LOOKING SOUTHEAST, 1917. This view shows the interurban tracks on Main Street. "Well Andy get a crowd and come down tomorrow," writes the sender of this card. "John Robinson will be here with his big show every body is looking forward to have a big time tell Paul to bring his mother and Ruth along after the show we can all go to the River and fish."

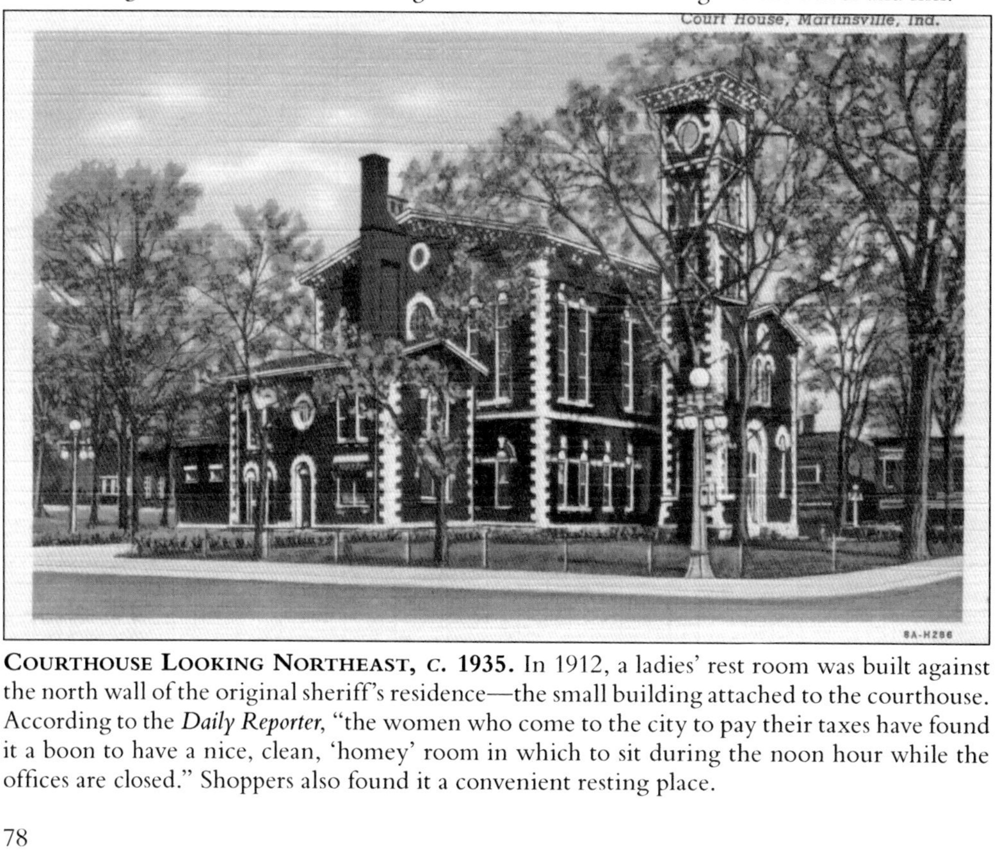

COURTHOUSE LOOKING NORTHEAST, C. 1935. In 1912, a ladies' rest room was built against the north wall of the original sheriff's residence—the small building attached to the courthouse. According to the *Daily Reporter*, "the women who come to the city to pay their taxes have found it a boon to have a nice, clean, 'homey' room in which to sit during the noon hour while the offices are closed." Shoppers also found it a convenient resting place.

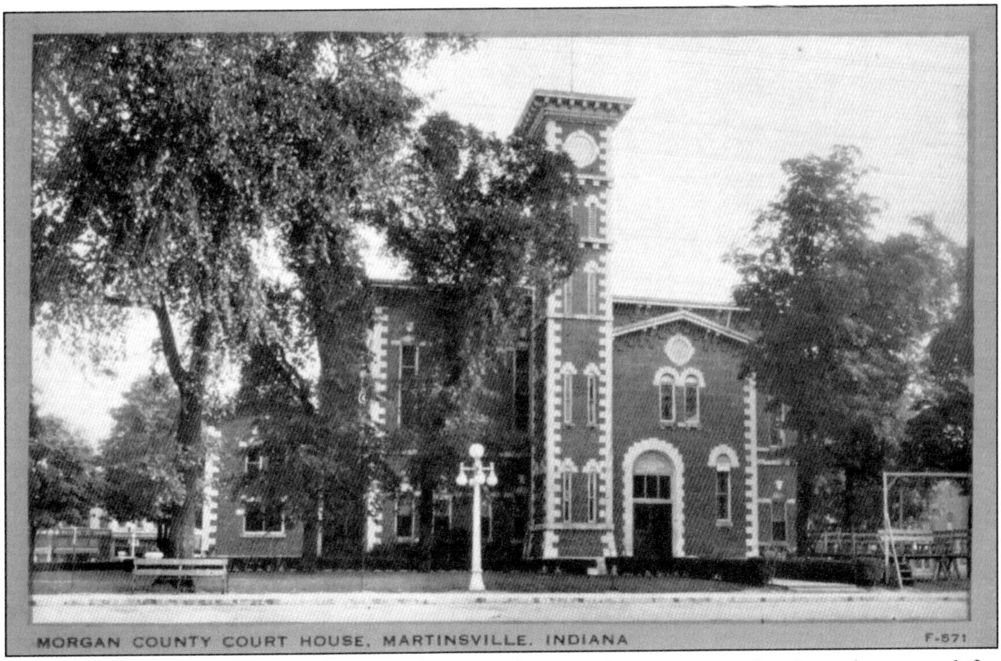

COURTHOUSE LOOKING NORTH, C. 1940. The courthouse square has long been used for community festivals and celebrations such as the 1922 centennial (see chapter 9) and since 1960, the Fall Foliage Festival. In this view, a raised platform is set up on the lawn. Today's streetlamps were selected because of their similarity to the historic cast metal lamps shown here. The campanile did not receive its intended clock until 1976.

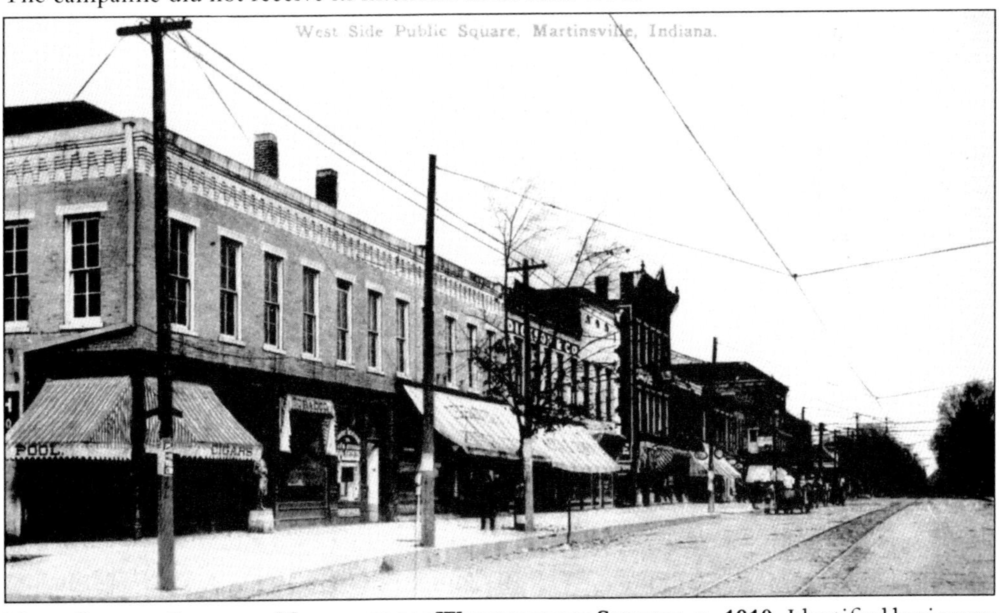

MAIN STREET LOOKING NORTH FROM WASHINGTON STREET, C. 1910. Identified businesses are J. E. Smith's tobacco and cigar shop and billiards and pool hall on the corner; Dessauer's clothing store (middle striped awning); and Dickson and Company men's clothing store (third striped awning). John M. Carleton's City Drug Store is located in the three-story building; the third floor is the Masonic lodge. The third floor was removed about 1915.

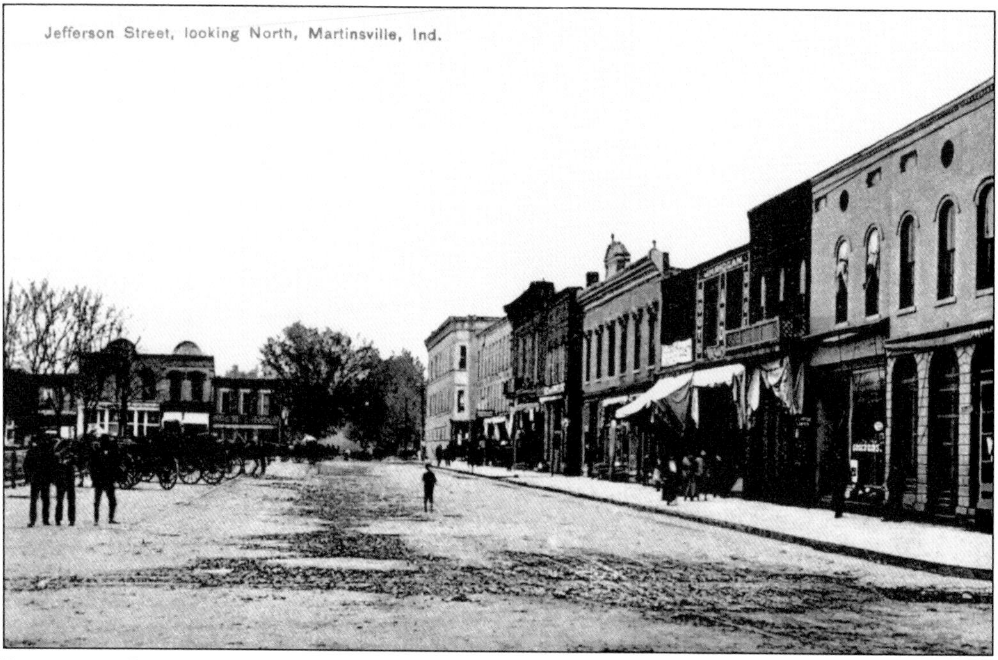

JEFFERSON STREET LOOKING NORTH FROM WASHINGTON STREET, *C.* 1910. These vintage downtown views show buildings not significantly different than they appear today. Visible businesses south of the alley are the post office at far right and J. M. Riggan boots and shoes (middle awning). Signs cannot be read on buildings north of the alley, but businesses known to exist at this time include Rossier jewelry and Toner's dry goods.

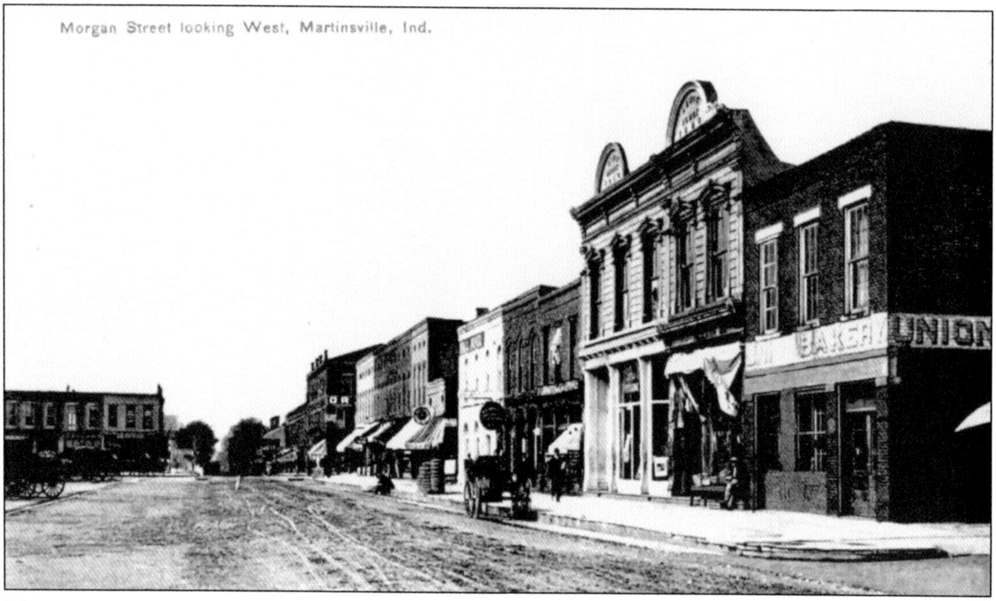

MORGAN STREET LOOKING WEST FROM JEFFERSON STREET, *C.* 1910. At the right is Union Bakery (1856–1937). Moving left, or west, are a grocery, Star Theatre (?), a furniture and stove store, Billy Mars's hardware store, and, in the white building, a harness shop. Across the alley are Nutter's cigar store, a restaurant, Blackstone Theatre, the Greek Candy Store, Nutter's newsstand, Stegner and Fuselman men's clothiers, and, on the corner, Prewitt's shoe store.

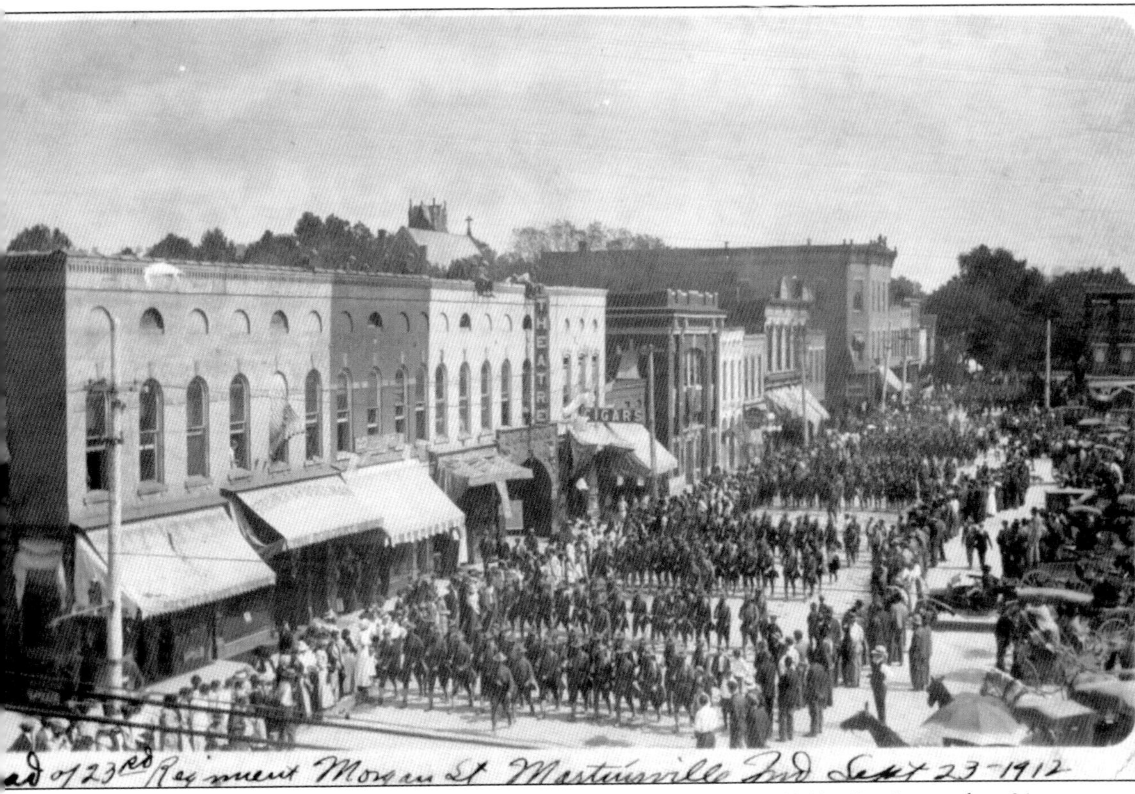

HEAD OF 23RD INDIANA REGIMENT, NORTH SIDE OF SQUARE, 1912. On September 21, 1912, this regiment left Fort Harrison for French Lick. After overnights in Indianapolis and Waverly, the troops reached Martinsville at 11:00 on the morning of September 23. While the officers dined at the Home Lawn Sanitarium, the soldiers made camp on the farm of Maj. Emmett F. Branch near the White River bridge. The regiment baseball team lost 8-12 in a game against the home team that afternoon, and the band played on the courthouse lawn that evening. The next morning, the regiment marched on to Gosport. Businesses from the left to the right include Prewitt's shoe store; the Toggery Shop owned by Frank Stegner and John Fuselman; Nutter's newsstand; the Greek Candy Store; Charles Blackstone's theatre and cigar store; a saloon; Citizens National Bank; Billy Mars's hardware store; Hill and Sadler grocery; and, on the corner, Union Bakery. Across Jefferson Street is the three-story Independent Order of Odd Fellows (IOOF) building. To its south is a three-story brick building that appears as the columned limestone-clad bank building in the next postcard.

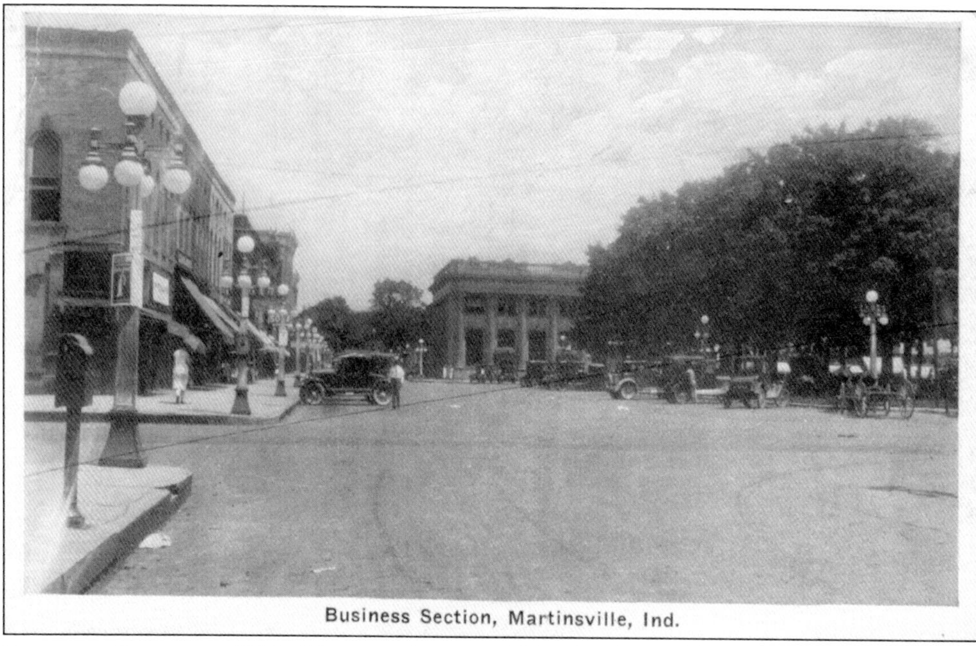

BUSINESS SECTION, 1926. The years between 1912, the date of the previous view, and 1926 were marked by significant changes in downtown Martinsville. Cars were replacing horses, the streets were paved with brick and lined with streetlamps, and in 1915–1916, the old building at the southeast corner of Morgan and Jefferson Streets, shown at the center, was reinvented both inside and out for the First National Bank and the Martinsville Trust Company.

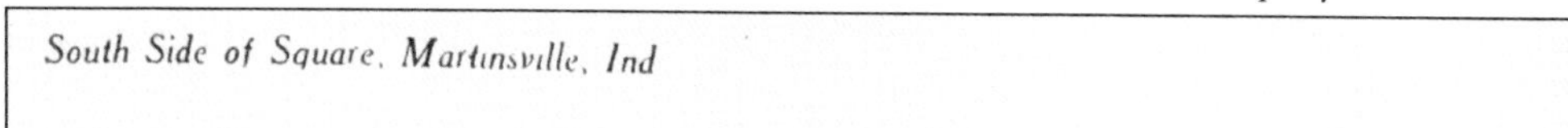

WASHINGTON STREET BETWEEN JEFFERSON AND MAIN STREETS, C. 1916. The square's south side was the last to develop, reaching maturity about 1915. At the right is the former Stevens house, made into a commercial building about 1915; dentist William S. Kinneman's office is upstairs. Behind the delivery car is James and Butler Grocery. To its left is Griffey and Johnson, tinners and roofers, and east of the alley, the Grace Theatre.

Five

BUILDINGS AND PEOPLE

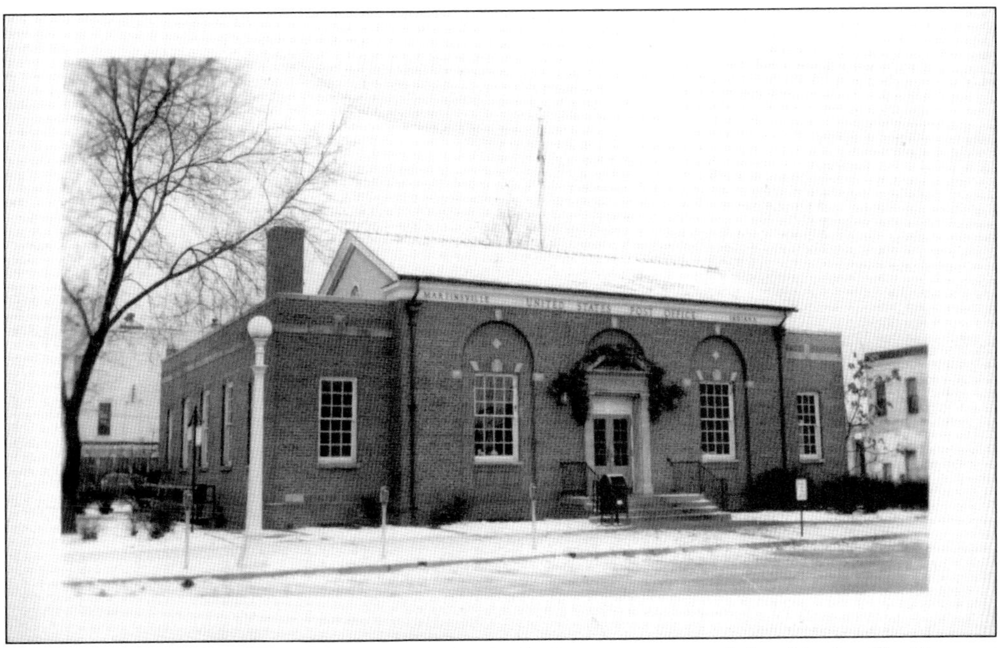

UNITED STATES POST OFFICE, C. 1940. Fred Finney, owner of the *Martinsville Democrat* newspaper and postmaster of Martinsville, campaigned for the construction of a new post office at the corner of Main and Washington Streets in 1935. (An identical building is found in Union City, Indiana.) The Martinsville post office was enlarged with the addition of a south wing in 1974. Behind the post office is the Colonial Sanitarium.

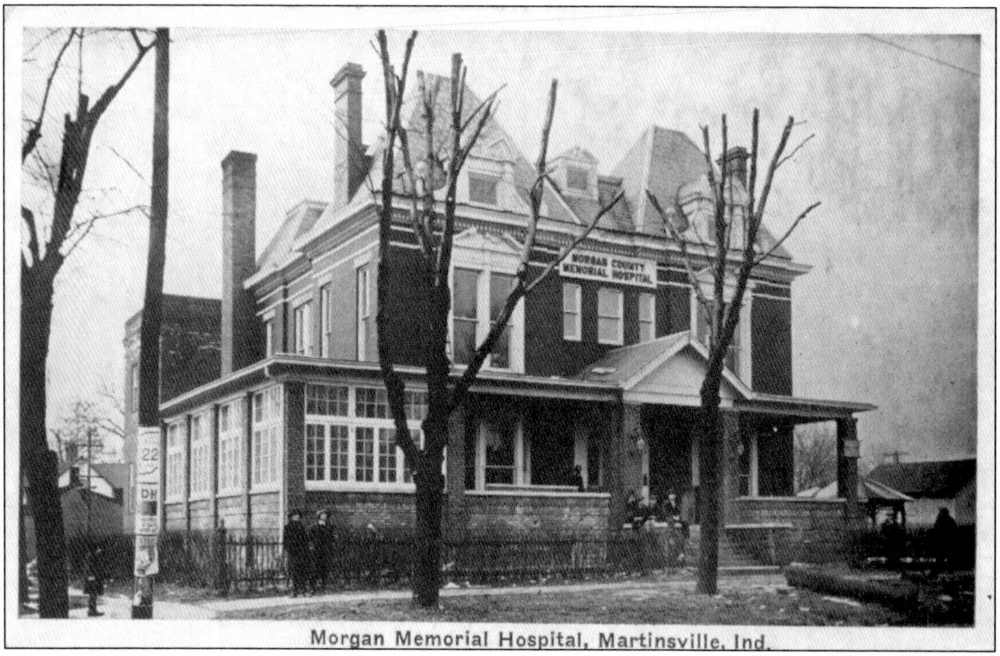

MORGAN COUNTY MEMORIAL HOSPITAL, c. 1925. In memory of his son Jack, killed in a bicycle accident in 1917, James W. Hussey bought and donated the John K. Mitchell homestead on South Main Street to county residents for use as a public hospital. A large rear addition was built in 1923. With the 1959 opening of a new hospital east of town, it became the county home. It was demolished in 1995.

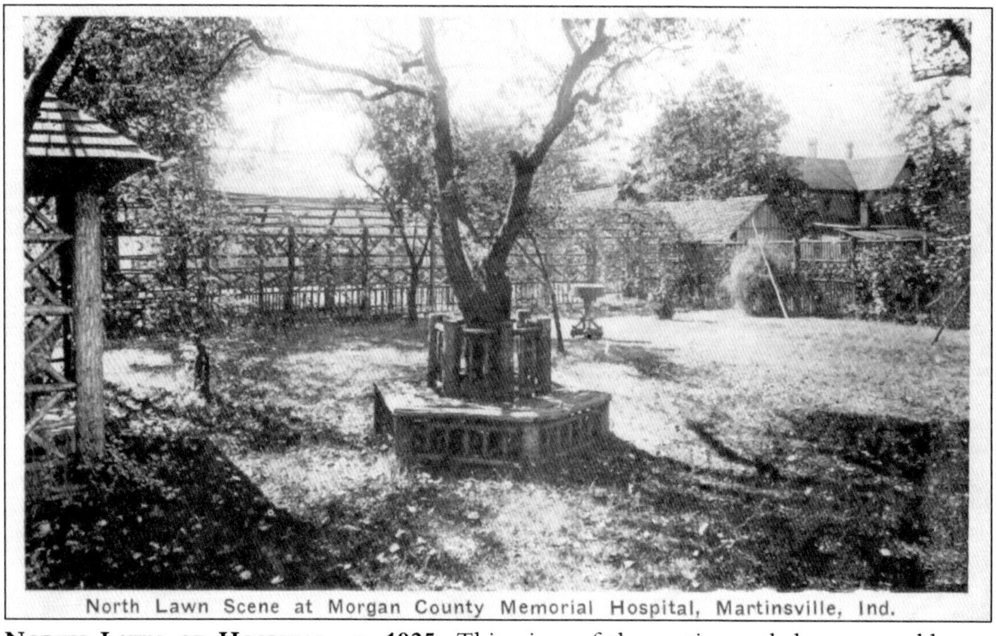

NORTH LAWN OF HOSPITAL, c. 1925. This view of the rustic north lawn resembles an advertisement for Martinsville's Old Hickory Furniture Company, owned by William H. Patton. The gazebo, trellised walkway, circular bench, and even the birdbath are all products of Old Hickory. The building seen at the right is the Morgan County sheriff's residence and jail.

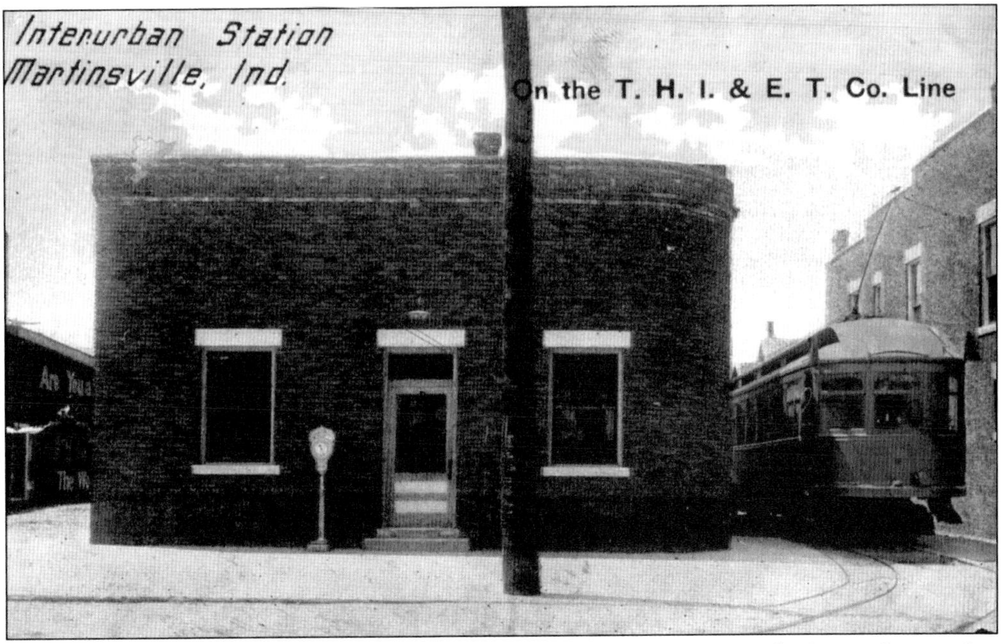

INTERURBAN STATION, C. 1910. Located at 154 North Main Street, the interurban station looked like this before 1911, when a carbarn was built behind and between it and the Eslinger Hotel, seen at the right in this view. Tracks and overhead wires ran down the middle of Main Street south to the line's terminus at Walnut Street. The building's rounded corner provided extra clearance for cars pulling alongside its north wall.

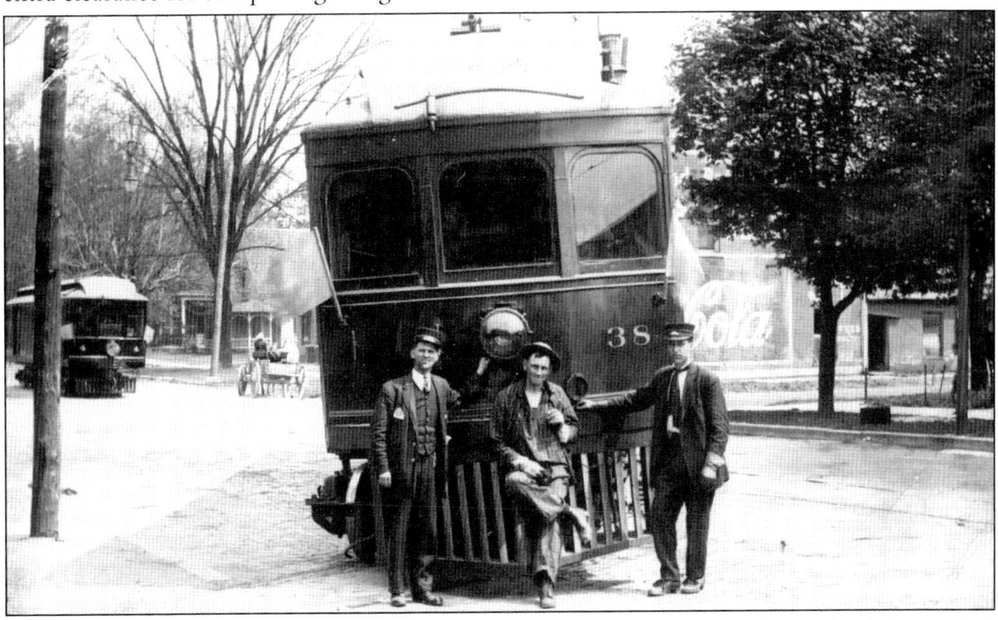

TERRE HAUTE, INDIANAPOLIS AND EASTERN TRACTION COMPANY CAR NO. 38, C. 1910. From 1902 to 1930, the interurban connected local residents with Indianapolis and points in between. Shown at the left of car No. 38, which is stopped at Walnut Street, is George Allen, a conductor for 20 years. He went on to become an attorney, county prosecutor, county clerk, and member of the Martinsville Common Council. Approaching from the north is car No. 4.

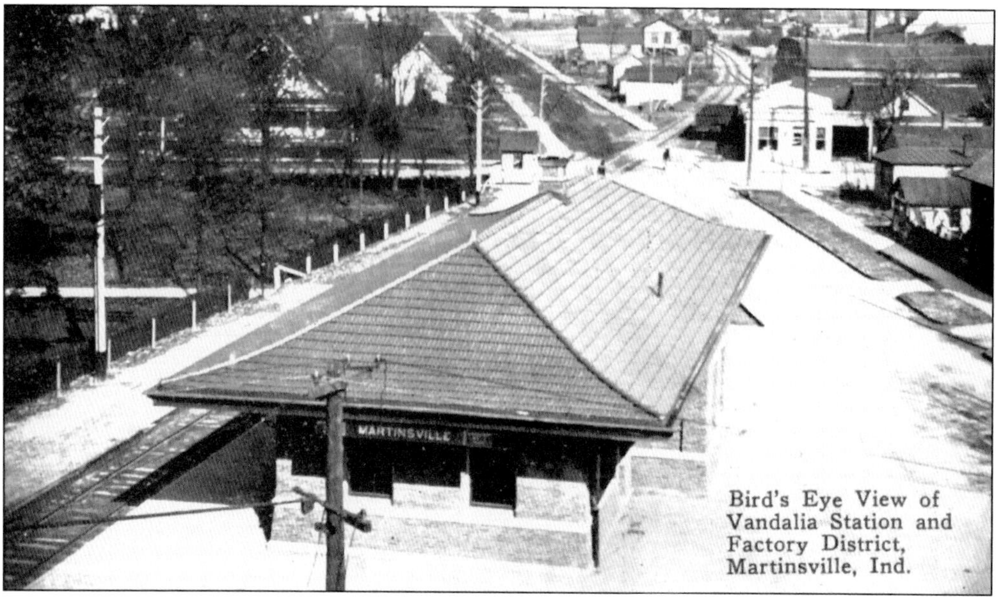

VANDALIA STATION, C. 1911. Martinsville's factory district spreads north and west from this railroad depot at Marion and Pike Streets. Built in 1910, the fashionable, craftsman-style station was the arrival and departure point for throngs of sanitarium guests who visited the "City of Mineral Water" every year. Located adjacent to the Martinsville Sanitarium, the depot signified a division between two worlds: labor versus leisure, vigor versus illness, and need versus affluence.

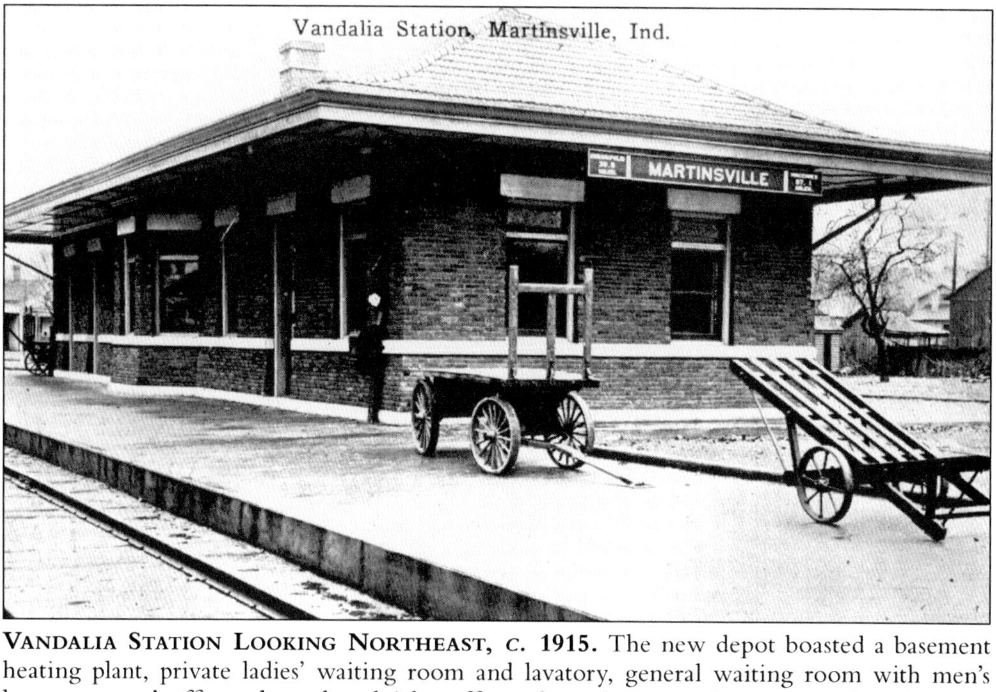

VANDALIA STATION LOOKING NORTHEAST, C. 1915. The new depot boasted a basement heating plant, private ladies' waiting room and lavatory, general waiting room with men's lavatory, agent's office, telegraph and ticket office, telegraph operator's apartment, large baggage room with lobby, and out front, grass plots and decorative brick paving. "Won't that be fine," extolled the *Daily Reporter*. "Think of the agreeable change that these changes will perfect!"

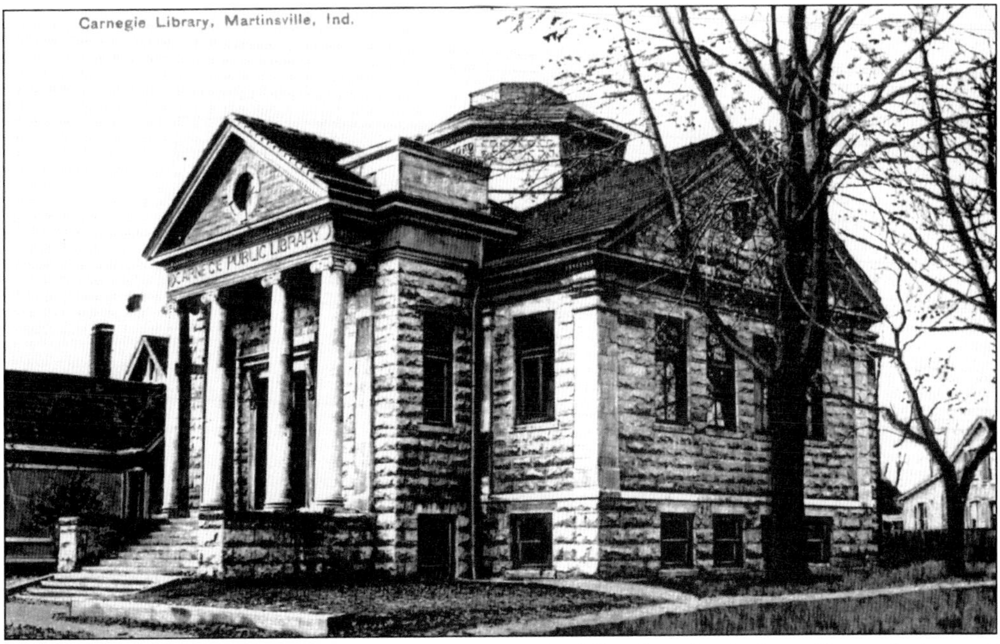

CARNEGIE PUBLIC LIBRARY, *c.* 1909. Pennsylvania philanthropist Andrew Carnegie donated $12,500 for the construction of Martinsville's public library. Local officials issued bonds for another $2,500 to upgrade the building from brick to Bedford limestone, which they considered a more suitable presentation to the city's "thousands of visitors from the best and most intelligent families of the United States."

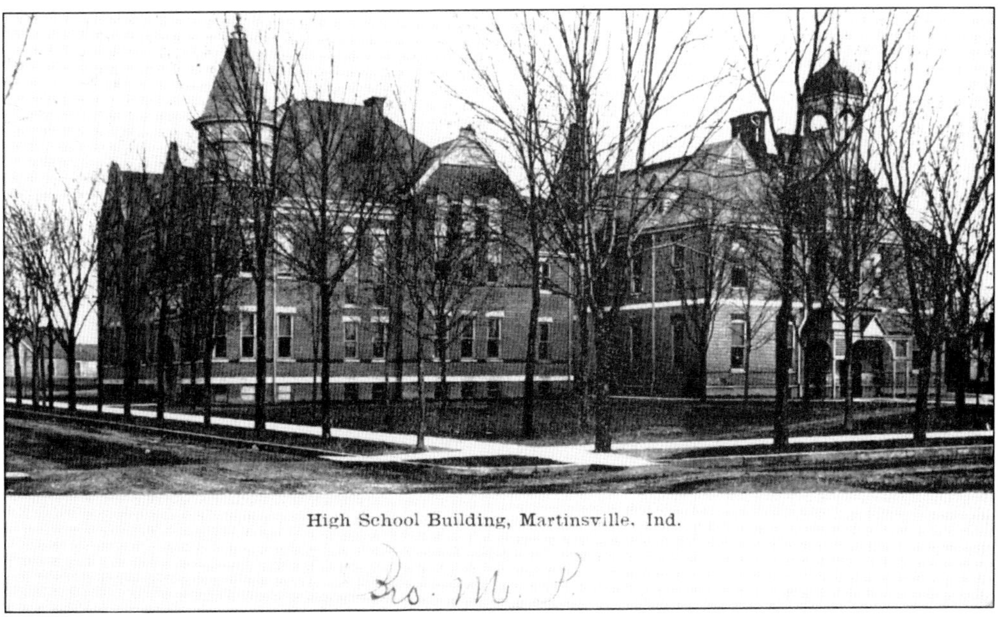

CENTRAL SCHOOL AND HIGH SCHOOL BUILDING, *c.* 1910. At the right is the original Central School for grades one through eight. At left is the 1900–1901 high school addition, which was superceded in 1914–1915 by a new building on Main Street. In February 1966, the last classes were held in the old Central School, and in November of the same year, it was demolished and replaced by the existing building.

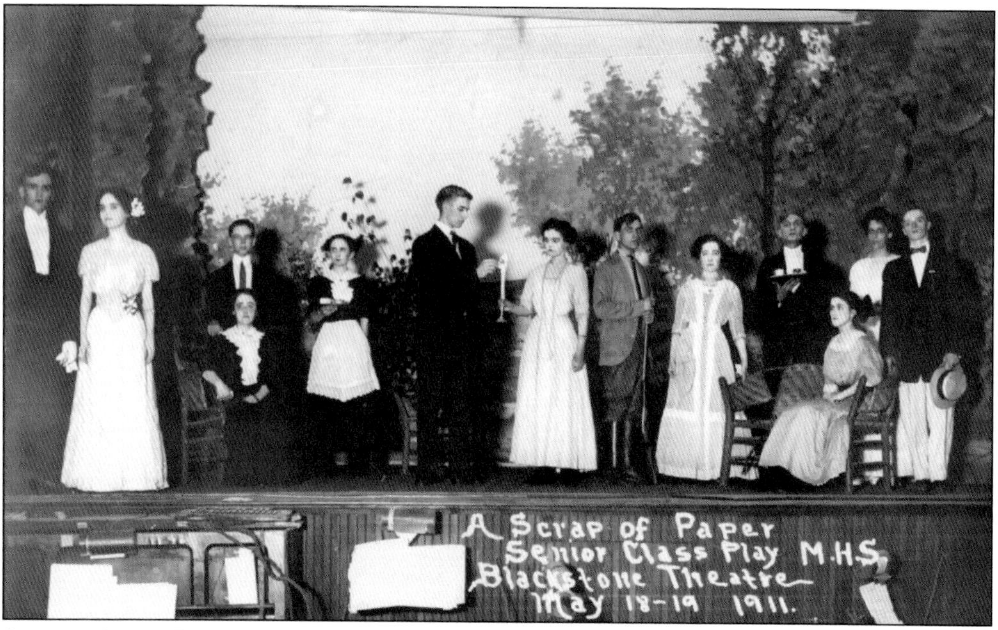

Senior Class Play, 1911. Directed by Leafy Branch, 12 Martinsville High School seniors performed a romantic, three-act comedy set in France. Pictured from left to right are Carl Mitchell, Faye Schuck, Raymond Cramer, Glendyn Hastings, Marie McKinley, Millard Overton, Edna Brown, Edda Brown, Iva Coffey, Walter Bailey, Grace Wallace, Leafy Branch, and Chester Jones. Located on Morgan Street, Blackstone Theatre can be seen in the postcard on page 81.

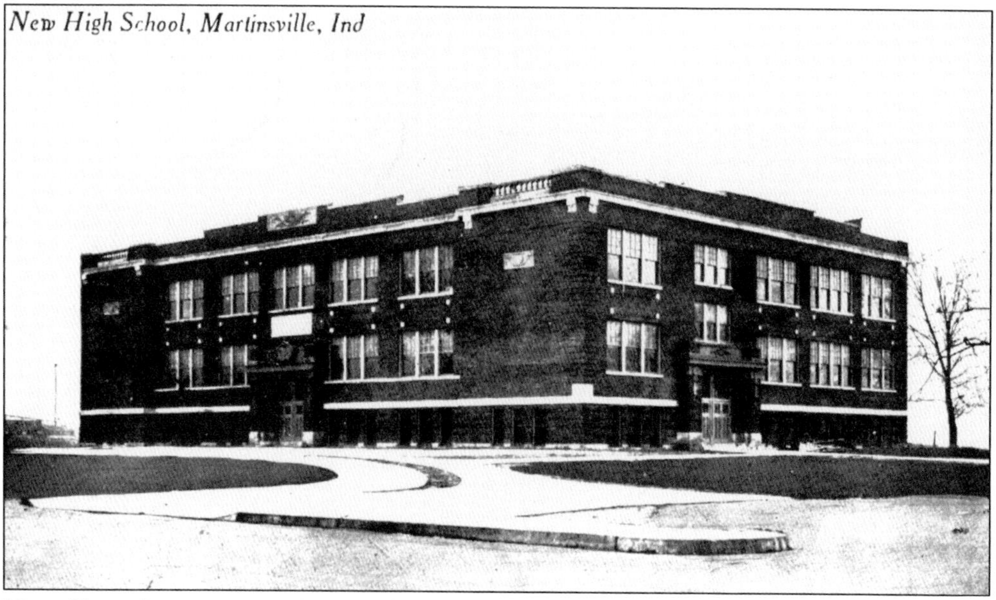

New High School, c. 1915. A thoroughly modern high school building was a point of tremendous community pride. This new neoclassical brick building graced the corner of Main and Garfield Streets and was seen by everyone passing through the city. Its proximity to downtown led to the success of many businesses popular with a teenage clientele, including the Martinsville Candy Kitchen. The building was demolished in 1979.

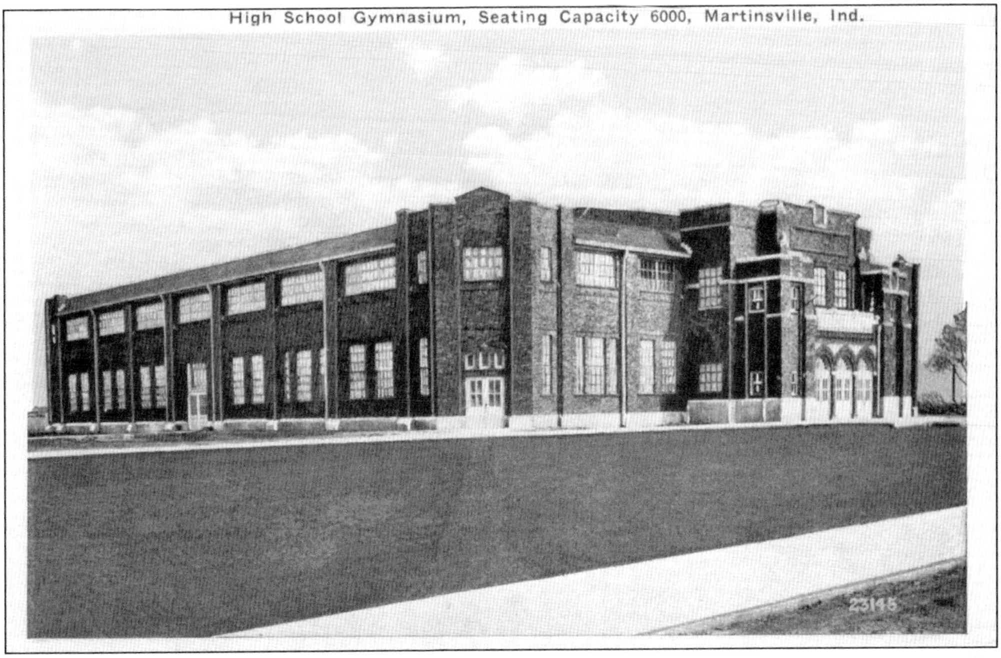

MARTINSVILLE HIGH SCHOOL GYMNASIUM, C. 1924. Erected in 1924, this gymnasium was the envy of the state. Its seating capacity of nearly 5,000 was greater than the city's population. Today the gymnasium is named for Glenn Curtis, who coached the Artesians to the 1924, 1927, and 1933 state basketball championships. Legendary college coach John R. Wooden played on the 1927 team.

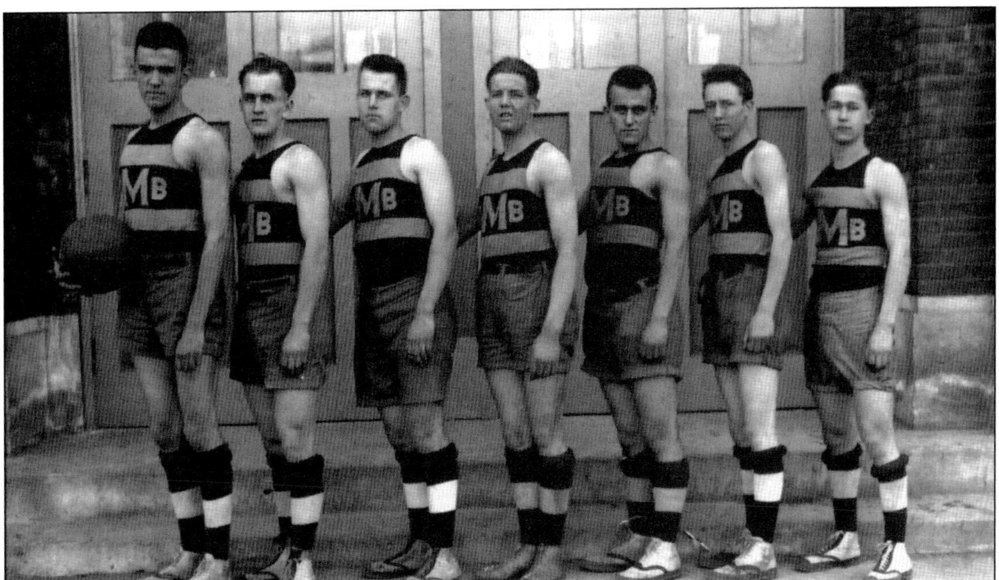

MARTINSVILLE HIGH SCHOOL BASKETBALL TEAM, 1914–1915. Coached by Claude Cohee, a teacher of algebra and geometry, and Emmett Poston, who replaced him late in the season, this team played in Martinsville's armory until the new high school on Main Street was completed in February 1915. From left to right are Shirley Kriner, Clyde "Dutch" Schmidt, Dewey Goss, Everett "Hobby" Shireman, Lawrence (Lary) Frye, Earle Woods, and Herman "Pete" Sanders.

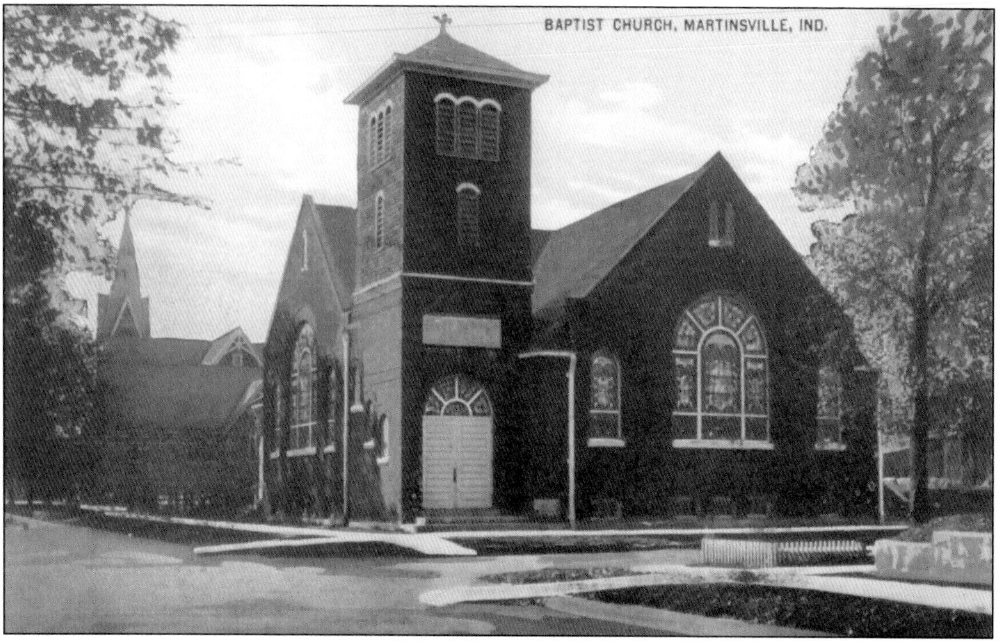

First Baptist Church, c. 1908. One of Martinsville's founding congregations, the Baptists purchased in 1881 a simple building at the northwest corner of Jefferson and Jackson Streets vacated by the Presbyterians. By 1901, it had been replaced by this Gothic Revival church. In 1963, the Baptists moved to their current building on Columbus Street, and this one was demolished for a parking lot. First Christian Church appears in the background.

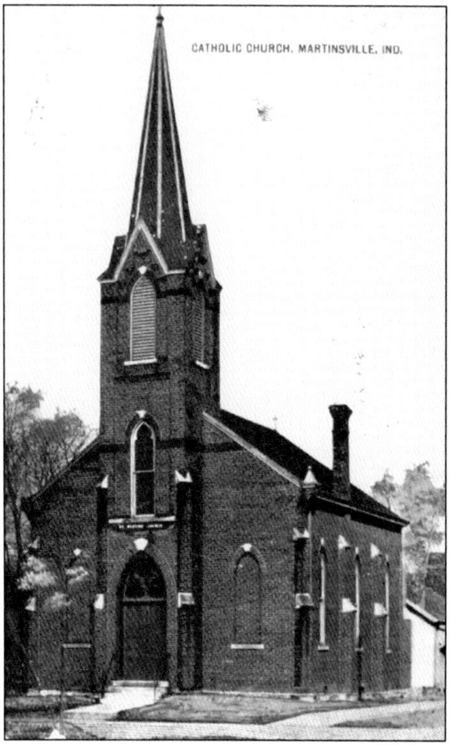

St. Martin of Tours Catholic Church, 1915. Located at the corner of Wayne and Pike Streets, this building was erected in 1891. The Catholics sold to the Lutherans in 1962 and moved into their current building on Harrison Street. "Here is where I attended church today," writes the sender of this card. "Heard a very good sermon too—but I am not ready to leave the church of my first choice yet."

FIRST CHRISTIAN CHURCH, 1908. When it was built in 1891, the Christian church was considered to be the most beautiful church structure in Martinsville. The elegant Gothic Revival–style building required tremendous financial commitment on the part of its 400 members, who included some of the wealthiest people in the city. They must have regarded the building as a public display of their strong faith.

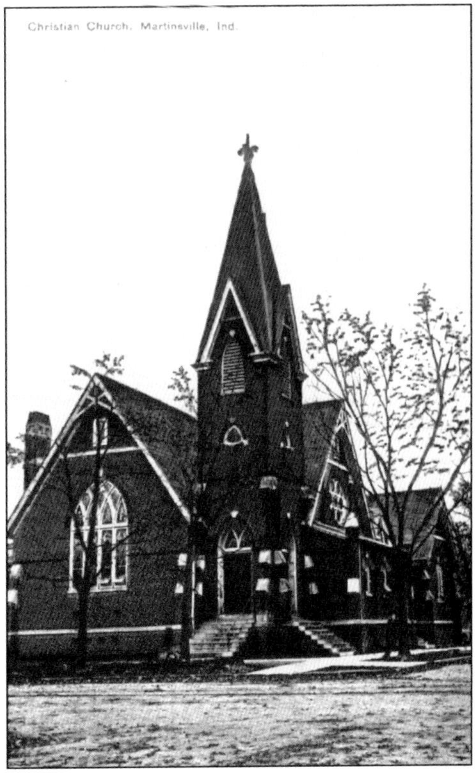

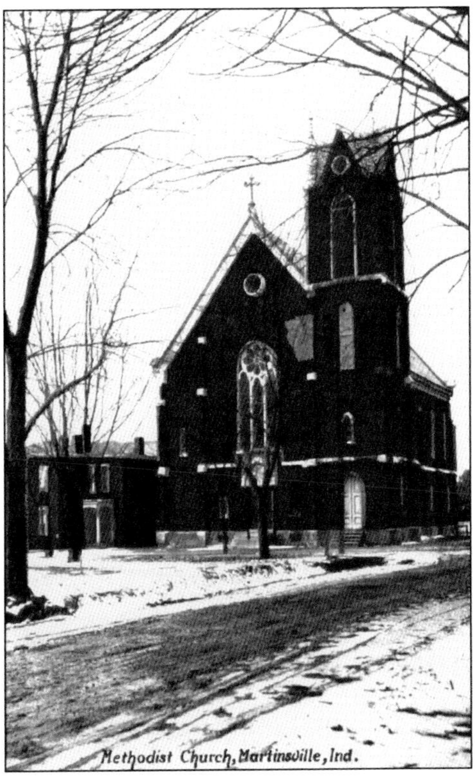

FIRST METHODIST CHURCH, c. 1908. Built 1872–1875, the church and parsonage shown here at Sycamore and Pike Streets were replaced in 1951. This was a period when city residents worshipped, worked, shopped, attended school, and visited friends and relatives in close proximity to where they lived. Today churches are often driving destinations. The Methodists' new facility north of Martinsville is expected to be completed in late 2008.

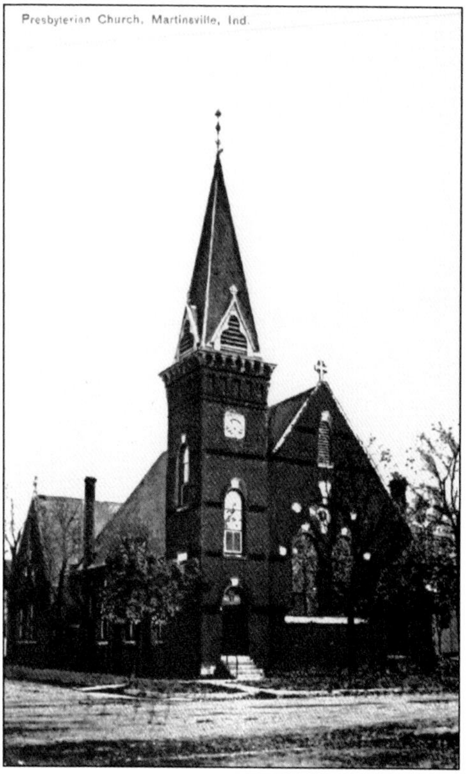

First Presbyterian Church, c. 1908. Standing at the corner of Washington and Sycamore Streets, the Presbyterian church was built in 1881. The church was popular with well-to-do, well-dressed sanitarium guests who would not dare go out without their mink stoles and hats. One Martinsville resident remembers, "We could always pick out the Home Lawn guests who attended . . . on Sunday morning by looking at their clothes."

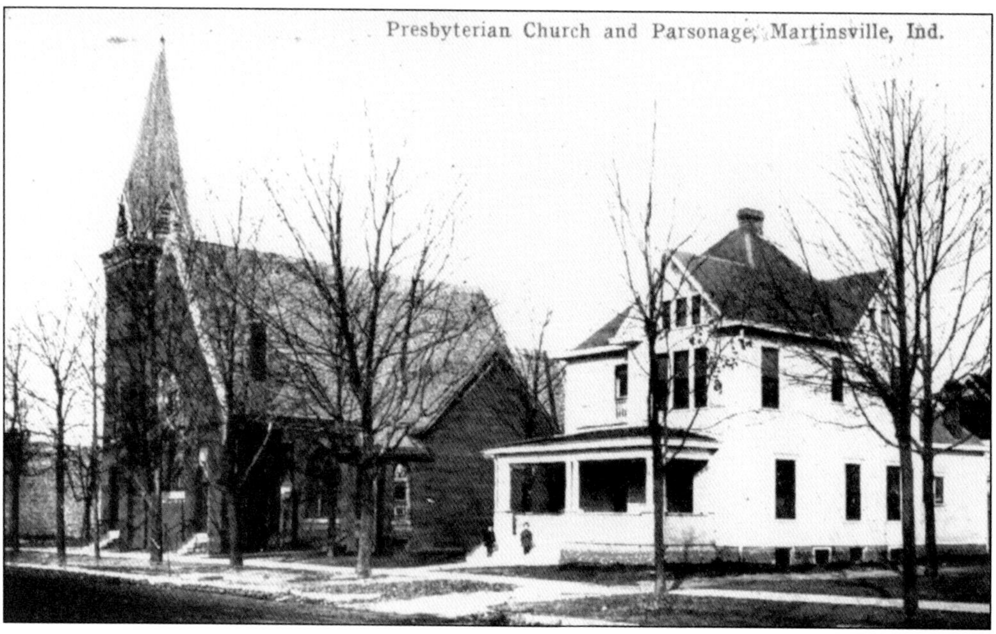

Presbyterian Church and Parsonage, c. 1907. The first occupants of the parsonage, built in 1907, were Rev. M. L. Gillespie, his wife, Mary, and their daughters Mildred and Mary—the winsome figures standing on the front steps. The parsonage became the church office in 1964 and was renamed MacDonald House after a longtime pastor. It was torn down in 2005 and replaced by Keller Hall.

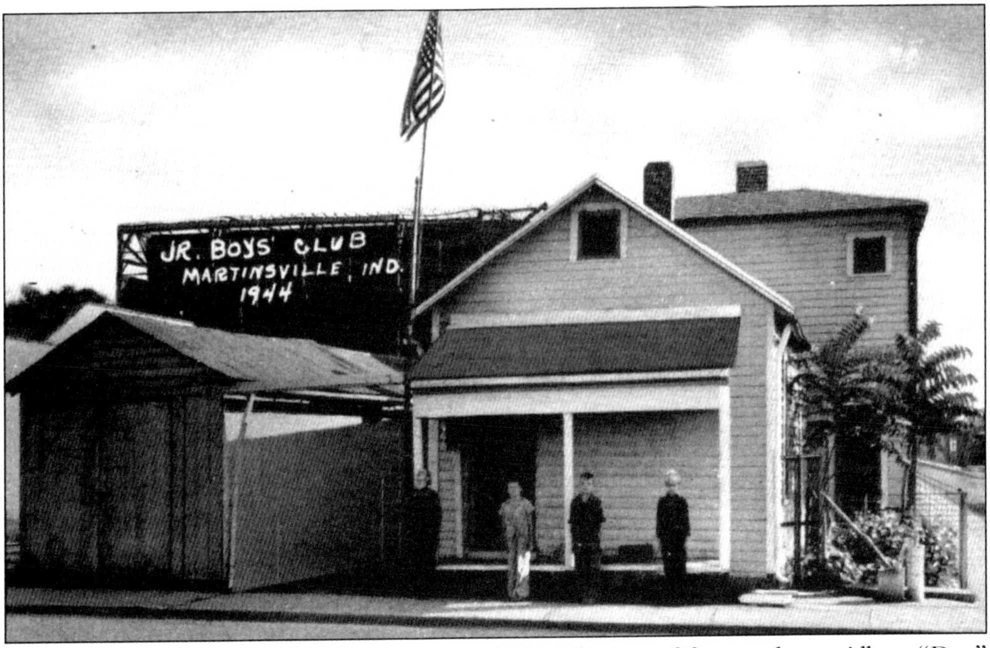

ALBERT MERRITT'S JUNIOR BOYS' CLUB, 1944. The son of former slaves, Albert "Doc" Merritt was employed as a porter at the Martinsville Sanitarium. In 1902, he began working with boys in the northwest part of the city. From 1926 to 1957, the Junior Boys' Club served hundreds of boys from the clubhouse at the southeast corner of Marion and Highland Streets.

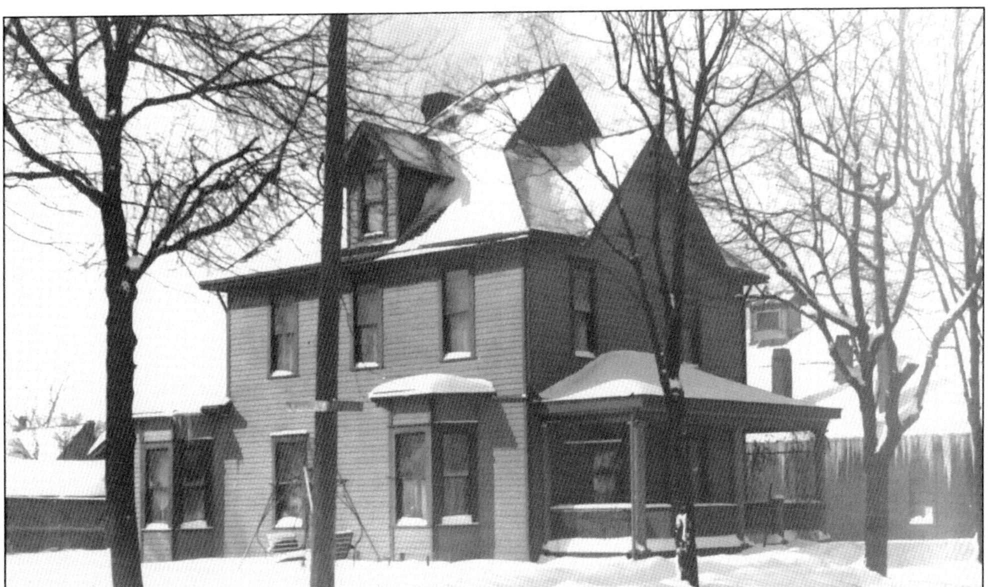

DAVID AND MARTHA COHN HOUSE, 119 WEST MORGAN STREET, C. 1910. This house still stands but is hardly recognizable as the one in this real-photo postcard. About 1916–1917, David Cohn, proprietor of the Hill House/Hill-Cohn Sanitarium, had the house extensively remodeled in the craftsman style with the front door on the east. See page 108 for a glimpse of the "new" house, with its fashionable brick facade, tile roof, and bracketed eaves.

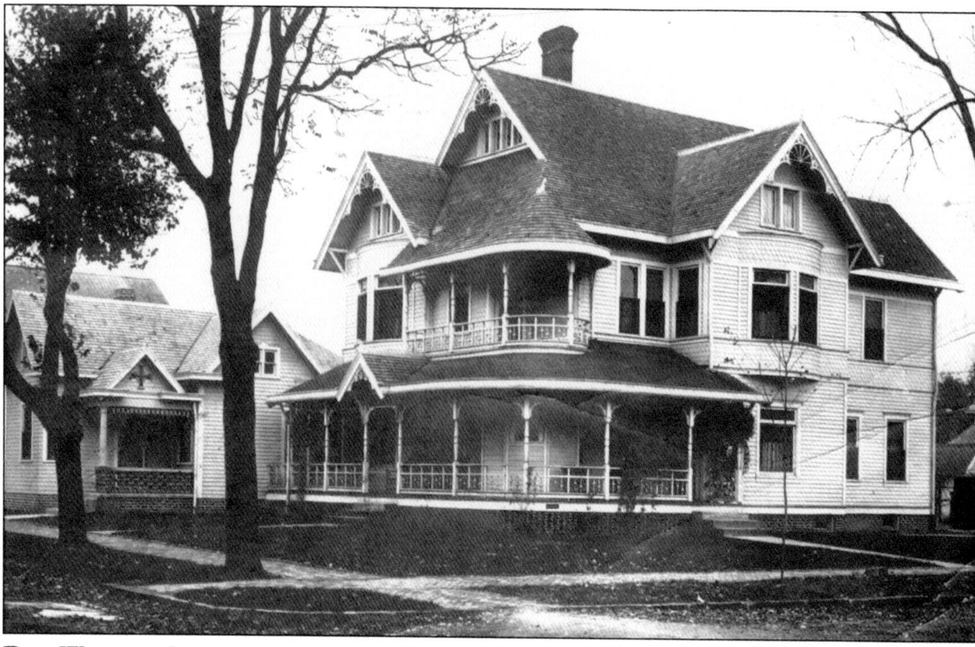

Dr. William J. and Catherine Sandy House, 1910. This stately Queen Anne–style house once stood on the southeast corner of Morgan and Sycamore Streets, behind First Presbyterian Church. A general practitioner, Dr. William J. Sandy had his office in the rear of the house. After his death in 1932, Catherine remained in the house until the early 1950s. The house was subsequently torn down and replaced by Standard Grocery, later IGA.

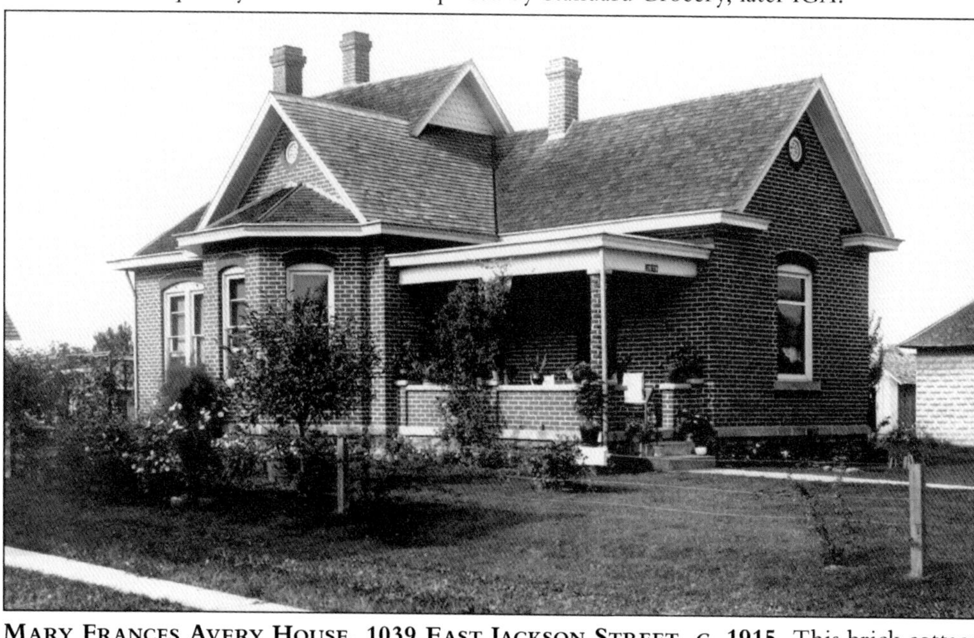

Mary Frances Avery House, 1039 East Jackson Street, c. 1915. This brick cottage was the longtime home of Mary Frances Avery, a housekeeper at the Home Lawn Sanitarium who died in 1951. Her great-grandson Eric Kersey, who lived in the house from 1954 to 1963, remembers family stories told about Mary Frances's beautiful flower beds. Eric enjoyed climbing the persimmon, walnut, cherry, and pawpaw trees that grew in the front yard.

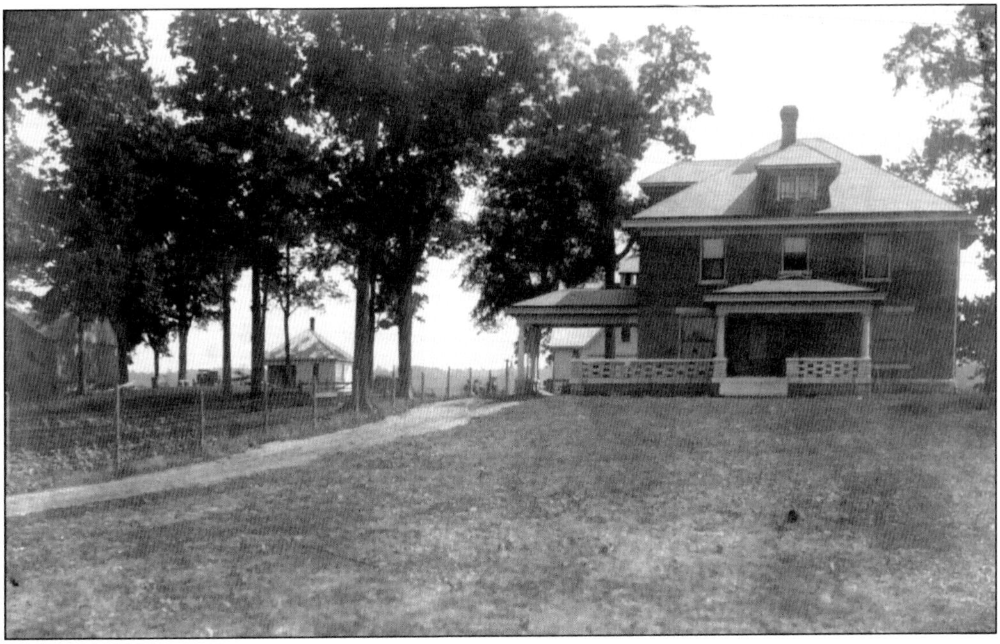

James S. and Palma Burton House, 309 Poston Road, 1909. This house was built for the Burtons in 1906. Primarily a farmer, James S. Burton engaged in the manufacture of brick in his early years, later becoming a street and highway contractor. His 14-year-old daughter, Katherine, penned this message to her Indianapolis cousin Fern McClure, "I don't see why you won't come down tomorrow there is a big circus so I thought you might come."

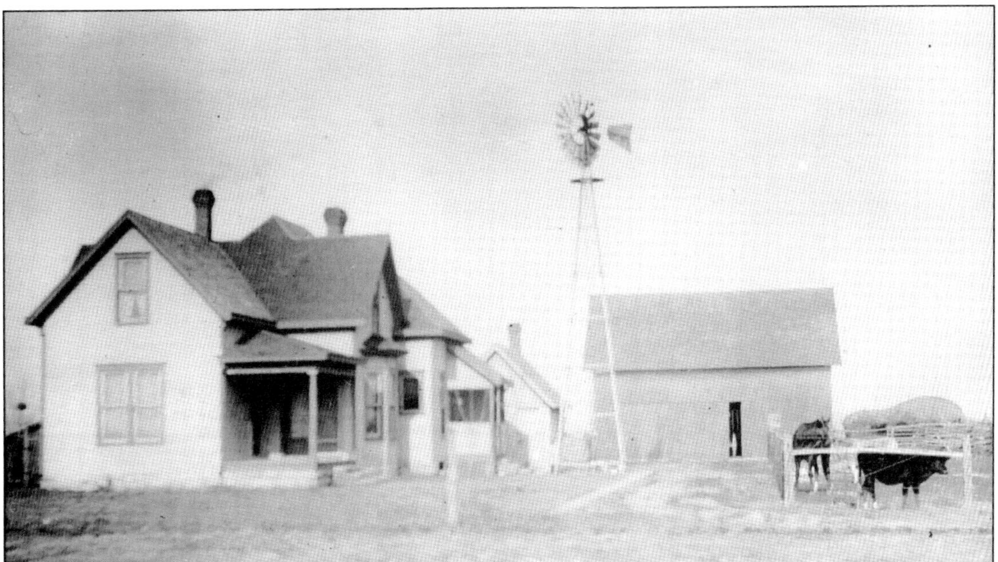

Perry and Eva Kirk House and Farm, 810 Hacker Drive, *c.* 1910. Perry Kirk was a farmer and house carpenter who built his own house, barn, and outbuildings on his property just west of Martinsville. When his youngest child, Otis Austin Kirk, married Beulah Bowman in 1941, this was the newlyweds' first home.

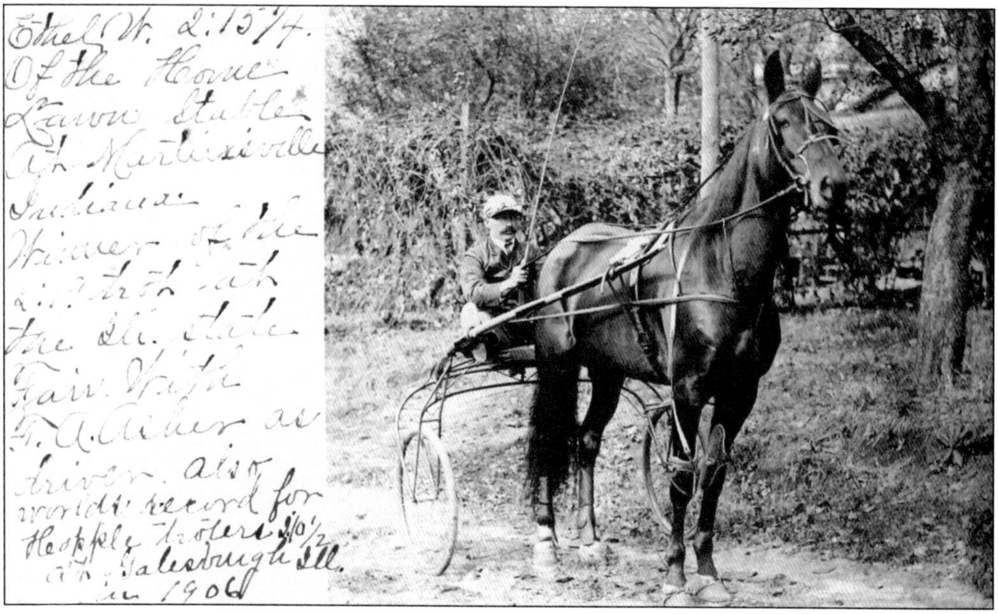

HOME LAWN HARNESS RACER AND TROTTER, C. 1906. Written in the margin at left is, "Ethel W. 2:15¼. Of the Home Lawn Stable At Martinsville, Indiana. Winner of the 2:19 trot at the Ill. State Fair. With F[erdinand] A. Asher as driver. Also worlds record for Hopple troters [*sic*] 2:10½ at Galesburg Ill. in 1906."

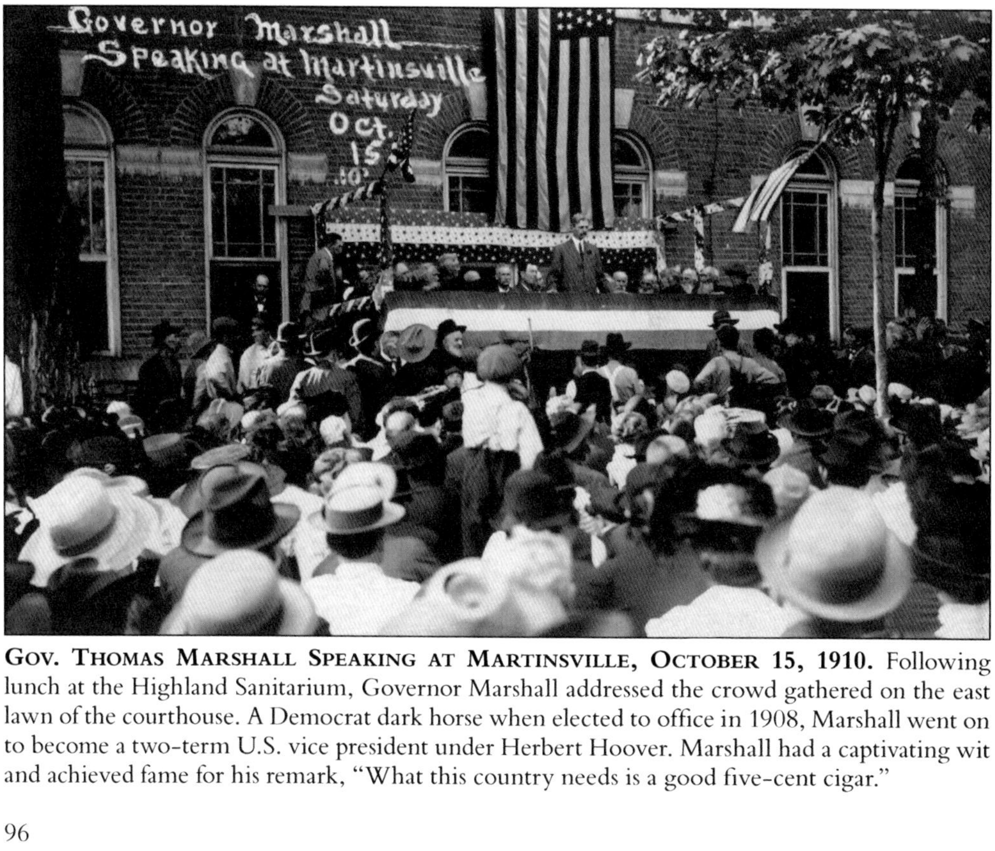

GOV. THOMAS MARSHALL SPEAKING AT MARTINSVILLE, OCTOBER 15, 1910. Following lunch at the Highland Sanitarium, Governor Marshall addressed the crowd gathered on the east lawn of the courthouse. A Democrat dark horse when elected to office in 1908, Marshall went on to become a two-term U.S. vice president under Herbert Hoover. Marshall had a captivating wit and achieved fame for his remark, "What this country needs is a good five-cent cigar."

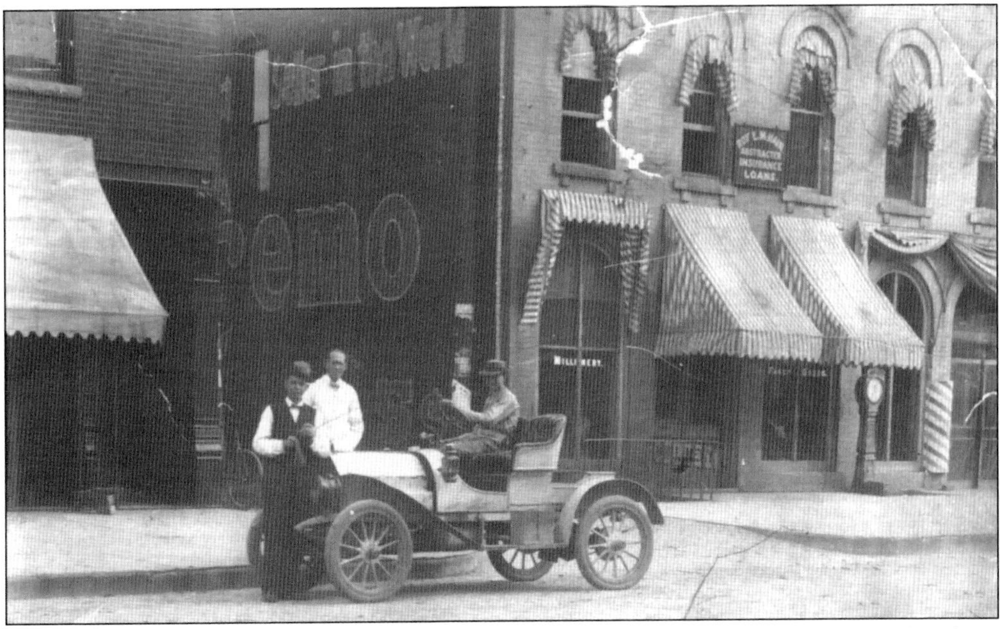

ROY MARTIN, *c.* 1915. A delivery boy for grocer C. W. Rose, Roy Martin is parked in front of the store at 153-163 North Main Street. A millinery shop is behind the car, with Roy D. McNair's abstract, insurance, and loan office above. Traces of the advertisement for Cremo 5¢ cigars remain on the wall yet today. Martin later owned the Shell service station at the end of East Morgan Street.

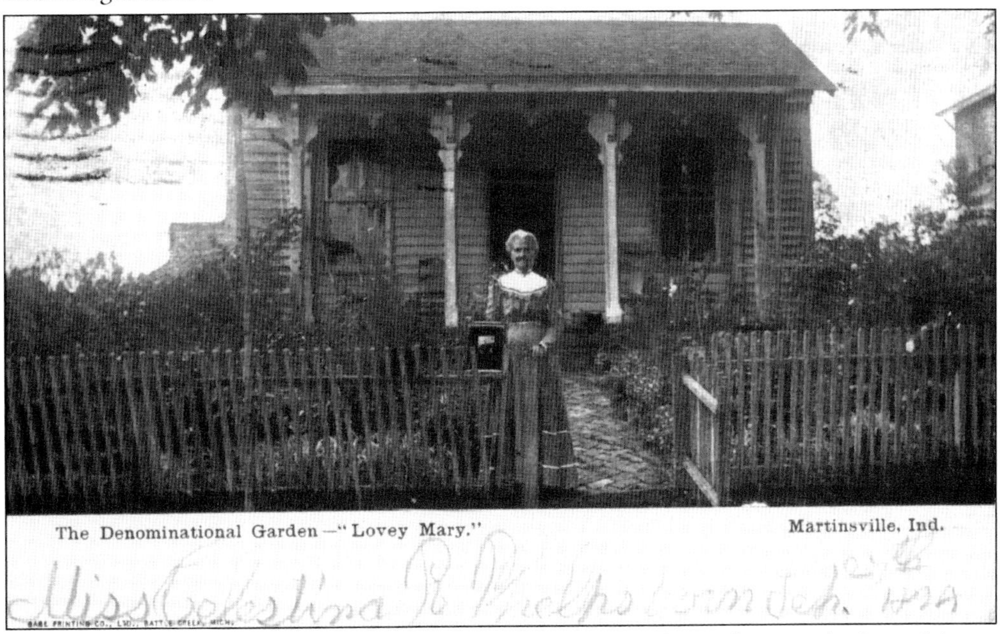

CELESTINA PHELPS, 1910. Celestina Phelps was fictionalized as a character in *Lovey Mary*, a popular novel by Alice Hegan Rice. The sender writes, "I called on Lovey Mary this afternoon and got this card from her with her autograph on it. She is 86, a cripple who cannot walk a step but a most interesting old woman. . . . If you have forgotten the book *Lovey Mary*, get it from the library."

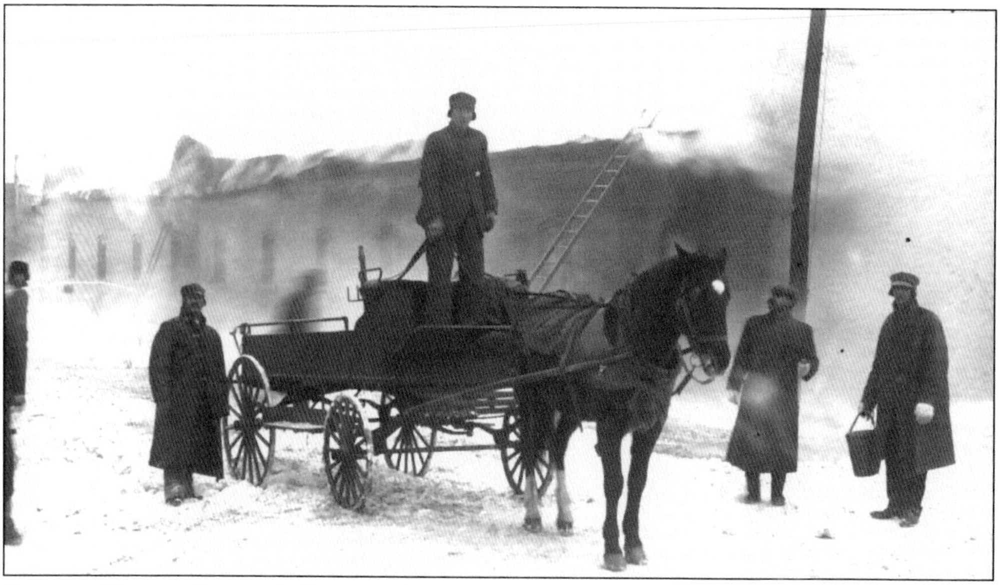

FIRE AT FRANK PHELPS'S LIVERY BARN, JANUARY 13, 1913. An overheated office stove sparked a blaze that reduced the livery to ashes. Subzero temperatures froze hydrants and hampered efforts of firefighters. Destroyed were an automobile, a 12-passenger buckboard and four-passenger cab belonging to Frank Phelps, a phaeton, a set of harnesses, and veterinary equipment and medicines belonging to Dr. Guy Porter, whose office was in the barn. (Photograph by Ennis Brothers.)

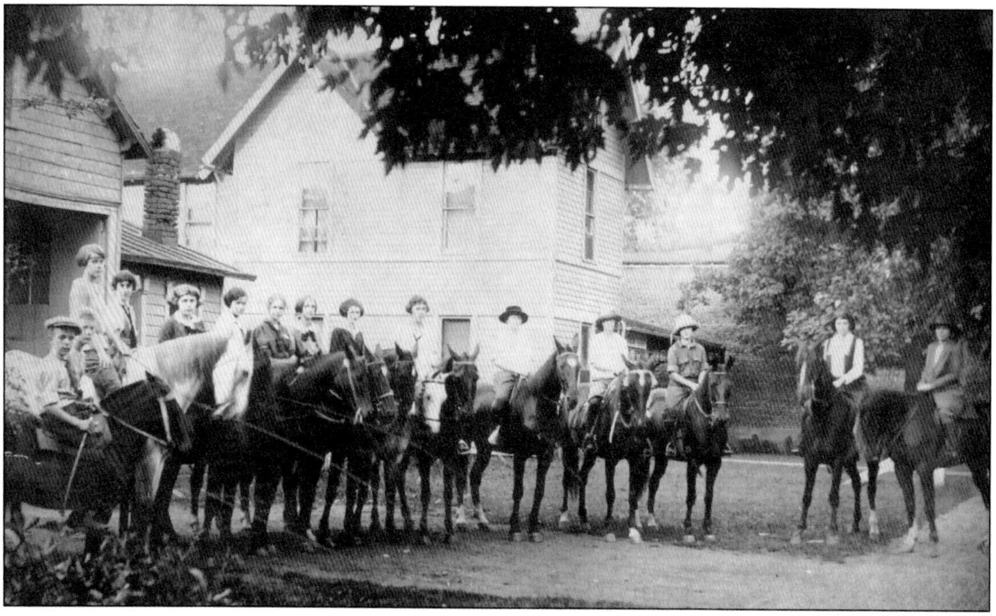

BAUHARD SALE BARN AND RIDING STABLE, *c.* 1915. Seen at the left, Bauhard's was located at 310 West Morgan Street. From left to right, the women are Margaret Hubbard Kivett, Mary Catherine Dickson Brown, Grace Rose, Harriet Stanger, Rosemary Hussey, Eileen Poston, Helen Lowder or Helen Terhune, Hannah Hubbard, Frances Petro Schnaiter, Dorothy Rudical, Ruth Bain, Harriet Sweet, and Rose Singleton. The Clifton boardinghouse is the two-story building in the center.

Six

Business and Industry

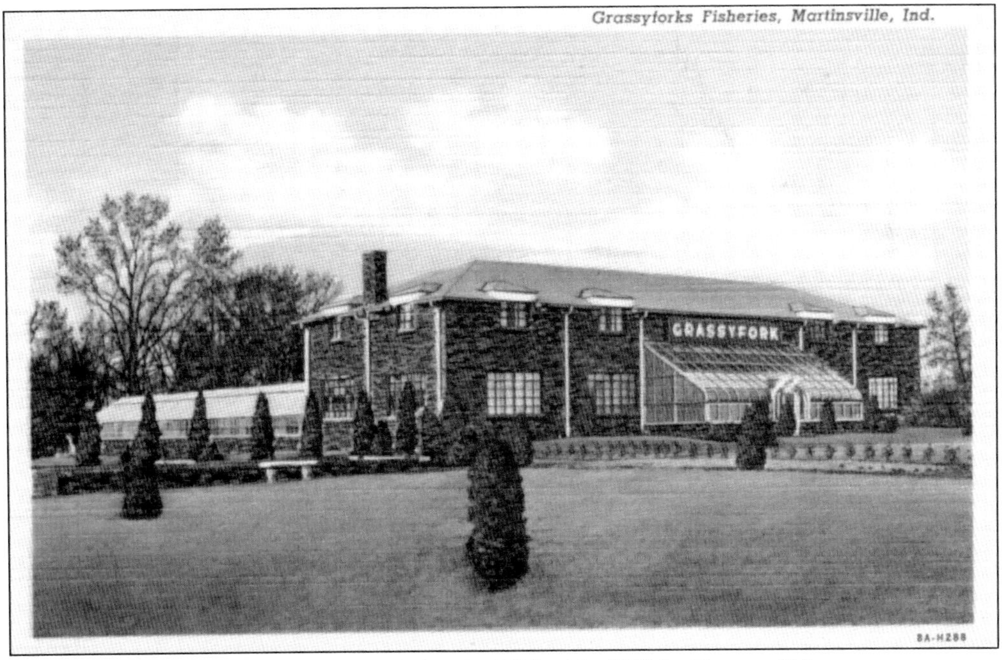

Display and Sales Building, c. 1936. Established in 1899 by Eugene Shireman on swampy farmland he had inherited, Grassyfork became, by World War II, the largest producer of goldfish and water lilies in the world. The industry expanded to include the breeding and sale of lilies and other water plants and the manufacture of fish food, aquariums, and aquarium accessories such as terra-cotta castles and bisque mermaids.

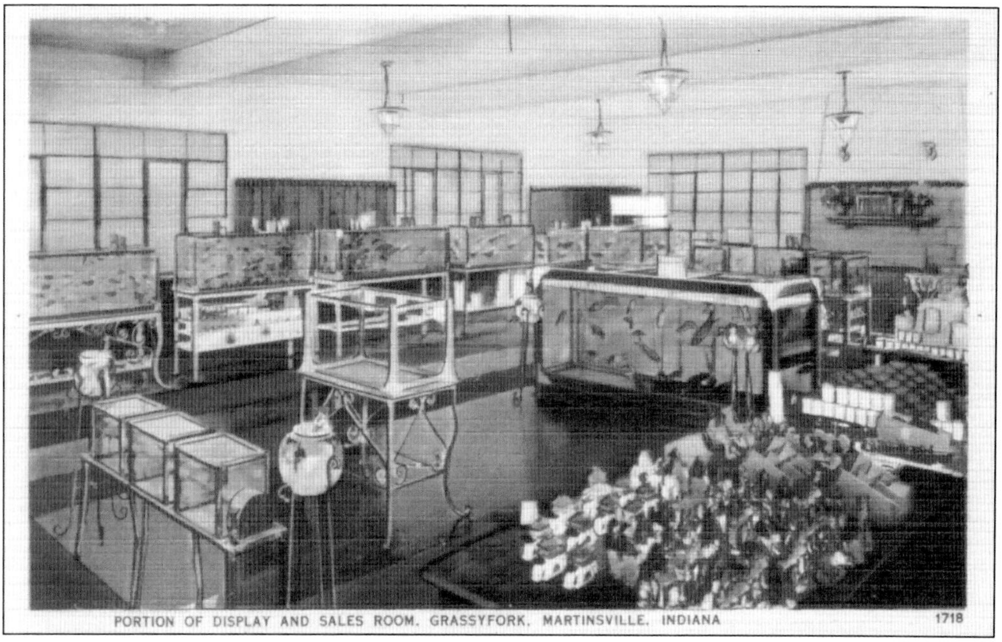

Display Salon, c. 1936. The grand opening of the display and sales building in May 1936 drew hundreds of local residents and motorists from five states. "The most vivid and colorful room of the building is the display salon where aquariums, stocked with a brilliant array of fish, are shown, along with aquarium fixtures and novelties," noted the *Daily Reporter.*

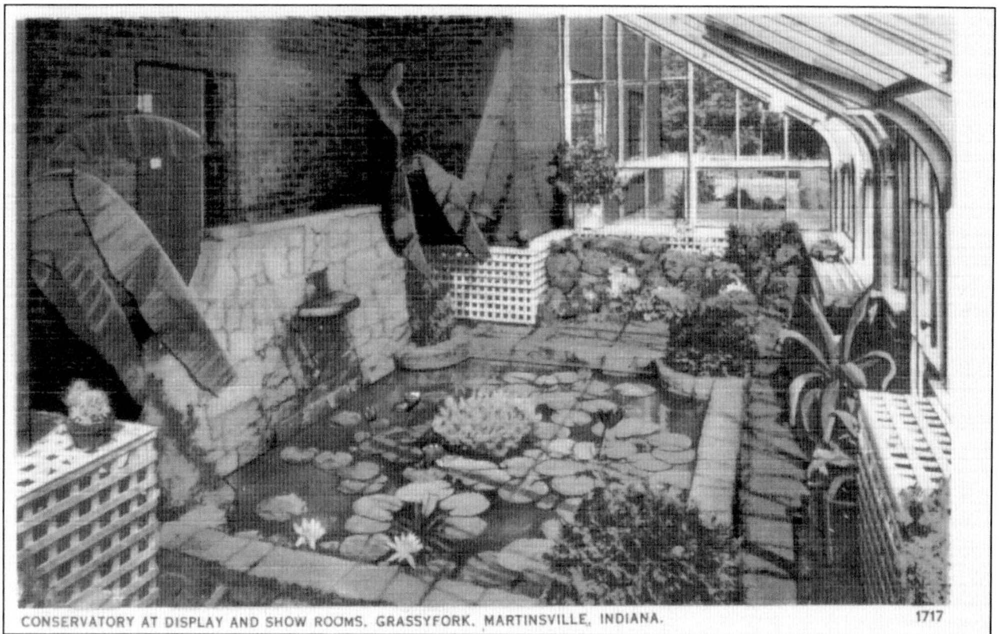

Conservatory, c. 1936. "Next in popularity [with grand opening visitors] seemed to be the conservatory with its artistically designed pool, rock path, and rock plants. The conservatory is entirely enclosed in glass, with a curved glass roof. An automatic fountain of new design adds to the beauty of the conservatory." Garden pools glimmering with Grassyfork's goldfish and tropical water lilies, lotus, and other aquatic plants became a nationwide fad.

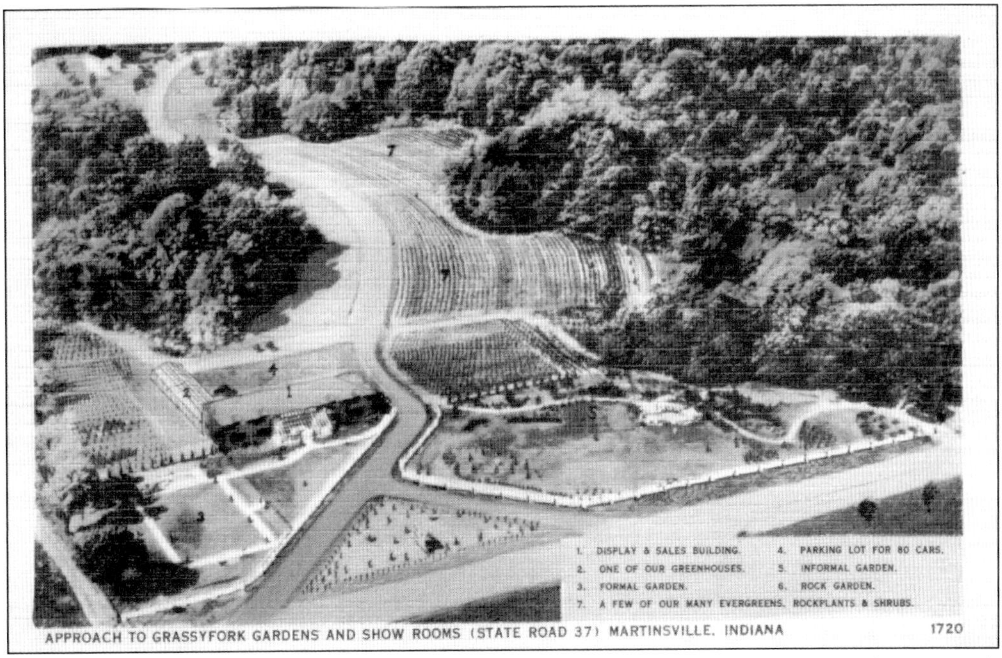

AIRPLANE VIEW, *C.* 1936. By the mid-1940s, Grassyfork covered 1,500 acres, with 645 ponds on seven farms. By 1950, 50 million goldfish were raised annually. The display and sales building appears left of center. Along the card's bottom is State Road 37, now East Morgan Street. The drive leading away from the display building continues to Hatchery No. 1 seen below.

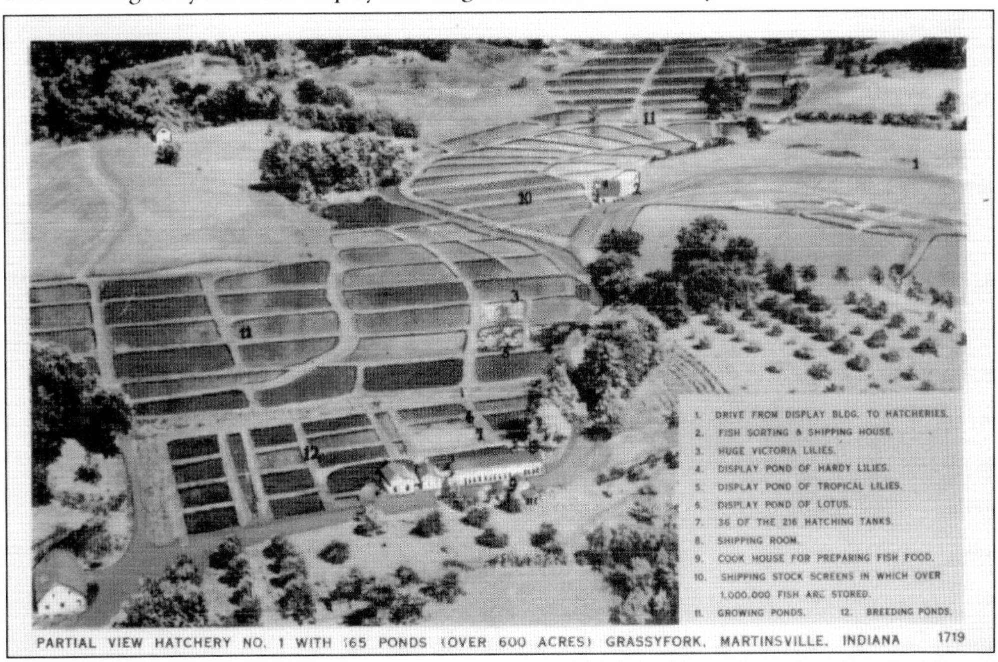

AIRPLANE VIEW OF HATCHERY NO. 1, *C.* 1936. Goldfish had been introduced to the United States only 20 years before Eugene Shireman hatched his fantastic plan. Shireman taught himself everything there was to know about raising goldfish. He developed his own feed, hatching tanks, breeding ponds, storage systems, and even a refrigerated truck for shipping.

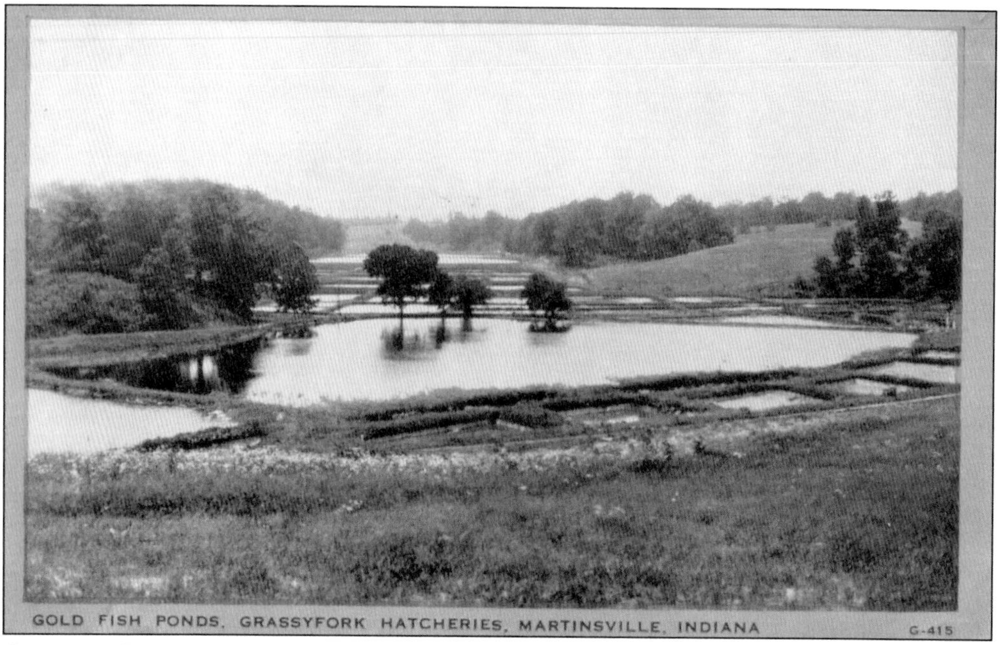

GOLDFISH PONDS, c. 1940. Expansion continued through the post–World War II years. Upon Eugene Shireman's death in 1960, Grassyfork was transferred to Stanley Byram, who had made his home with Shireman for many years and been groomed as his successor. A year later, 200,000 visitors made their way to Grassyfork. Purchases of local grain to be made into fish food and employment of 25–30 people provided additional stimulus to the local economy.

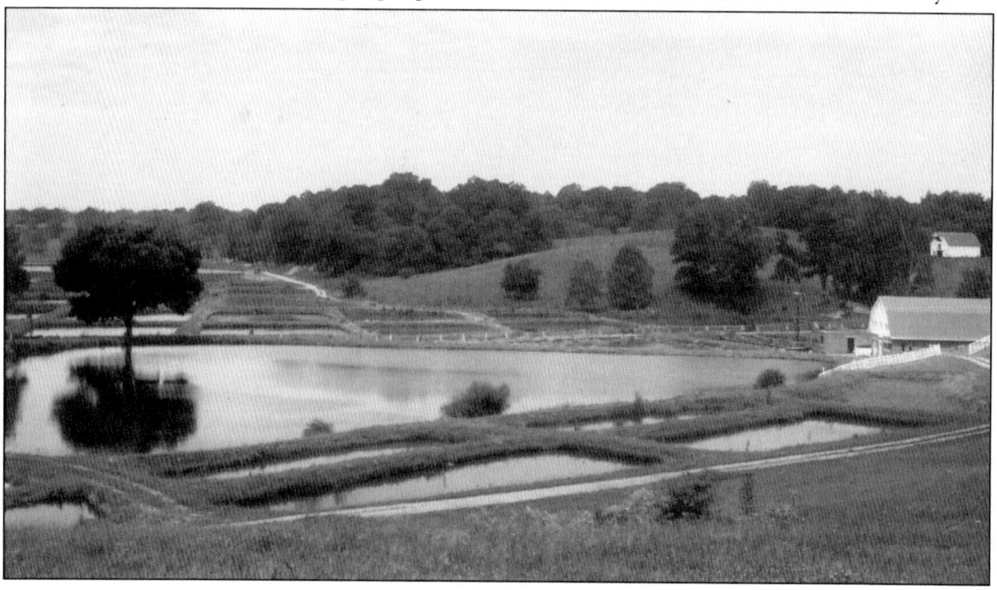

VIEW OF HATCHERIES FROM WHAT IS NOW GRASSYFORK LANE, c. 1965. In May 1970, Byram sold the 1,100 acres comprising Grassyfork Fisheries to Ozark Fisheries of Ozark, Missouri. One year later, Pres. F. Lawrence Balliere platted and began developing the Shireman Estates subdivision. Within a few years, the display room was closed and retail sales and public tours discontinued. Today Grassyfork produces approximately 25,000 goldfish and koi annually in 350 ponds on three sites.

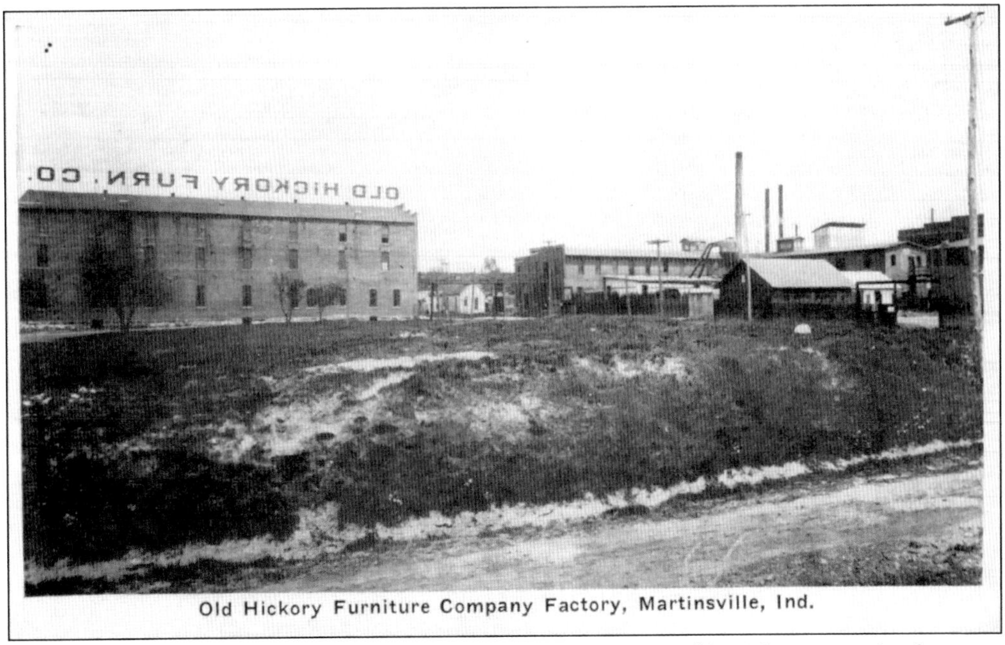

OLD HICKORY FACTORY, *C.* 1925. Established about 1892, Old Hickory was the foremost producer of Indiana rustic hickory furniture and accessory pieces. In 1900, it moved into this new plant on Cherry Street. Initially only chairs were made, but by 1921, under the ownership of William H. Patton, the company was producing a variety of pieces, and its name was changed from Old Hickory Chair Company to Old Hickory Furniture Company.

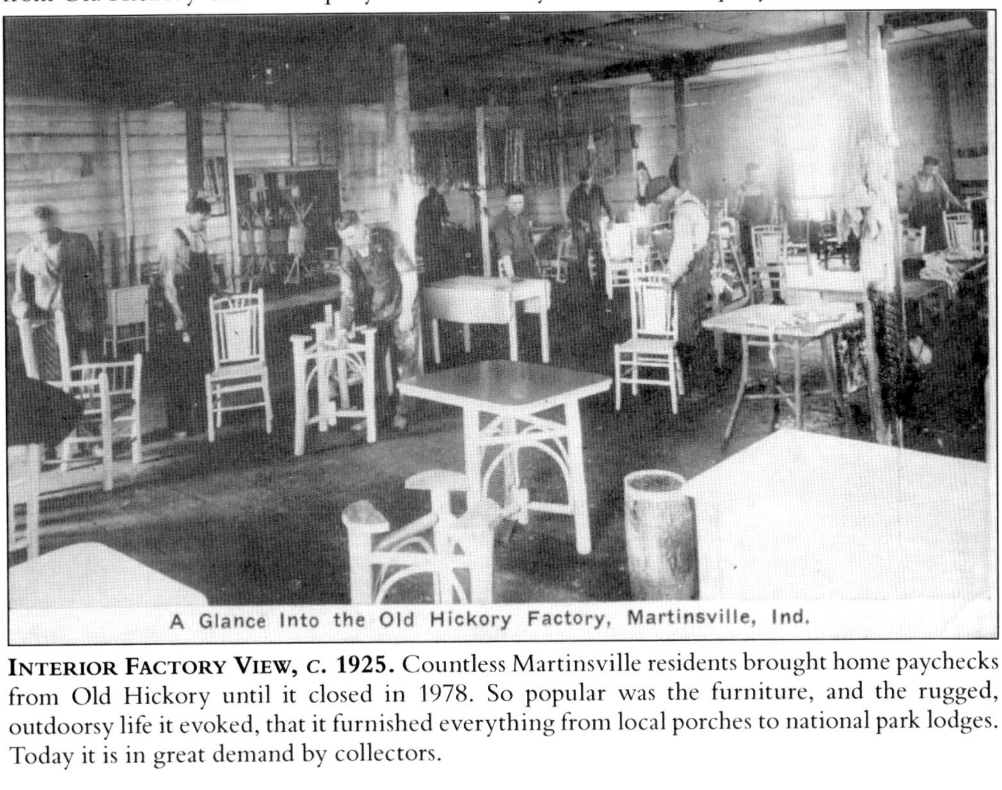

INTERIOR FACTORY VIEW, *C.* 1925. Countless Martinsville residents brought home paychecks from Old Hickory until it closed in 1978. So popular was the furniture, and the rugged, outdoorsy life it evoked, that it furnished everything from local porches to national park lodges. Today it is in great demand by collectors.

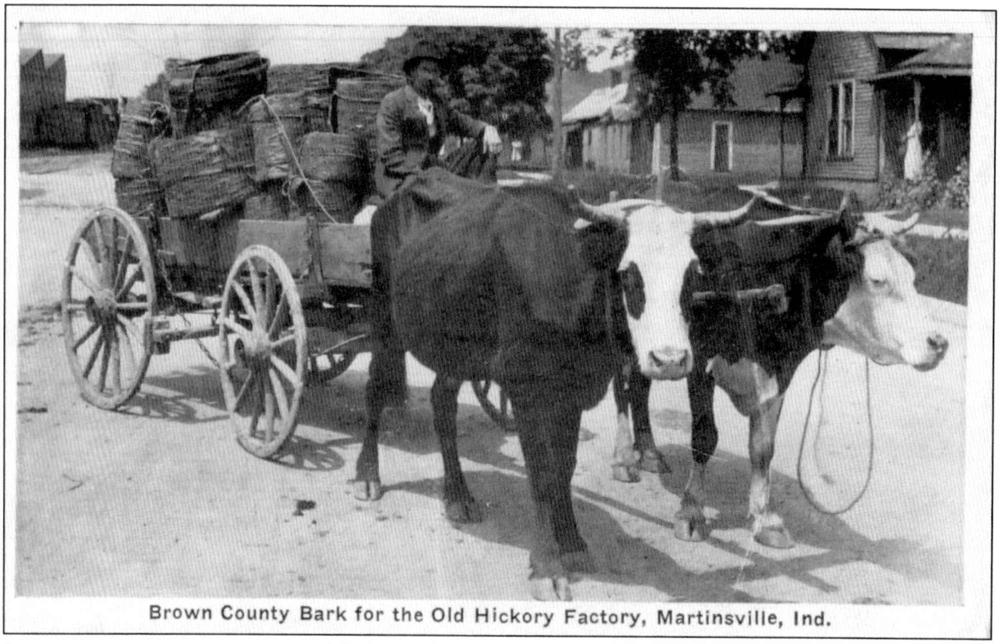

BRINGING IN THE BARK, C. 1925. Bark was harvested in Brown County and hauled to the factory. Soaked in large vats, the bark became pliable so that it could be split and woven into chair seats and backs and panels on furniture pieces. When bark became scarce, it was replaced with rattan. When rattan became impossible to get during World War II, chairs were made with spindles and wood slats.

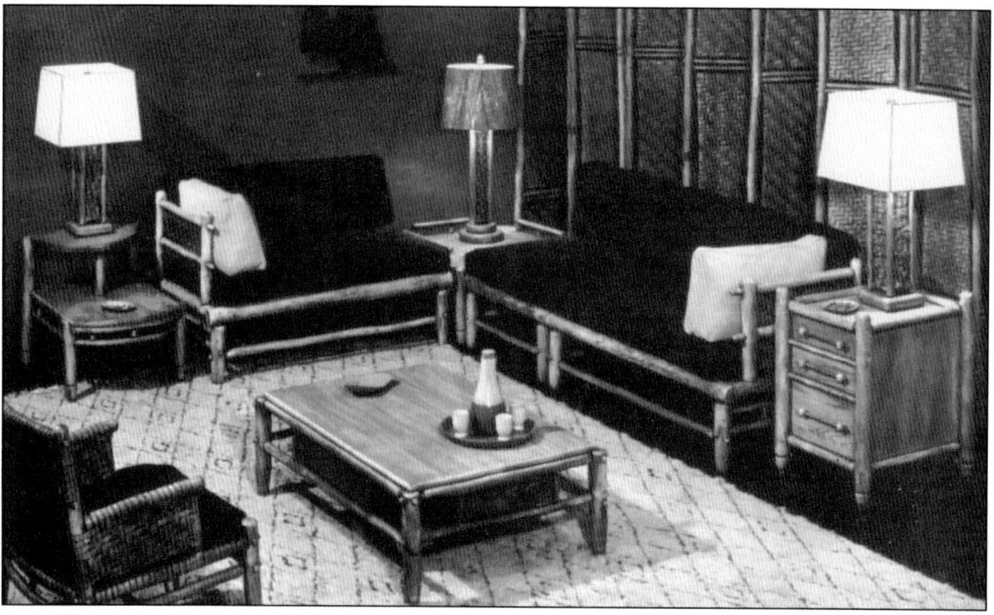

OLD HICKORY SIMPATICO LINE, C. 1960. The caption on this card reads, "A new, completely co-ordinated line of seating, storage, table and decorative units. As the name implies, Simpatico is truly congenial—casual in the modern manner. Simpatico is an important addition to our collection of Authentic Normandy French Farmhouse, American Provincial and Hickory Rustic Furniture. Showrooms: Chicago, New York, Los Angeles, San Francisco, Houston."

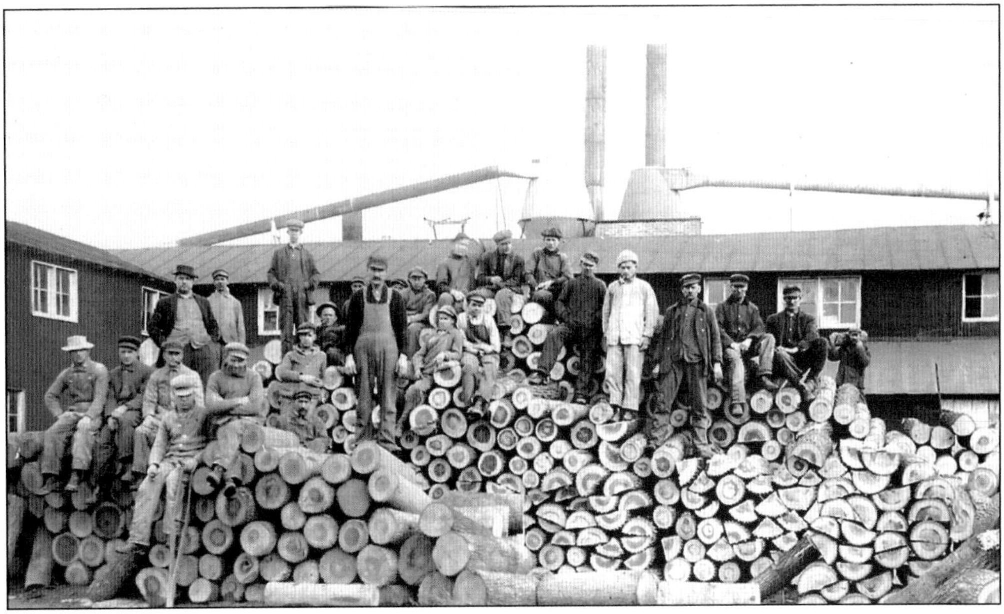

WORKERS AT DAVIS COOPERAGE, 1913. The "Bucket Factory" on South Ohio Street was established in 1888 by the Bierbusse family, who first went into business in Germany in 1869. Sold to the Ault Wooden Ware Company of Cincinnati in 1897, the plant became known by the name of its manager, Henry C. Davis. Production expanded from oak kegs to include buckets, pails, ice-cream tubs, chicken coops, and other woodenware products.

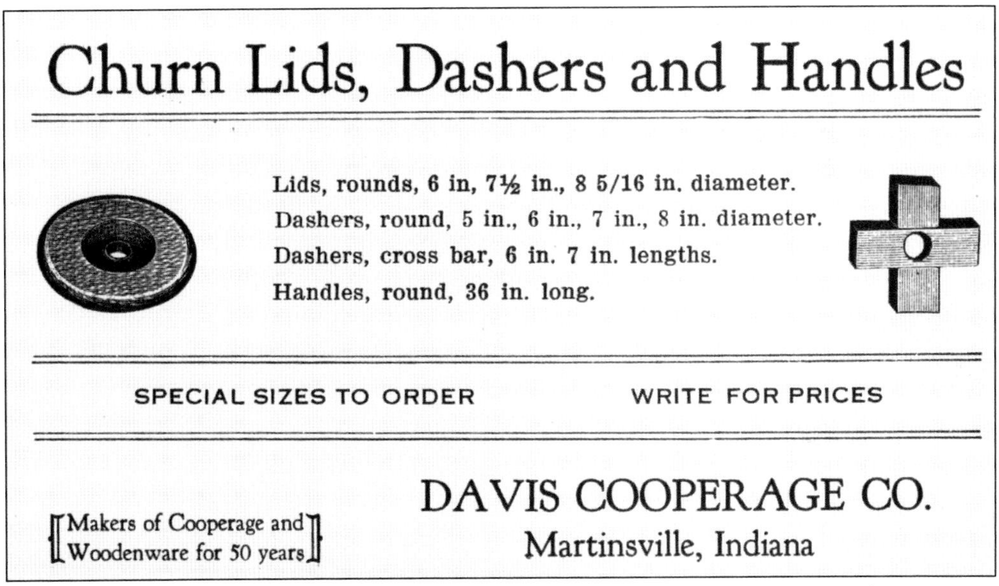

DAVIS COOPERAGE, C. 1919. James W. Hussey, an Ault manager, purchased the plant in 1929. At the peak of operations in the 1920s and 1930s, 300 people worked 10 hours a day. As plastic, glass, and metal gradually replaced wood, oak kegs again became the sole product. When it closed in 1980, the bucket factory was the last cooperage in the Western Hemisphere making oak kegs smaller than five gallons.

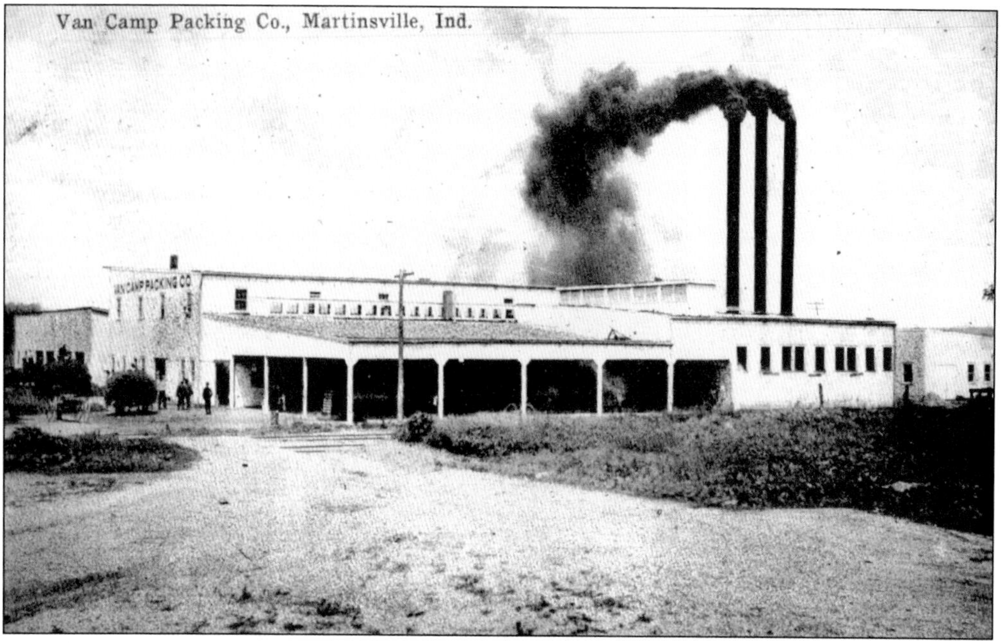

VAN CAMP PACKING COMPANY LOOKING NORTHWEST, 1910. Located on the north side of Douglas Street, Van Camp, built in 1903, began as a small receiving station for tomatoes. By 1940 it had grown into a huge packing plant with an annual payroll of more than $70,000. Round-the-clock shifts were needed to process tomatoes into ketchup, canned tomatoes, chili sauce, and tomato juice. Cabbage, peas, and pumpkins were also processed.

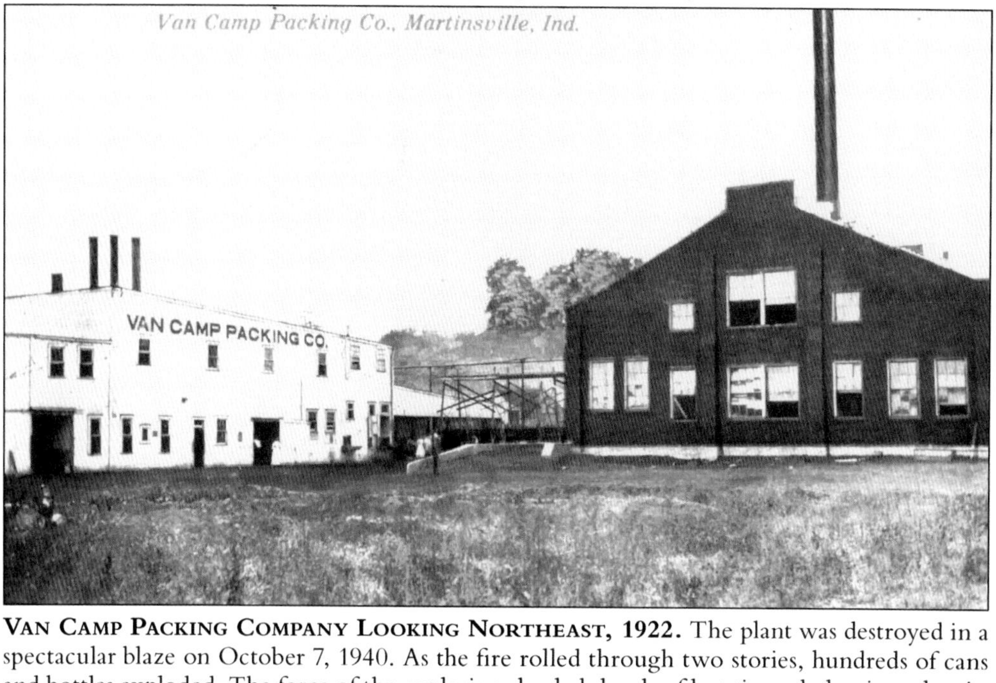

VAN CAMP PACKING COMPANY LOOKING NORTHEAST, 1922. The plant was destroyed in a spectacular blaze on October 7, 1940. As the fire rolled through two stories, hundreds of cans and bottles exploded. The force of the explosions hurled shards of hot tin and glass into the air. The memories of older residents who viewed the fire as children are to this day infused with the smell of tomatoes and sauerkraut.

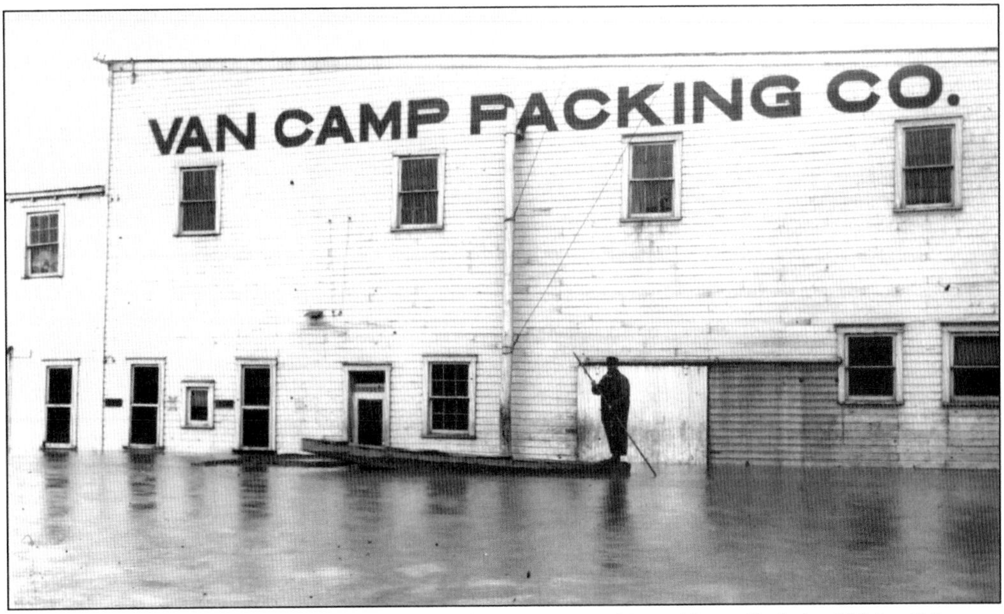

VAN CAMP IN FLOOD, 1916. Heavy rain from January 27 to 29 swelled the White River to overflowing. Flood levels were approximately three feet below that of the great flood of 1913, forcing the interruption of rail and interurban service and sending the residents of Martinsville's northwest side scrambling once again to dry out their homes and belongings. This photograph was taken on January 31, 1916.

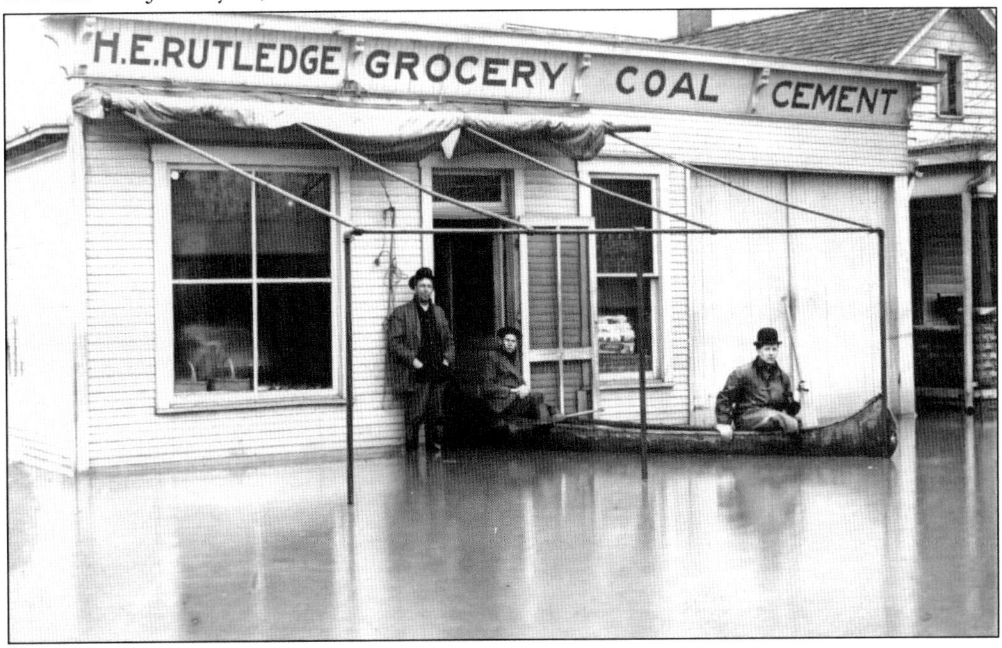

RUTLEDGE GROCERY, COAL, AND CEMENT, 1913. For many years, Hugh "Gert" Rutledge operated a grocery and coal delivery business at the northeast corner of Harrison and Marion Streets, shown here during the 1913 flood. Born in 1870, Rutledge appears as a player in an 1892 photograph of the Martinsville baseball team, was a veteran of the Spanish-American War, and served as city treasurer—he was a Democrat—when Martinsville City Hall was built in 1917.

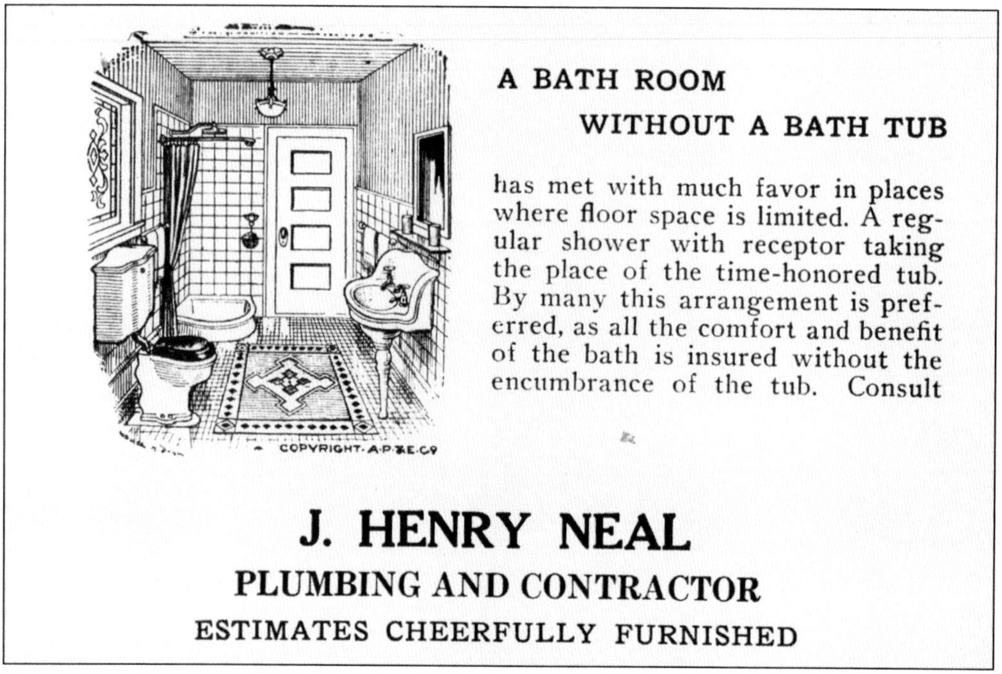

PUBLICITY CARD, c. 1915. Born in 1893, Henry Neal was self-employed as a plumber for a few years before partnering with Jesse H. Finchum in a plumbing and heating contracting business. Married to Mary Barger in 1911, Henry was the father of five children when he died suddenly of an abscessed kidney at the age of 33.

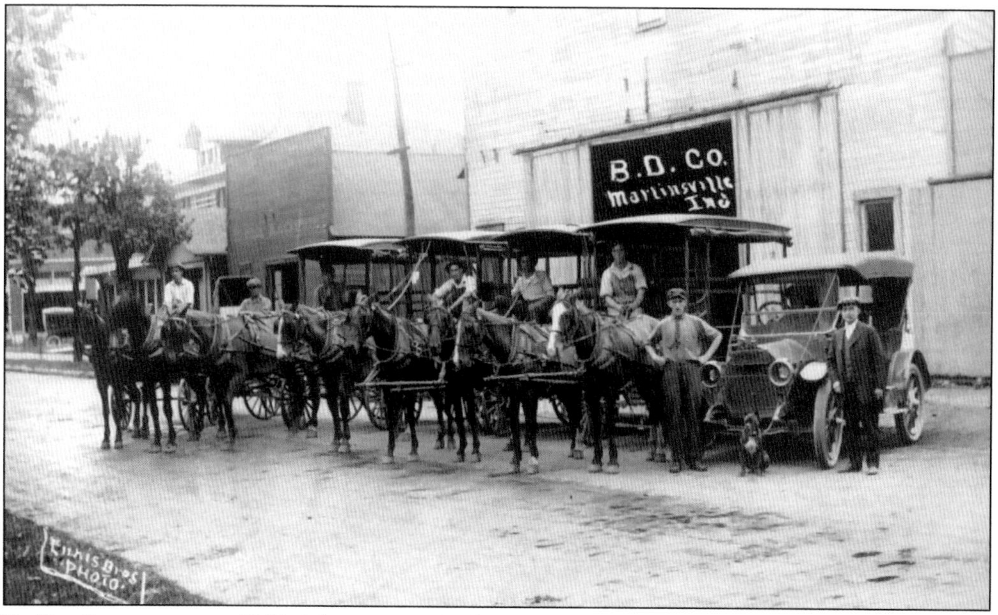

B. D. COMPANY, c. 1917. The owner(s) of this livery on West Morgan Street is unknown. Prior to the completion of city hall in 1917, this building served as a fire station. At the far left, at the corner of Mulberry Street, are the Martinsville Auto Company and the David Cohn house. The small, gabled building behind the tree is Michael Cohn's photography studio. The frame false-fronted building is a blacksmith shop.

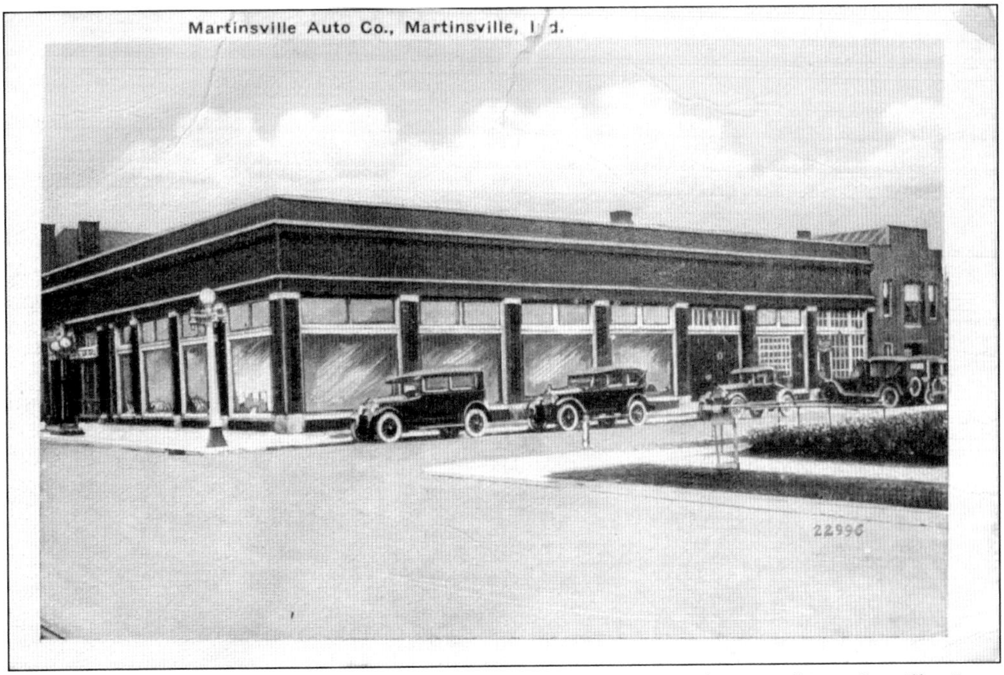

MARTINSVILLE AUTO COMPANY, *C.* 1920. This showroom, home of Martinsville Auto Company (1904–1975), was built in 1915. When owner William E. Clark retired in 1944, his was the oldest Buick dealership in Indiana and the fourth oldest in the United States.

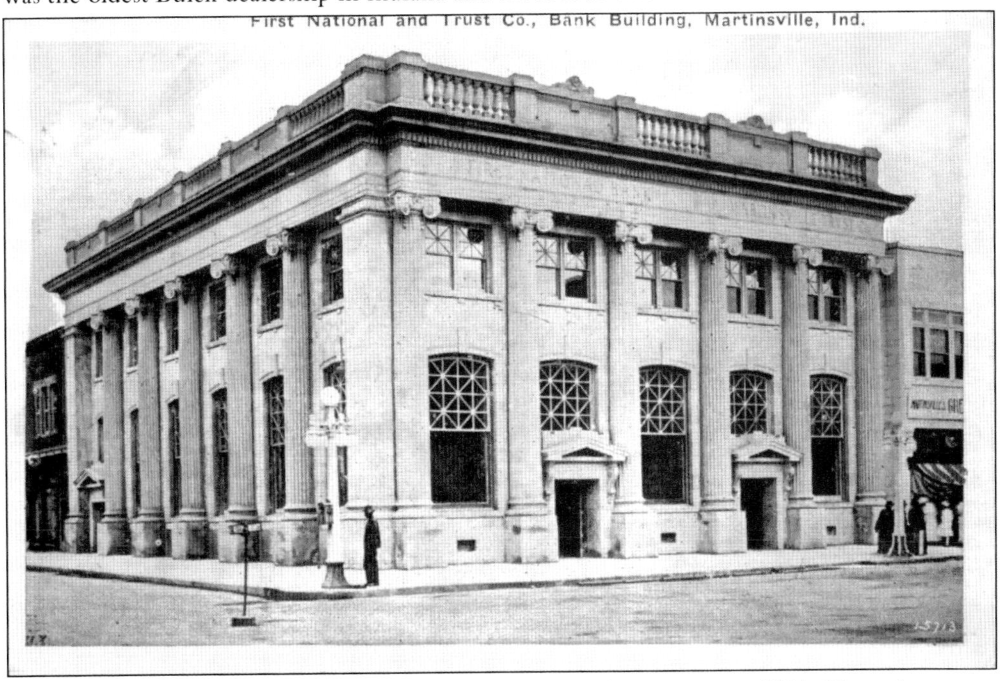

FIRST NATIONAL BANK AND MARTINSVILLE TRUST COMPANY, *C.* 1916. The columns on this building erected in 1916 were quarried at Stinesville, brought to Martinsville by train, and hauled to the site on horse-drawn flatbeds. The building exists yet today, but the two banks that shared it crashed and closed during the Depression.

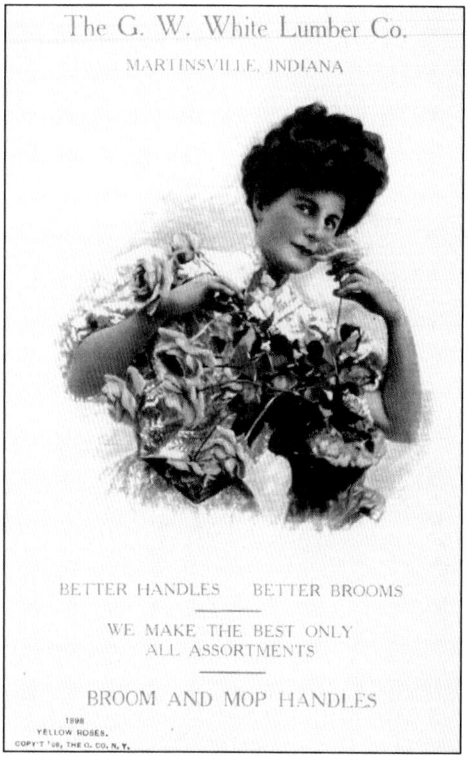

G. W. WHITE LUMBER COMPANY, *C.* 1915. This card has a copyright date of 1906. Little is known about this company and manufacturer of broom and mop handles. Its owner was George W. White, who is identified in the 1910 federal census as a lumber dealer living at 539 East Morgan Street. His sawmill was located at 359 South Sycamore Street.

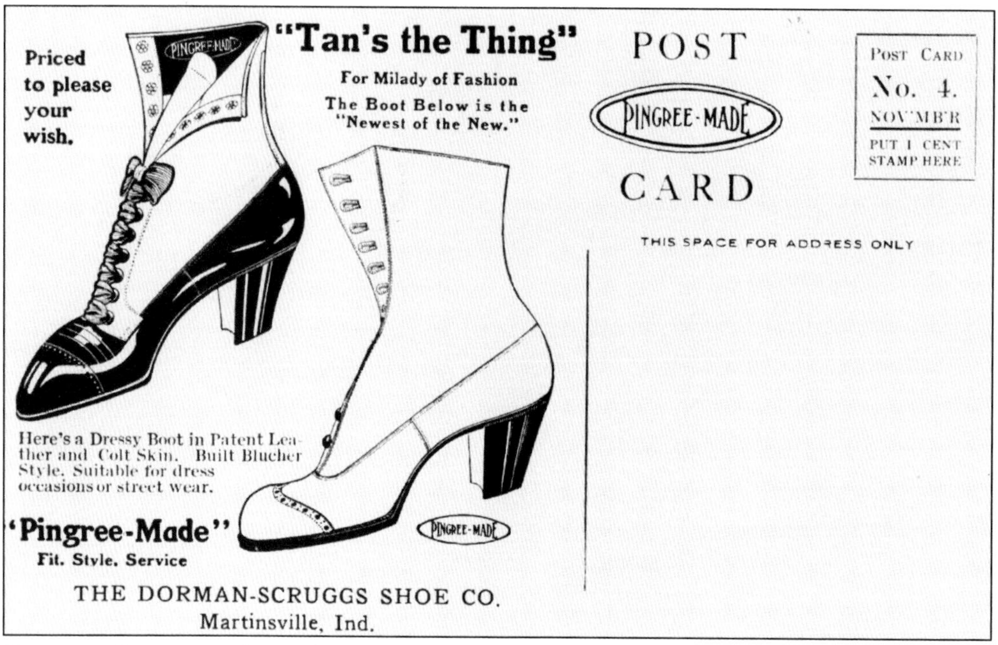

DORMAN-SCRUGGS SHOE COMPANY, *C.* 1911. A Mooresville dry goods merchant from 1887 to 1919, George R. Scruggs established a shoe store on Martinsville's square with partner Ivan Dorman. Managed by Scruggs's son, Fred, the business operated for a few years. An advertisement in the 1912 Martinsville High School annual promises, "We sell the very best values for the price, no matter what the price. 'When you see it in our Add, It's So.'"

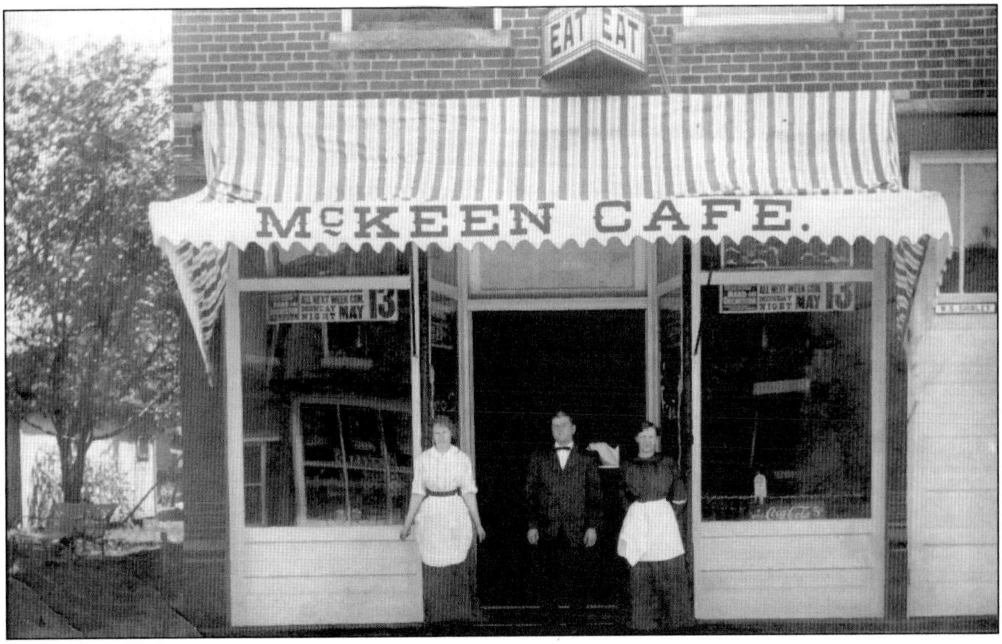

McKeen Cafe, 171 North Main Street, 1912. This little café operated as McKeen's from about 1912 to 1915. The window posters advertise the six-day vaudeville run of the Harris-Parkinson Stock Company. McKeen's became the White Star Restaurant and eventually Callis Cafe, owned and operated by John and Catherine Callis. In 1932, Callis Cafe moved to the north side of the courthouse square and became a favorite local eatery.

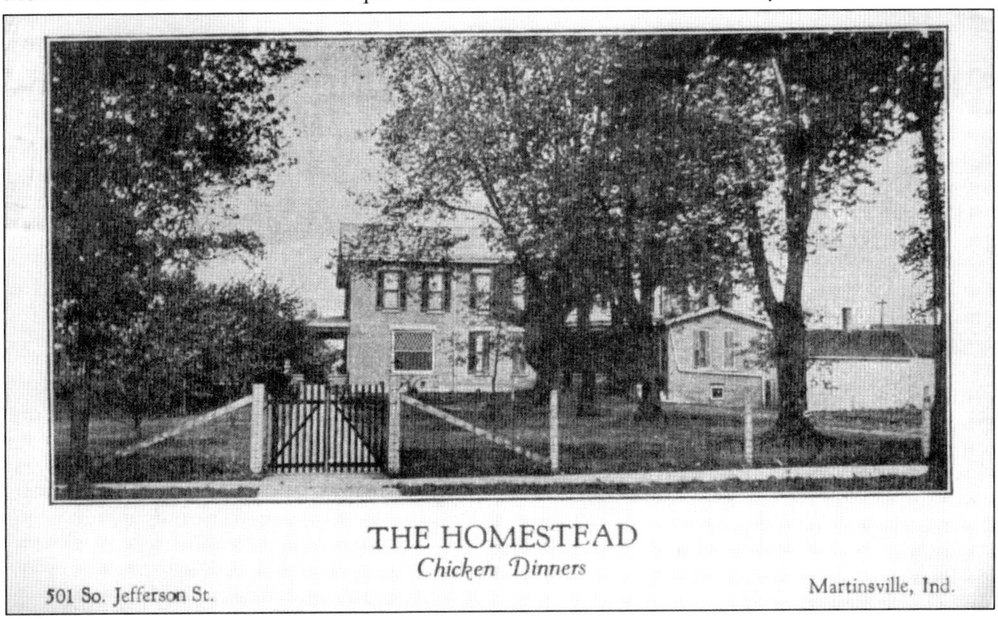

The Homestead, 1933. Following the death of her husband in Kansas City in 1932, Anna May Dickson Adsit returned to Martinsville and opened up the family home for public dining. About her debut on July 23, the *Daily Reporter* noted that 44 guests "thoroughly enjoyed a chicken dinner. The service, excellent menu, and the delightful society made the event a charming occasion for the guests."

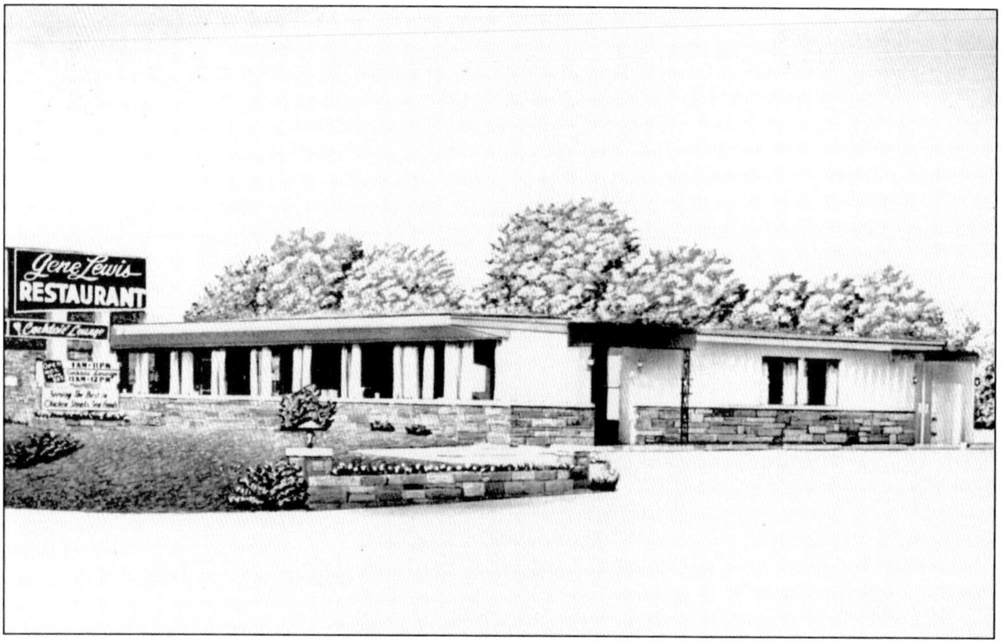

GENE LEWIS RESTAURANT, *c.* 1970. Established by Gene and Virginia "Gin" Lewis about 1959, the original restaurant, a glass-fronted roadside box, burned when the charbroiler ignited the roof. Seen here, the rebuilt and expanded Gene Lewis Restaurant and Knight's Cocktail Lounge was never as successful as the original, and the Lewises sold out to another local restaurateur. Following yet another fire, it became home to Morgan County Insurance and other businesses.

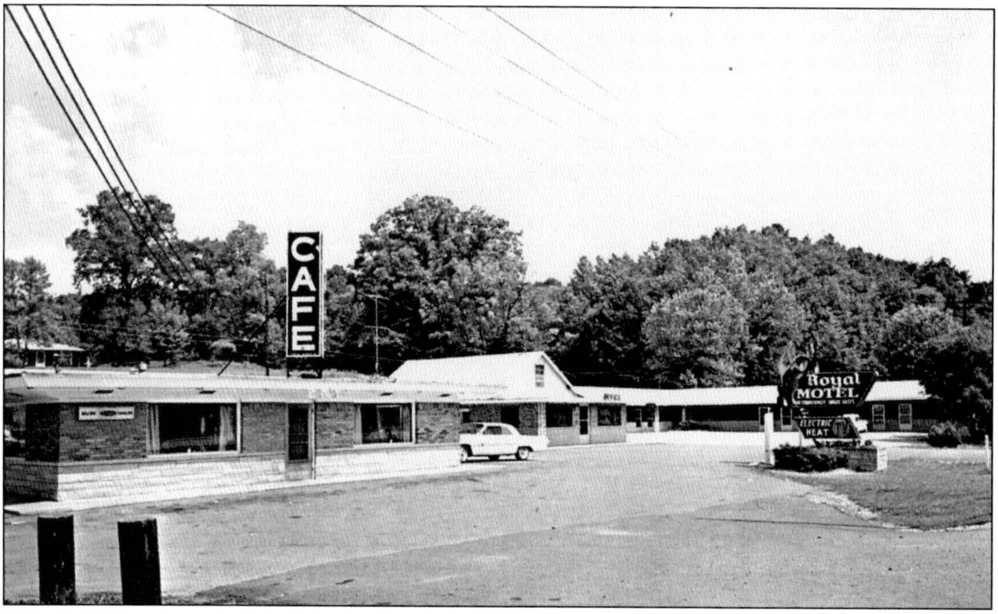

ROYAL MOTEL AND CAFE, *c.* 1960. This motel is still located on State Road 67 near the 39 Bypass. The café, owned and operated by Charles "Bobby" and Shirley Ewing from 1960 to 1970, was well known for its home cooking. Duane Blaschke, who ran the motel for 21 years, remembers that it was a home cooking kind of restaurant serving excellent biscuits and gravy and fried brain sandwiches. The café closed in 1979.

Seven

THE FLOOD OF 1913 AND THE 1922 CENTENNIAL

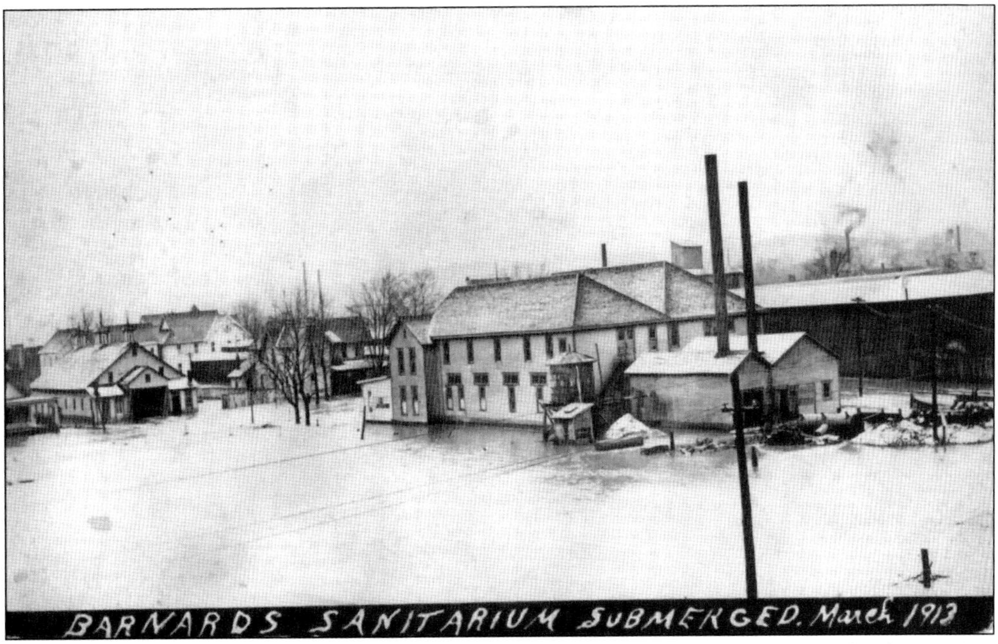

LOOKING NORTHEAST FROM HUBBARD'S MILL, 1913. Torrential rains caused White River to escape its banks, flooding the northwest part of Martinsville on March 24 and 25, 1913. The rear of Barnard's Sanitarium is in the foreground. Across the street is Melvin Bauhard's sale barn. The dark building at the right is A. R. Shireman and Son, drayers and dealers in wood and coal. This and the following flood views with the black bottom border were photographed by Ennis Brothers. Some say the flood of June 7, 2008, rivaled that of 1913.

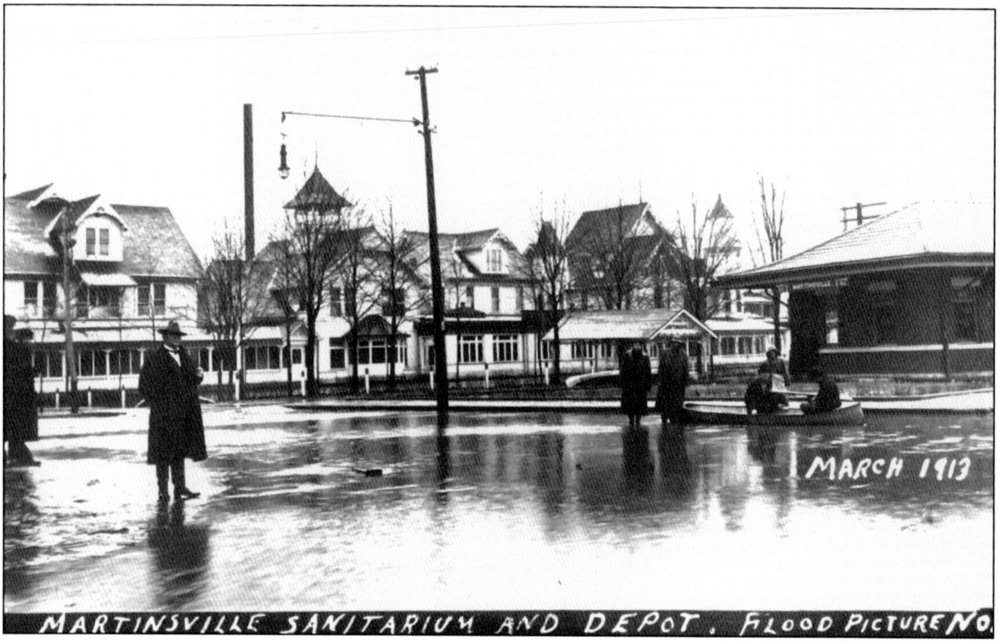

LOOKING NORTHWEST FROM PIKE STREET, 1913. Some sanitarium guests were transferred to other sanitariums and private homes throughout the city. Others chose to ride out the flood along with employees, many of whom lived in the flooded district. Standing in the left foreground is George McClellan "Colonel Mac" Isenhower, a well-known auctioneer who with his wife, Stella, operated a successful real estate, insurance, and loan business.

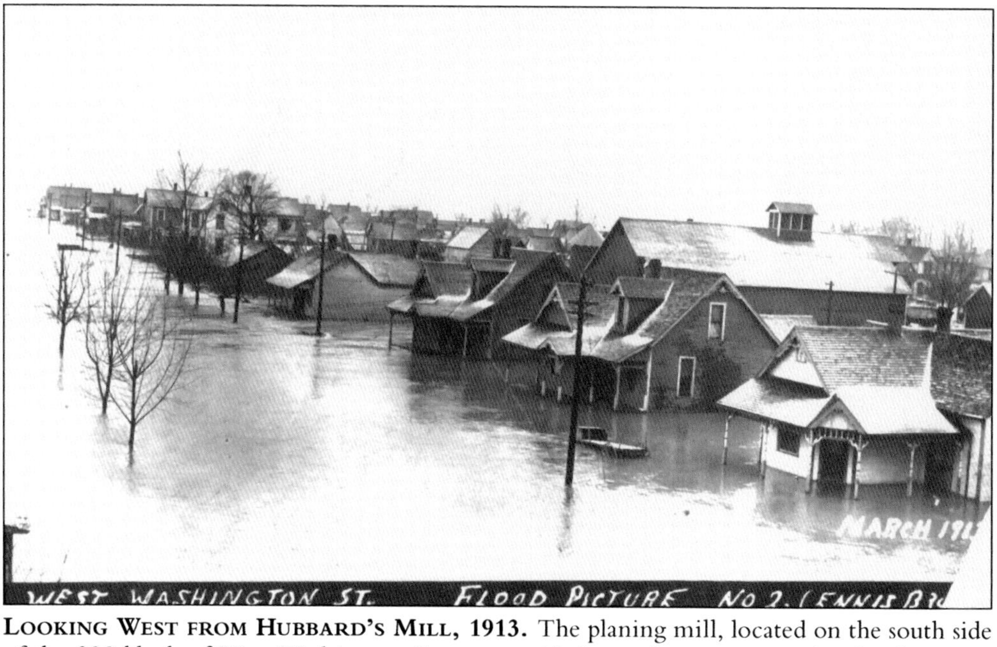

LOOKING WEST FROM HUBBARD'S MILL, 1913. The planing mill, located on the south side of the 300 block of West Washington Street, provided a perfect vantage point for the Ennis Brothers photographers to capture views of the flood. The address of the white house in the right foreground is 360 West Washington Street. The house stands yet today. The large gabled building with a cupola is a private stable.

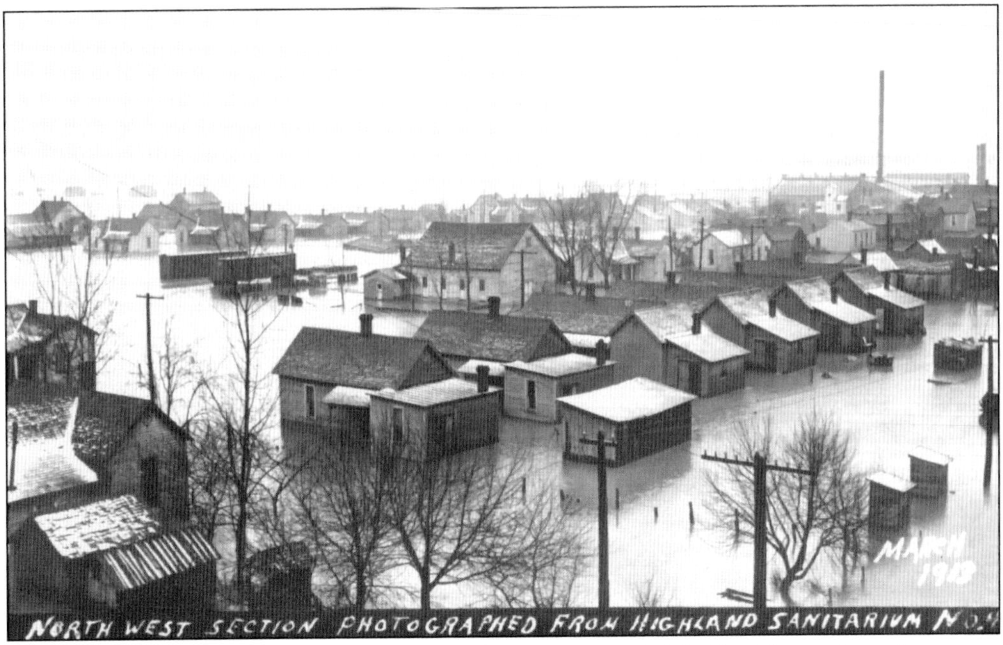

LOOKING NORTHWEST FROM HIGHLAND SANITARIUM, 1913. The identical small cottages seen from the rear are located on the east side of the 500 block of North Mulberry Street. At the center of this view is the Centenary Methodist Episcopal Church. The tall smokestack at right identifies the Van Camp Packing Company. Note also the stranded railcars behind the church and the two backyard privies in the right foreground.

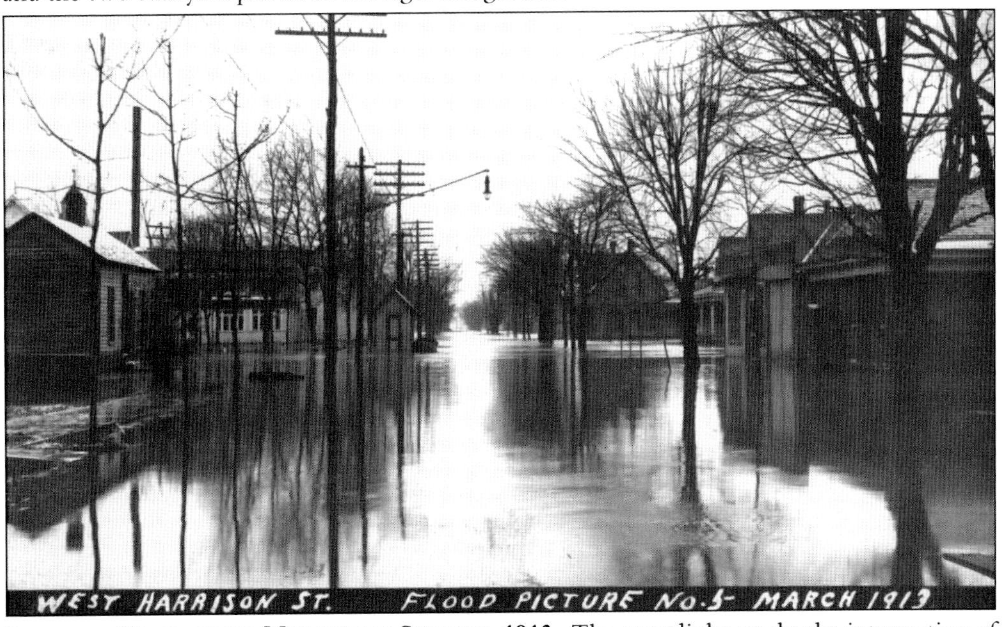

LOOKING WEST FROM MULBERRY STREET, 1913. The streetlight marks the intersection of Harrison and Marion Streets. At the southwest corner is the Martinsville Sanitarium. Doubting that the floodwaters would rise much higher, many people opted to stay with their houses and belongings. By day two of the flood, four feet of water covered some areas and the need for rescue exceeded the number of available boats.

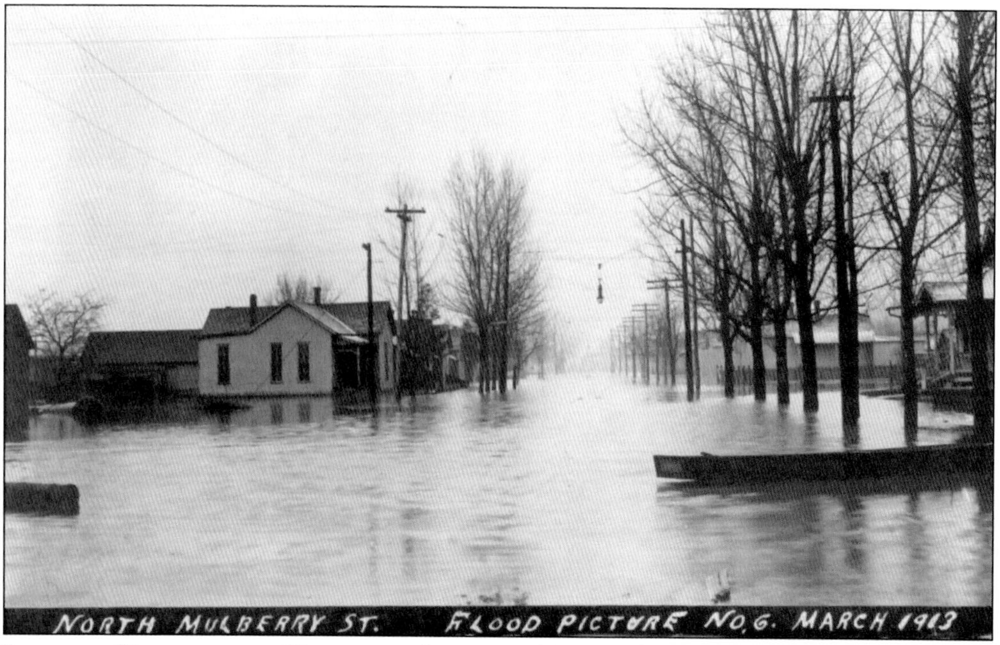

LOOKING NORTH FROM HARRISON STREET, 1913. By day three, Mayor C. H. Hastings advised residents to eat sparingly because of the possible shortage of food. Damage to rail and interurban lines, bridges, and roads prevented travel by anything but boats. Telegraph, telephone, and mail service was interrupted, and newspaper delivery was halted. Martinsville seemed cut off from the world. The house at the left is 410 North Mulberry Street.

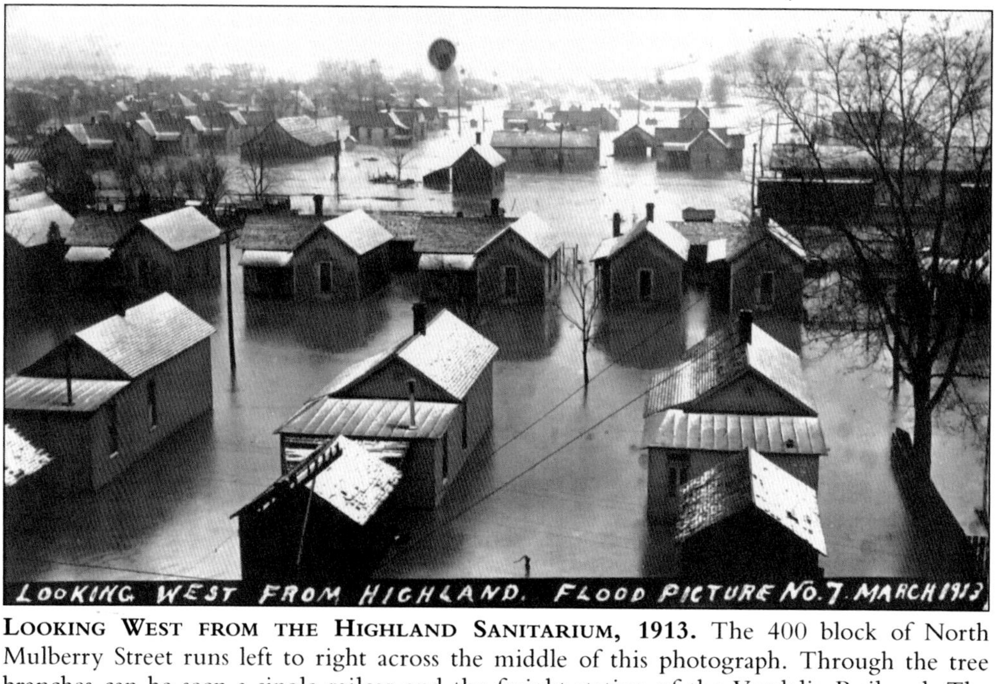

LOOKING WEST FROM THE HIGHLAND SANITARIUM, 1913. The 400 block of North Mulberry Street runs left to right across the middle of this photograph. Through the tree branches can be seen a single railcar and the freight station of the Vandalia Railroad. The three shotgun cottages in the foreground were later torn down for expansion of the Highland Sanitarium on Main Street.

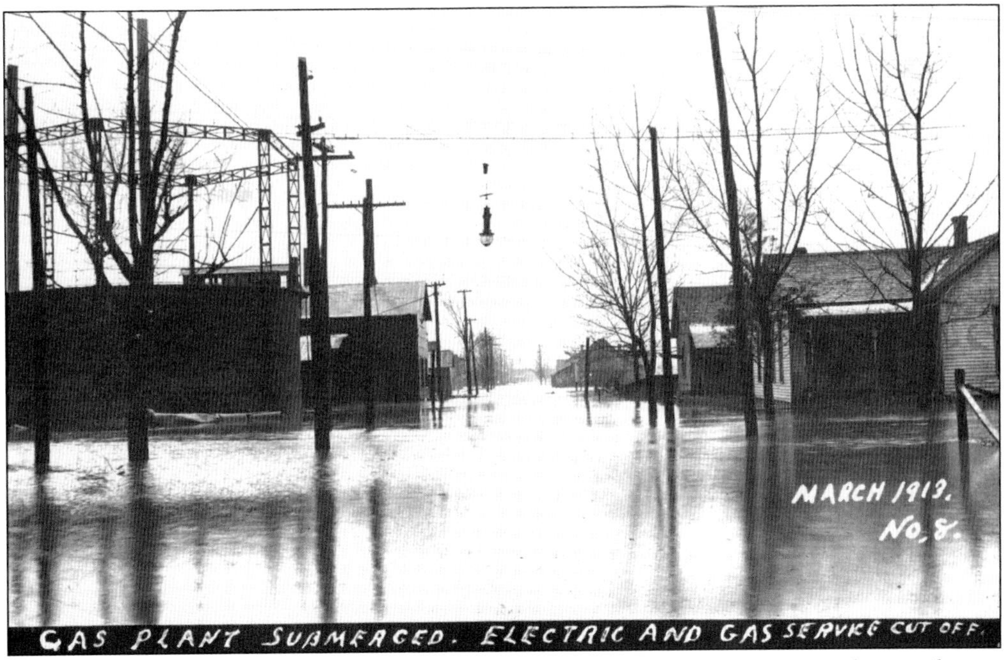

HIGHLAND STREET LOOKING WEST FROM MULBERRY STREET, 1913. Workers at the gas and electric plant fought to keep the engine room dry. Electric service was cut off at 10:00 on the evening of day one. Gas in the round storage tank was exhausted by noon the following day. With a single load of coal left to power the plant, service to customers was restricted to the hours between noon and midnight.

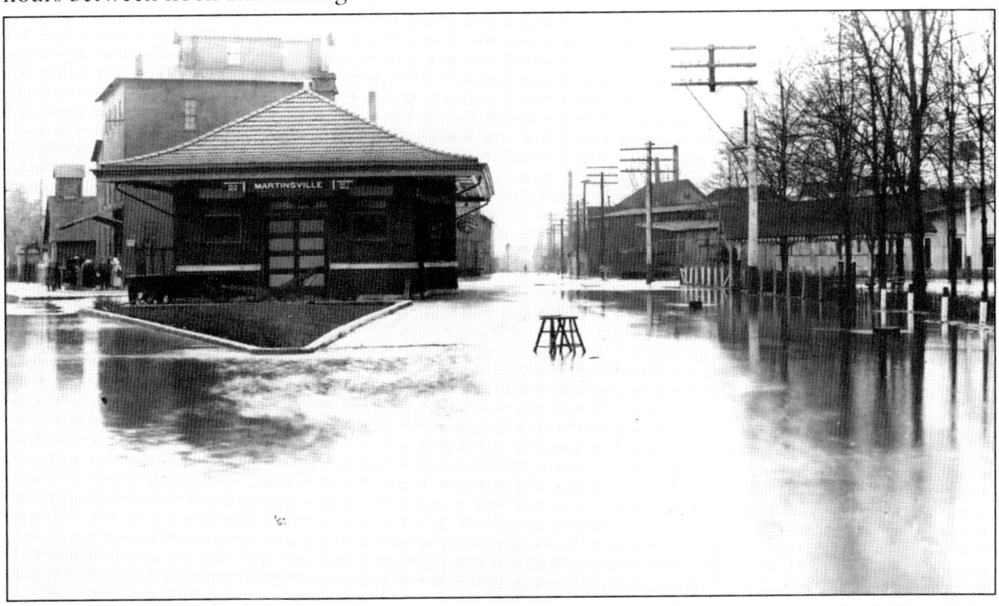

VANDALIA DEPOT LOOKING SOUTH, 1913. Here is a view of Marion Street (at left) and the submerged line of the Vandalia Railroad, which passes the station on its right and continues south through Martinsville's west side. Towering above the depot is Branch Grain and Seed Company. The open structure at right is the train wait station belonging to the Martinsville Sanitarium. Behind it, one block to the south, is Barnard's Sanitarium.

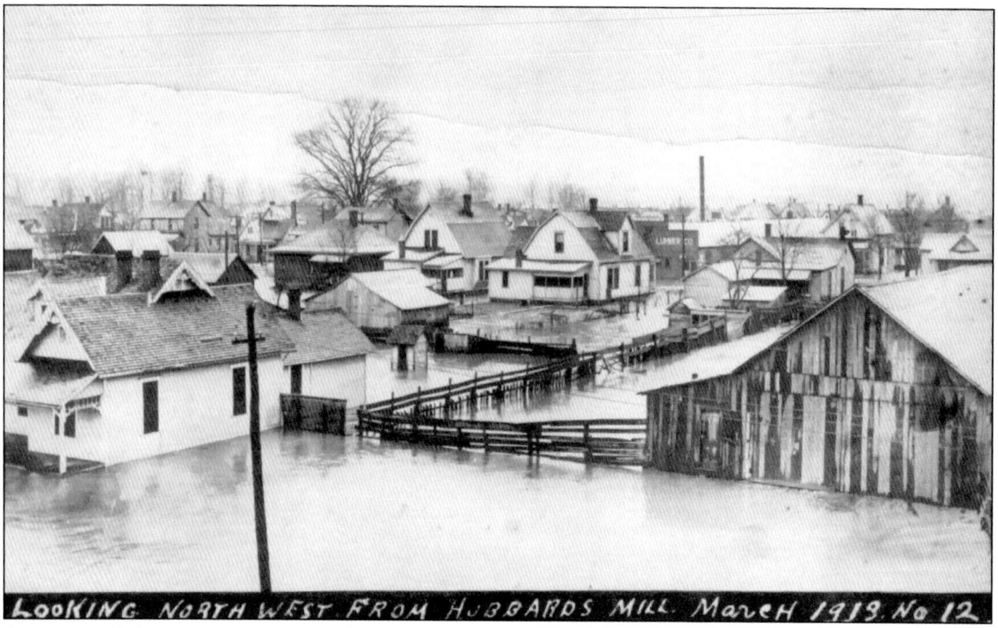

LOOKING NORTHWEST FROM HUBBARD'S MILL, 1913. The two gambrel-roofed houses at the center of this view are located at 385 and 387 West Morgan Street. Across Morgan Street is the Deming Lumber Company, which survived the flood but was destroyed by fire in November 1914. The white house in the left foreground is at 370 West Washington Street. It exists yet today.

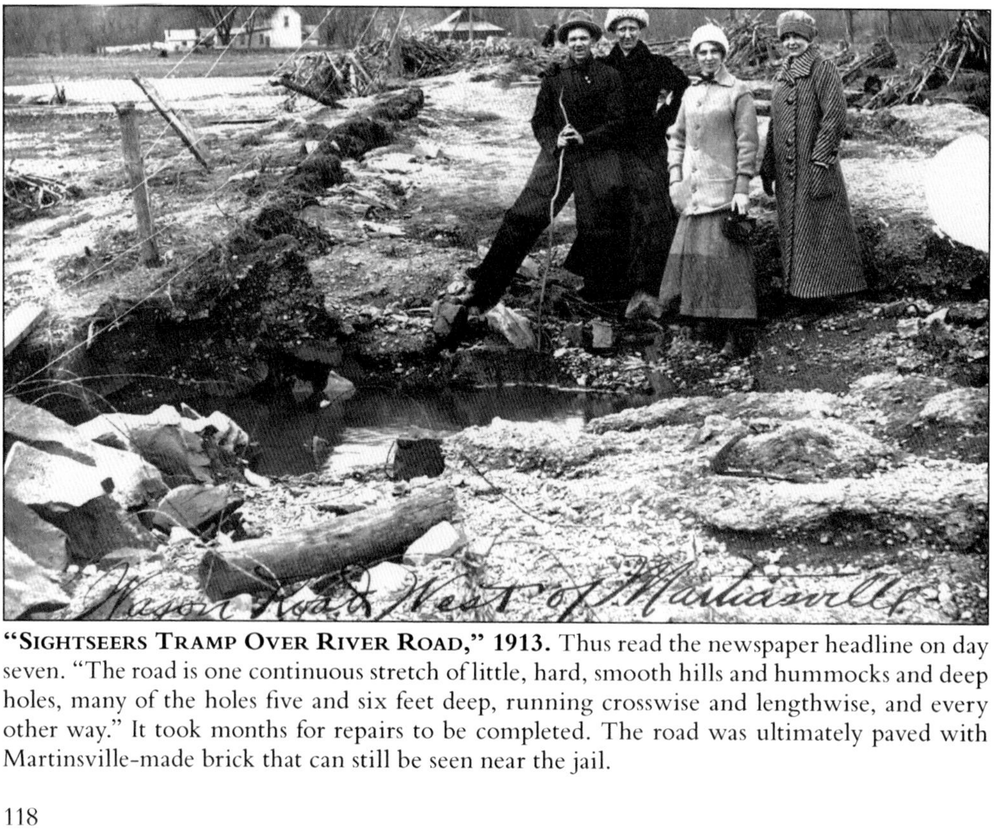

"SIGHTSEERS TRAMP OVER RIVER ROAD," 1913. Thus read the newspaper headline on day seven. "The road is one continuous stretch of little, hard, smooth hills and hummocks and deep holes, many of the holes five and six feet deep, running crosswise and lengthwise, and every other way." It took months for repairs to be completed. The road was ultimately paved with Martinsville-made brick that can still be seen near the jail.

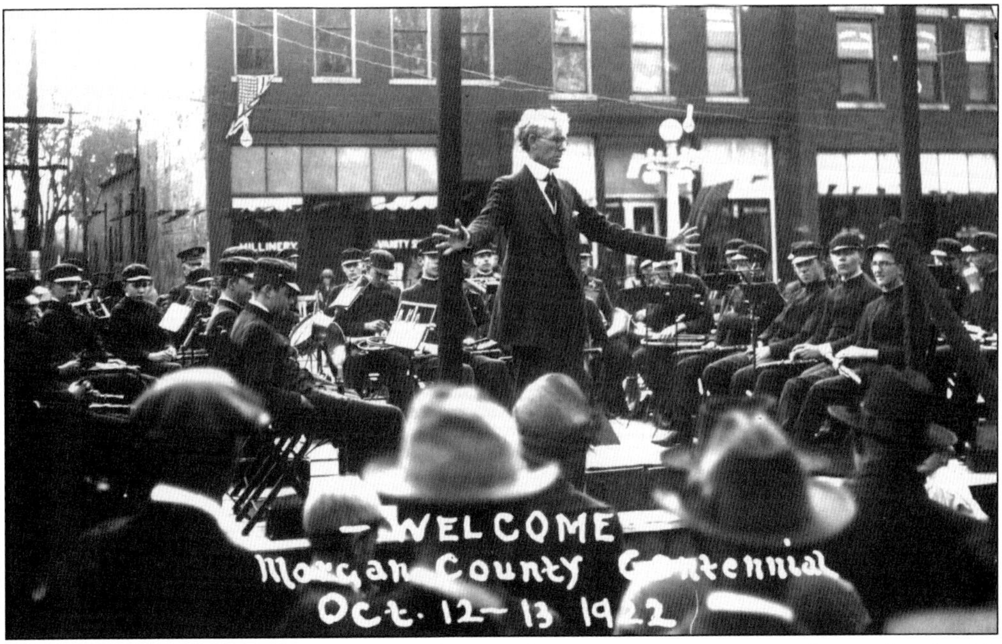

LT. GOV. EMMETT F. BRANCH, 1922. "It is an honor to welcome you to the one hundredth birthday of the best county in the best state in the best country in the world," exclaimed Lt. Gov. Emmett F. Branch from a bandstand on the south lawn of the courthouse. A lifelong Martinsville resident, Branch served as governor of Indiana from 1924 to 1925, taking over the final term of Warren T. McCray, who resigned.

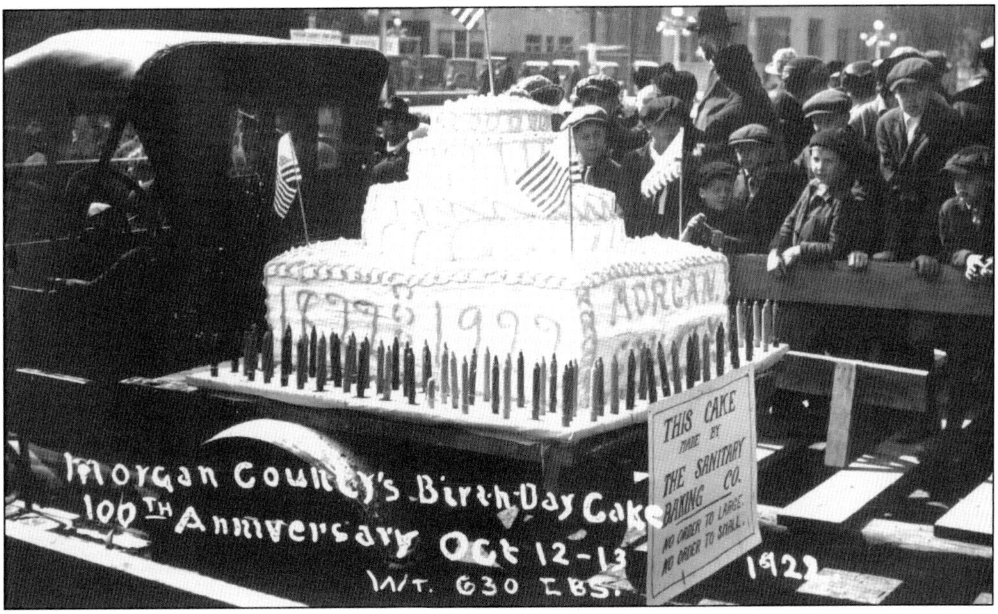

A 630-POUND BIRTHDAY CAKE WITH 100 CANDLES, 1922. Declared delicious, this mammoth cake was made by Hugh Dillon, owner of the Sanitary Bakery, whose misspelled sign boasted "No order to large, no order to small." The cake was served at the Morgan County basket dinner held on the opening day of the two-day event. The photograph on this book's back cover is thought to show the serving tables on Jefferson Street.

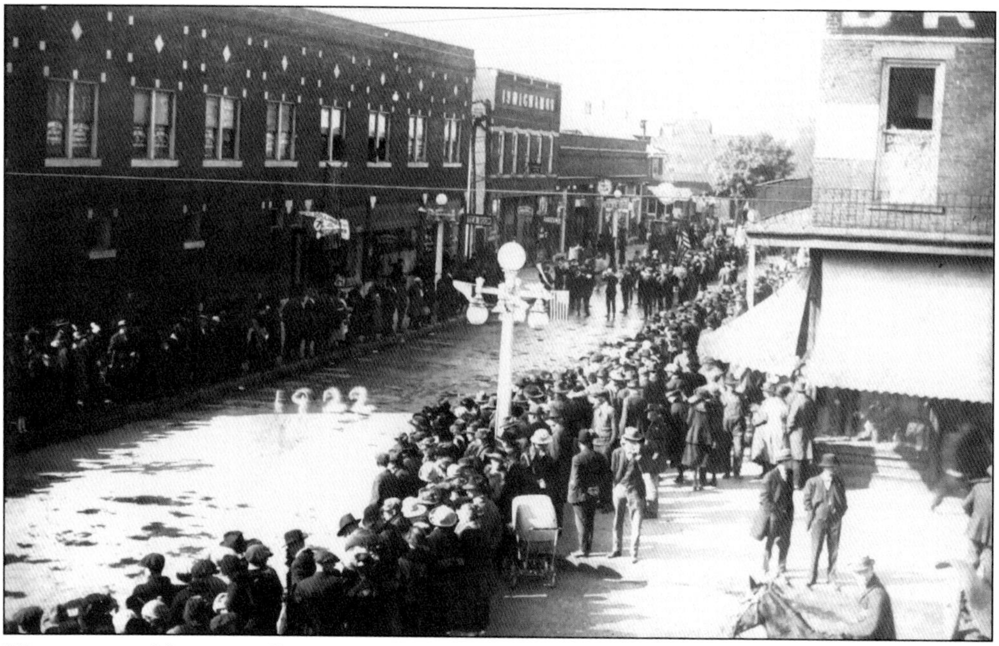

WHITELAND MILITARY BAND ENTERING SQUARE FROM WEST MORGAN STREET, 1922. One of the most famous musical organizations of the state in its day, the Whiteland Military Band led off the parade of schoolchildren that opened the celebration's second day. The Corner Drug Store is in the right foreground. At left center is the Wigwam, the second-floor lodge of the Seminole Tribe of the Improved Order of Red Men.

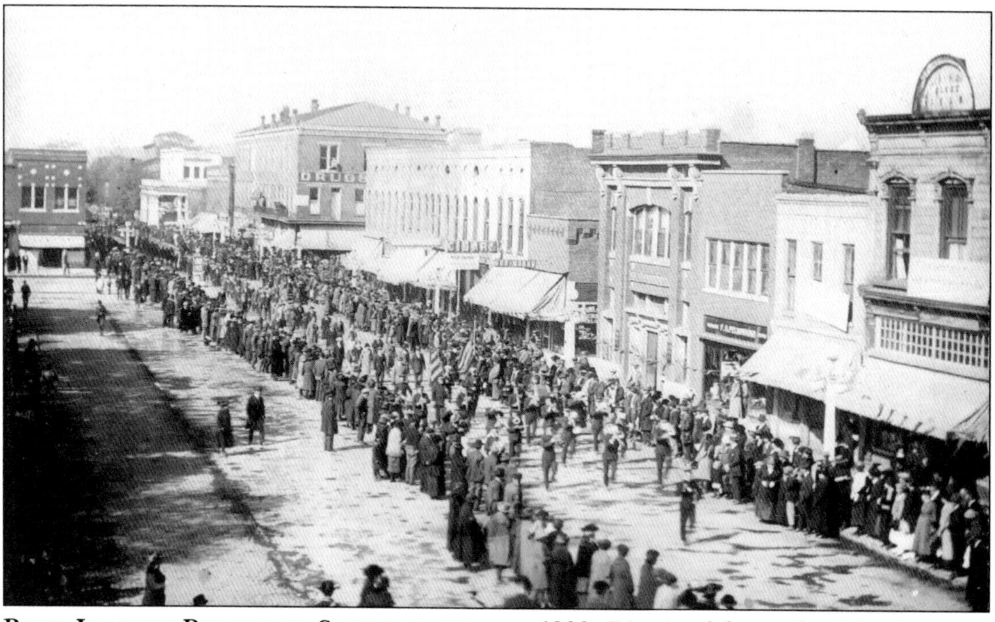

BAND LEADING PARADE OF SCHOOLCHILDREN, 1922. Dismissed from school for the grand event, hundreds of county schoolchildren marched through Martinsville. "It was an interesting and impressive sight as these future citizens of the county paraded before their parents, relatives and friends, a sight that will not soon be forgotten," wrote the *Daily Reporter.* Following the parade, the children competed in contests such as the oat bag throw and shoe scramble.

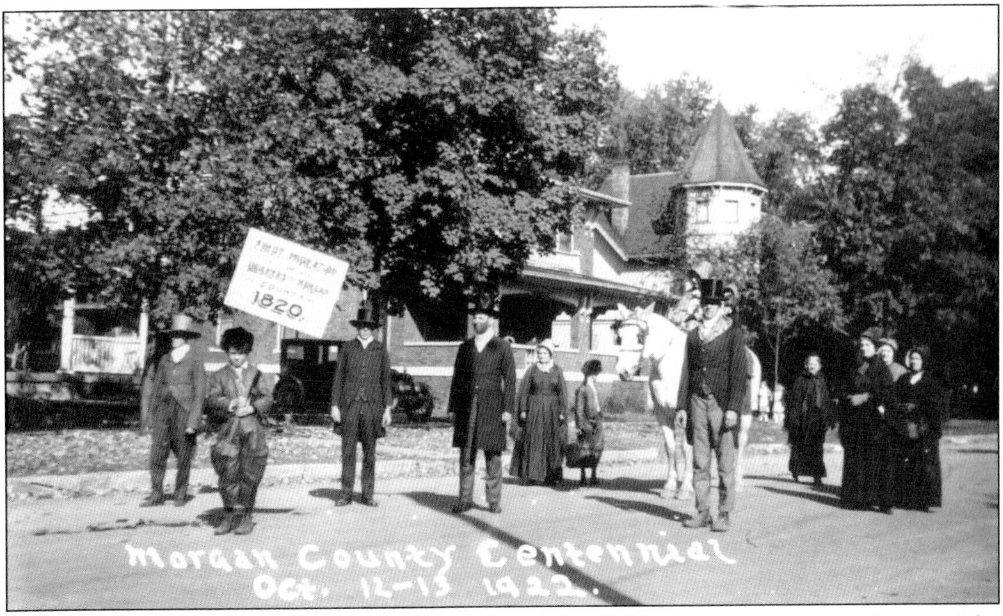

"SPIRIT OF THE PIONEERS," PAGEANT PARADE, 1922. The pageant parade was "the crowning feature of the big celebration," according to the *Daily Reporter.* Representing the "First Migration of Quakers to Morgan County, 1820" these Mooresville residents "dressed in the style of the Quakers of the early days," including homespun coats, silk dresses, and hats worn by their grandparents.

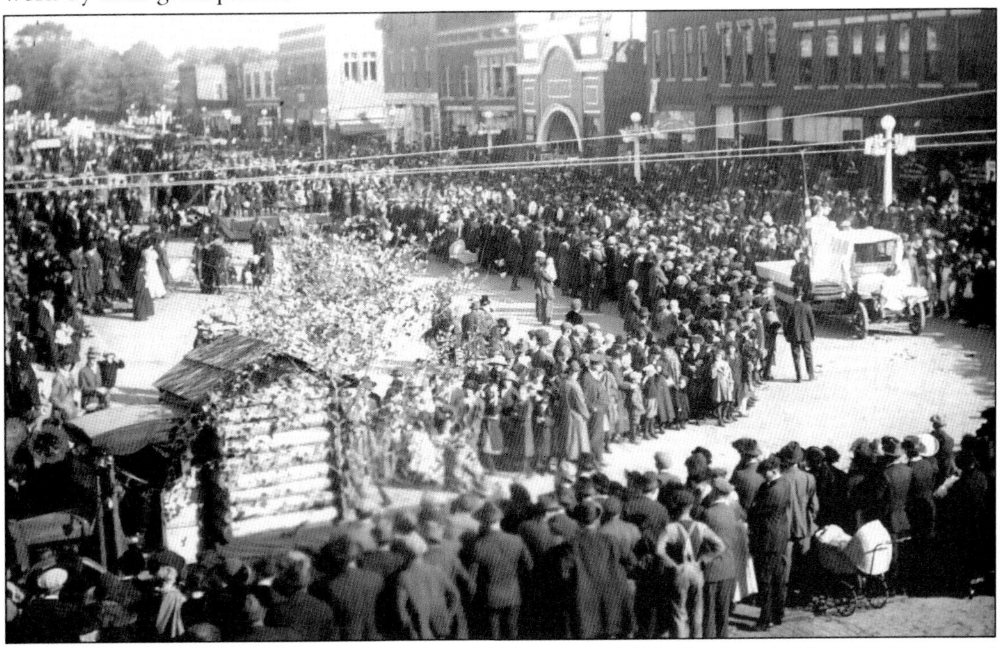

FLOAT FROM BROWN TOWNSHIP, PAGEANT PARADE, 1922. As directed by Carrie Scott of Mooresville, the pageant parade included floats from Morgan County's various communities. This log cabin represents "Samuel Moore's trading station, which stood on a hill a short distance south of Mooresville in the early days, and from which Mooresville derived its name." The float that follows features Miss Columbia, representing patriotism.

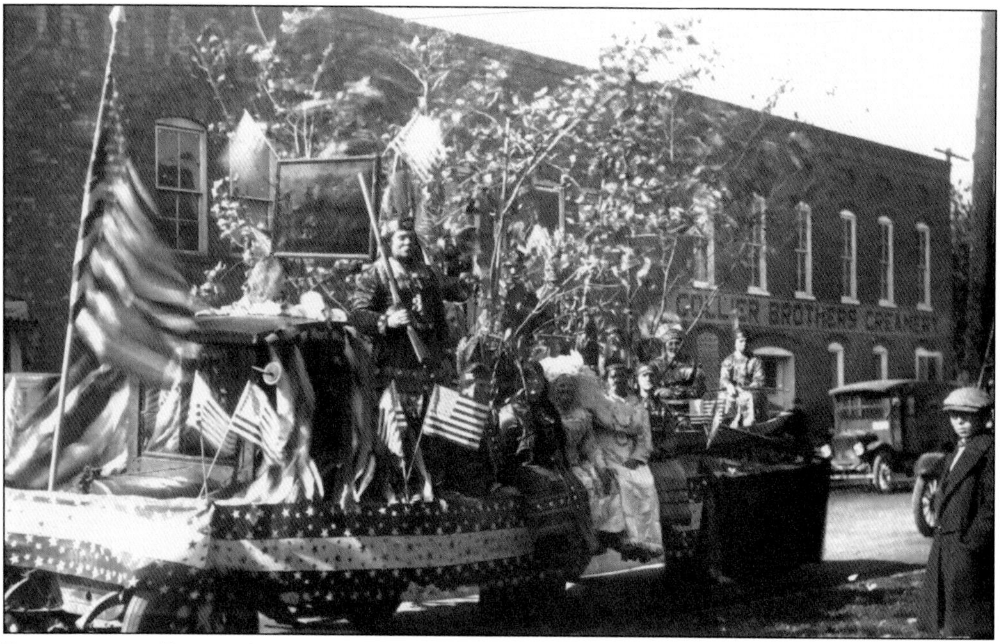

POCAHONTAS LODGE NO. 33, PAGEANT PARADE, 1922. The women's auxiliary of the Red Men passed in front of Collier Brothers Creamery at the corner of Washington and Sycamore Streets. Their float concluded the parade. Afterward, centennial celebrants enjoyed a band concert on the courthouse's south lawn. Collier Brothers produced milk, ice cream, cream, and cottage cheese from 1916 to 1955. The building was torn down in 1962.

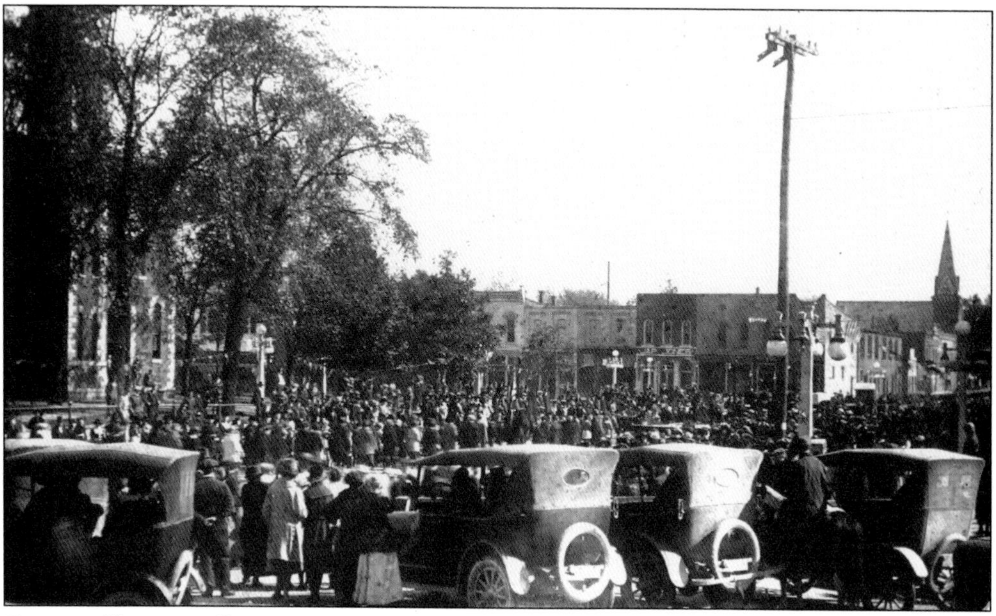

CROWD VIEWING PARADE, 1922. The pageant parade was captured by an Indianapolis filmmaker. "What a sensation this picture will create when the second centennial celebration is held one hundred years from now," enthused the *Daily Reporter*. "The generation of that time will doubtless have many a good laugh [at our] costumes. Possibly abbreviation of wearing apparel will go on [and] they will think it strange that people ever wore anything at all."

Martinsville

The poets and sages, both the small and the great,
Have sung of the glory of our Nation and State.
But language is hardly sufficient to tell
All the glory rung out from 'Old Liberty Bell.'
But this unfinished tale, we will leave to the pen
Of the scholar and poet, who will tell it again.
And while we are waiting their story to hear,
We will turn to the City, that we all love so dear.
In the White River Valley, nestled close to the hill,
In this fair little City, yes, our own Martinsville.
Its fame has already reached the ends of the earth,
For its waters, long known for medicinal worth.
And thousands who suffer with pains and with aches
From Ocean to Ocean, from the Gulf to the Lakes,
Come here every year, with the fervent belief
That the Martinsville Water will bring them relief.
They are not disappointed, though their stay may be short.
And they join in the praise of this 'Great Health Resort.'
For they're glad unto others, the story to tell,
Of the waters that surely make sick people well.
Yes its fame is increasing, so the years come and go,
Of the blessing that waits, in the City so fair,
Which the rich and the poor are invited to share.
Then our Business Men, Merchants, and the Men of the Bank
Are second to none, in the very front rank.
They merit support, from each one and all;
In summer and winter; in the spring and the fall:
We make the best brick, and the best wooden-ware;
We're the home of the goldfish, and the 'Old Hickory Chair.'
And wherever the earth is kissed by the sun,
And civilized blood in the human veins run,
We may see our own products, or the fish in the bowl;
And the thoughts of our City gives a thrill to the soul.
And in every hand those that toil throughout the day,
In the field or the office, or in house either way,
May come home at evening, to forget every care
And quietly rest in an "Old Hickory Chair.'
We cannot do justice to out theme of to-day,
Though, we can hope someone else, in the near future may,
But since that our fame has encircled the earth,
May we all be aware of our City's own worth.
And boost for it always, both at home and abroad
And forever its name and its virtues applaud:
For its glory is ours, to enjoy to the fill,
Then boost and keep boosting for 'Oh! Martinsville.'

***MARTINSVILLE* BY M. A. BLUNK.** Blunk's poem, celebrating Martinsville with prideful boosterism, appeared in the *Martinsville Democrat* in 1923.

INDEX